FDI Qualities Review of Canada

ACCELERATING INCLUSIVE AND SUSTAINABLE GROWTH

OECD

BETTER POLICIES FOR BETTER LIVES

Please cite this publication as:
OECD (2024), *FDI Qualities Review of Canada: Accelerating Inclusive and Sustainable Growth*, OECD Publishing, Paris, https://doi.org/10.1787/273d99ec-en.

ISBN 978-92-64-80637-5 (print)
ISBN 978-92-64-59631-3 (PDF)
ISBN 978-92-64-34281-1 (HTML)
ISBN 978-92-64-77201-4 (epub)

Photo credits: Cover © Invest In Canada.

Corrigenda to OECD publications may be found on line at: www.oecd.org/about/publishing/corrigenda.htm.

Foreword

This *FDI Qualities Review of Canada* provides an assessment of how foreign direct investment (FDI) contributes to Canada's sustainable development. The review uses OECD and non-OECD data sources and draws on the qualitative insights from an OECD business consultation on the corporate sustainability practices of a group of domestic and foreign companies operating in Canada. It provides initial policy considerations to improve the impact of FDI on inclusive and sustainable growth in Canada.

The report comprises five chapters. Chapter 1 provides an overview of the main challenges for sustainable development in Canada, analyses recent FDI trends, and presents a summary of the main findings of the study, which show the role that FDI currently plays in supporting sustainable development. Chapter 2 examines the impact of FDI on trade and GVC integration, productivity and innovation. Chapter 3 analyses the impact of FDI on employment creation, job quality, and skill development. Chapter 4 assesses how FDI influences diversity and inclusion of vulnerable workers (women, indigenous peoples, foreign workers from disadvantaged backgrounds, and people with disabilities) in the labour market. Finally, Chapter 5 provides an evaluation of how FDI contributes to Canada's net-zero transition.

The review has been prepared by the OECD in close co-ordination with Invest in Canada. It is part of a series of *FDI Qualities Reviews*, supporting the implementation of the *OECD Council Recommendation on FDI Qualities for Sustainable Development,* adopted by OECD Ministers in 2022. The FDI Qualities Reviews, conducted so far in Ireland (2021), Jordan (2022), Portugal (2022), Slovak Republic (2022), Austria (2023), Chile (2023), and Croatia (2023), shed light on how FDI contributes to a country's sustainable development priorities. They help identify areas where such impact can be improved and provide tailored policy advice.

The FDI Qualities Review of Canada was prepared by a team led by Letizia Montinari and comprising Fares Al-Hussami, Derek Carnegie, Stratos Kamenis, Katharina Laengle, Iris Mantovani, and Mertol Ozaltan of the Investment Division in the OECD Directorate for Financial and Enterprise Affairs, under the overall guidance of Ana Novik, Head of the Investment Division and Martin Wermelinger, Head of Sustainable Investment Unit. Invest in Canada was instrumental in providing guidance and feedback to the OECD team. Statistics Canada provided, for the purpose of this review, unique data on skills shortages faced by foreign and Canadian companies. The report benefited from discussions with and comments from Ben Conigrave and Philip Hemmings from the OECD Economics Department, and Stephen Thomsen from the OECD Investment Division. An earlier version of this report was shared for comments with the OECD Investment Committee.

Table of contents

FIGURES

TABLES

Abbreviations and acronyms

AI	Artificial Intelligence
CAD	Canadian dollar
CSD	Canadian survey of disability
GERD	Gross expenditure on research and development
EU	European Union
FDI	Foreign direct investment
GDP	Gross domestic product
GFA	Global framework agreements
GHG	Greenhouse gas
GVC	Global value chains
HRM	Human resources management
IBA	Impact and benefit agreement
ICT	Information and Communications Technologies
IT	Information Technologies
M&A	Merger and acquisition
MNE	Multinational enterprise
OECD	Organisation for Economic Co-operation and Development
PFI	Policy framework for investment
PHRI	Population Health Research Institute
R&D	Research & Development
SDG	Sustainable development goal
SME	Small- and medium-sized enterprise
SPE	Special purpose entity
STEM	Science, technology, engineering, and mathematics
USD	United States dollar
VC	Venture capital

Executive summary

Canada must continue pursuing its sustainable development agenda and address pressing challenges, including weak productivity growth, persistent socio-economic inequalities, and the need to reduce net greenhouse gas emissions to zero by 2050, as set out in its ambitious environmental plan. Canada has historically been open to investment and trade. The stock of foreign direct investment (FDI) as a percentage of gross domestic product (GDP), highlighting the economic importance of foreign investment, has increased over time and is higher than that of most other OECD countries. The largest share of FDI is found in services, particularly in the management of companies and enterprises, finance and insurance and trade. Some manufacturing sectors, particularly chemicals, food and beverages, petroleum and coal products), and gas and oil extraction have also received significant foreign investment, particularly in the form of expansions and new establishments of foreign companies (i.e. greenfield FDI). Other sectors such as manufacturing, agriculture, utilities, and construction attract relatively lower levels of FDI in Canada. The majority of greenfield FDI projects are situated in Ontario, Alberta, British Columbia, and Quebec, which are the most densely populated provinces and centres of economic activity.

FDI supports Canada's important sustainable development goals. FDI is an important driver of exports, particularly of products at earlier stages in production such as oil and gas extraction, but also of transport equipment, ICT and electronics. Affiliates of foreign multinational enterprises (MNEs) in Canada account for more than half of merchandise and commercial services exports and are more involved in GVCs than domestic firms, especially in terms of backward linkages. They are on average more productive and innovative than Canadian firms and can thus provide an important boost to domestic labour productivity, which in Canada has lagged behind that of other major OECD economies. Moreover, compared to Canadian firms, foreign firms are more engaged in R&D and product and process innovations and joint product development with other firms. They also create significant buy and sell links with domestic firms, including many Canadian small and medium enterprises (SMEs), which can encourage positive productivity spillovers through technology transfer and greater integration into GVCs. Further diversifying FDI in more innovative and knowledge-intensive sectors can boost the positive impact of international investment on productivity, innovation, and integration in GVCs.

Foreign firms in Canada also make an important contribution to job creation and upskilling. In 2020, foreign firms were responsible for about 13% of employment, despite accounting for less than 1% of active firms. While FDI has a lower job creation potential than the OECD average (1.3 jobs per USD million invested – half the OECD average), many are jobs in technology- and knowledge-intensive occupations offering high wages and stable employment contracts (i.e., full-time, permanent jobs). However, FDI is concentrated in sectors with falling collective bargaining coverage rates as shown in Chapter 3. Workers' representations can support better working conditions in MNEs and help companies adapt to a rapidly changing world of work. Foreign employers in Canada face skills imbalances in digital, tech-related and trades skills, although less than domestic firms. As MNEs, they rely on their large size and global experience to deploy more effective strategies to scout talent and train workers. Aligning the investment promotion, employment and skills development strategies, further facilitating partnerships between foreign firms and education providers, encouraging international labour mobility across subsidiaries of an MNE, and integrating FDI into mechanisms that assess and anticipate future skills needs will help ensure that the impact of FDI is more widespread and positive.

The extent to which foreign firms operating in Canada contribute to enhanced diversity and inclusion of vulnerable groups, particularly women, Indigenous peoples, foreign workers from disadvantaged backgrounds, and people with disabilities in Canada's labour market cannot be determined with the limited data available for this report. Foreign firms are generally more prevalent in sectors where these vulnerable groups tend to be less represented, such as mining and energy, business services and manufacturing. The results of an OECD business consultation provides preliminary evidence that foreign companies seem to put less priority on having a diverse and inclusive workforce compared to Canadian peers. This is denoted by their lower shares of workers from these vulnerable groups (except for foreign workers), including in management positions, compared to Canadian companies. Foreign companies are also less likely to use inclusive work practices in the workplace than Canadian companies. On the other hand, foreign companies seem to attach more importance to formal training and have a higher proportion of employees from vulnerable groups who have received training, compared to Canadian companies. Improving the representation of these vulnerable groups of workers in sectors where Canada attracts or wants to attract more FDI will ensure that the job opportunities created by foreign companies benefit all segments of the population.

FDI has also the potential to help Canada achieve its ambitious plan to reduce the economy's net emissions to zero by 2050. Canada has made great progress in phasing out coal-fired power, achieving among the highest shares of zero-emission electricity in the OECD. It is a clean technology pioneer when it comes to developing breakthrough technologies that will help decarbonise heavy industries. Yet, the Canadian economy remains carbon-intensive due to oil and gas extraction, road transport, and residential heating. FDI has the potential to provide financial and technological resources to accelerate Canada's green transition. However, it remains concentrated in relatively more carbon-intensive activities compared to domestic investment, especially in the mining, chemical and pharmaceutical sectors. Furthermore, fossil fuels still account for a large share of FDI (84%) in Canada's energy sector and investment in green R&D is modest compared to FDI in other forms of R&D. Accelerated electrification of key sectors and electricity grid upgrades will be crucial for Canada to achieve its ambitious climate commitments. Attracting more FDI in green sectors and technologies can help reduce GHG emissions and develop the green skills needed to achieve these environmental goals.

1 Overview

This chapter provides an overview of Canada's current state of sustainable development and discusses how FDI can contribute to Canada's sustainable growth. It provides a summary of key findings from the assessment of the impact of FDI on trade, productivity and innovation; employment, job quality and skills; diversity and inclusion of vulnerable groups; and the transition to a net-zero emissions economy.

1.1. FDI can support Canada's sustainable development trajectory

1.1.1. Canada faces several pressing sustainability challenges

The Canadian economy has recovered quickly after the COVID-19 crisis, with real GDP growth exceeding pre-pandemic levels in 2021 (Figure 1.1, Panel A) (OECD, 2023[1]). Yet, Canada is facing several pressing socio-economic and environmental challenges. These include weak productivity growth, significant labour market imbalances, persistent socio-economic inequalities, an ageing population, and the need to reduce net greenhouse gas emissions.

Figure 1.1. The Canadian economy has recovered rapidly after the recent shocks

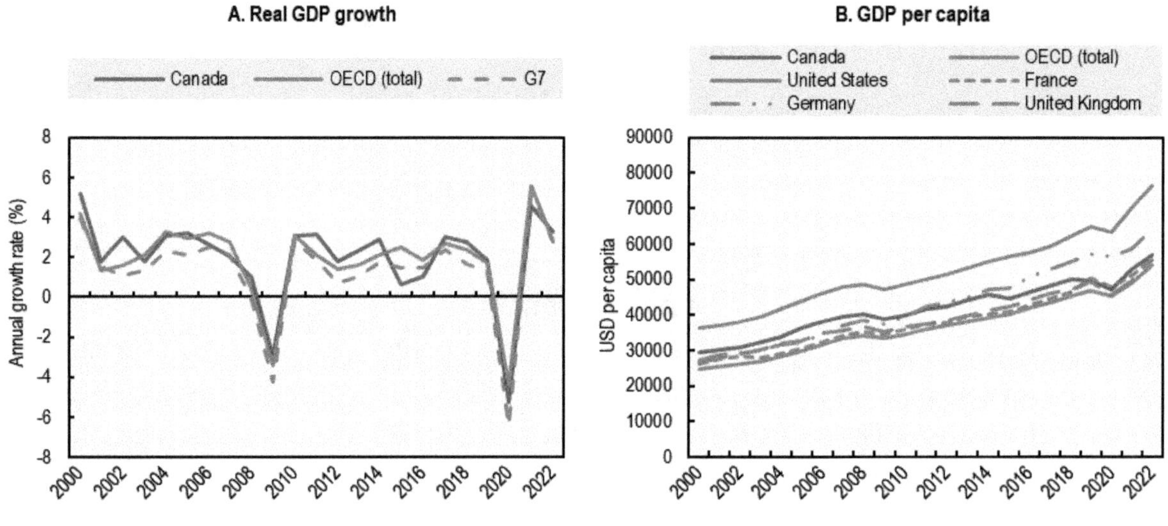

Source: OECD National Accounts (2023[2]), https://stats.oecd.org/

In recent years, Canada's GDP per capita has grown in step with that of OECD countries, including several leading economies such as France and the United Kingdom. However, the gap with some G7 economies such as the United States and Germany has widened (Figure 1.1, Panel B), partly reflecting weak productivity performance. Canada's productivity measured in terms of GDP per hour worked is similar to the OECD average, but about 20% below the average of G7 countries. In recent years, the Canadian economy has demonstrated a limited ability to increase output through innovation (OECD, 2023[1]). Gross domestic spending on R&D, an indicator of the resources invested in R&D by all residents (companies, research institutes, university, government laboratories, etc.), accounts for only 1.7% of GDP in Canada, compared to the 2.7% OECD average and the 2.3% G7 average.

The labour market recovered rapidly after the COVID-19 crisis. Canada has one of the highest employment rates in the OECD area and among the G7 countries. Canada also has the most highly educated workforce in the world: 62% of the workforce aged 25 to an OECD average of 40%. The pandemic, however, has exacerbated existing skills shortages in several sectors, especially in medium-skilled occupations (e.g., electricians, mechanics) (OECD, 2020[3]). Canada also has a high percentage of workers who have a qualification or field of study that does not match the requirements of their job, also known as skill mismatches (38% compared to the 34% OECD average and the 32% G7 average) (OECD, 2020[4]). Such skills mismatches are particularly severe in manufacturing, wholesale and retail trade, and scientific services. In addition, in Canada as in the rest of the OECD and G7 countries, the ageing population poses a further challenge to sustainable growth due to strong pressures on public spending (Crowe et al., 2022[5]).

The demographic old-age dependency is expected to reach 45 in 2050 (meaning 45 individuals aged 65 and over per 100 persons of working age).

The pandemic has also exacerbated pre-existing socio-economic gaps within the population and highlighted the vulnerabilities of some disadvantaged groups in the labour market (OECD, 2021[6]). However, Canada took important steps including through new legislation (e.g. the 2021 Pay Equity Act) and leadership development programs that help address the remaining gender pay gap. In Canada, the difference between men's and women's median annual earnings relative to men's median annual earnings is 17%, compared to the OECD average of 12% and the G7 average of 15%. Indigenous people also remain marginalised in many socio-economic dimensions. For instance, labour force participation of Indigenous people is 7 percentage points lower than that non-Indigenous people. Canada has one of the largest shares of foreign-born population among OECD countries, particularly immigrants (i.e., foreign-born people with permanent resident status). Although immigrants contribute significantly to economic growth, recent immigrants in particular tend to have lower-skilled jobs than the Canadian-born even with the same educational qualifications (Statistics Canada, 2022[7]).

Canada has an ambitious plan to reduce 2005 levels of greenhouse gas (GHG) emissions by 40--45% by 2030 and has committed to achieving net zero emissions by 2050 (Government of Canada, 2023[8]). Its GHG emissions per capita are higher than the OECD average (15.6 tonnes of CO2 equivalent per capita, compared to an OECD average of 8.5 tonnes of CO2 equivalent per capita). Canada's current energy and economic profile presents both challenges and opportunities for achieving these environmental GHG reduction targets, given its status as a large energy producer, consumer and exporter. Energy is fundamental to the Canadian economy and is a major source of capital investment and trade flows, as well as a key generator of middle-class jobs, including for Indigenous peoples (IEA, 2022[9]). Canada is also a leader in the production of renewable energy, particularly hydropower, which is key to reducing GHG emissions. Renewable energy sources (excluding solid biofuels) currently provide about 13% of Canada's total primary energy supply, compared to about 8% in the OECD and 7% in G7 countries.

1.1.2. The importance of FDI and trade to the Canadian economy has increased in the past decades

Canada has historically been open to investment and trade. The importance of foreign direct investment (FDI) for Canada, as measured by the stock of FDI relative to gross domestic product (GDP), is well above the average for OECD countries and some leading economies such as the United States, Germany and France (Figure 1.2, Panel A). Similar to what has been observed in other countries, this ratio has increased over the last decade. In 2021, the ratio of FDI stock to GDP reached 72%, the highest value since the global financial crisis of 2008--09. Between 2021 and 2022, the ratio of FDI to stock decreased slightly (OECD, 2023[10]). In 2007, there was a strong surge in FDI flows in Canada, similar to that observed in many other countries. In Canada, this was mainly due to a series of cross-border M&As in the mining sector, stimulated by its strong economic growth, tax cuts and competitive business environment (UNCTAD, 2007[11]). Thereafter, FDI flows were largely stable and high (with a few outliers during crisis years), contributing to a growing importance of FDI for Canada's economy.

Figure 1.2. The FDI stock to GDP ratio has increased in the past decade

FDI stock to GDP (%)

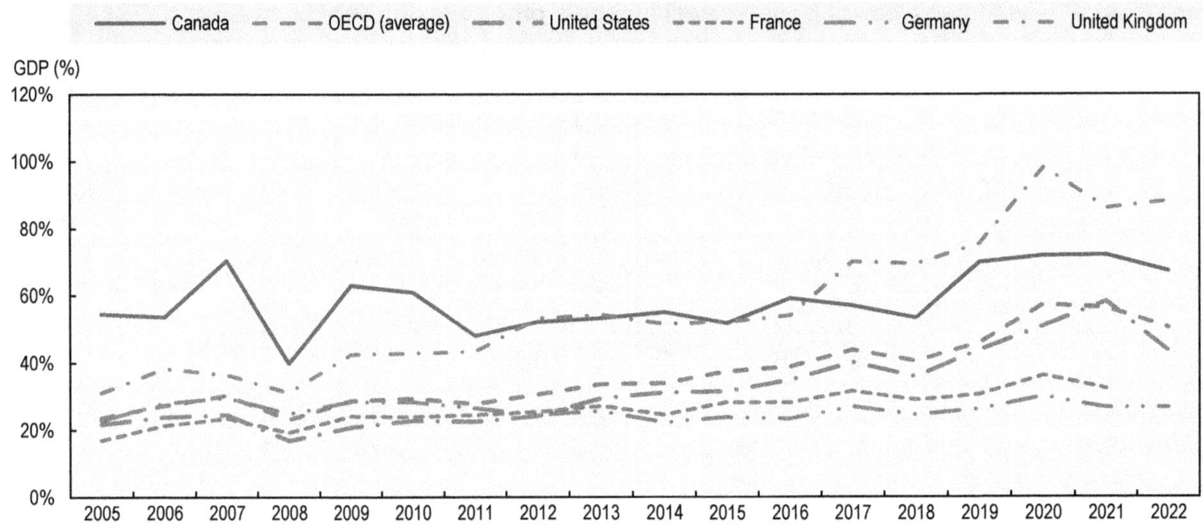

Source: OECD FDI Statistics (2023[12]), https://stats.oecd.org/

Canada's reliance on international trade has also grown over the past decade. The ratio of trade (gross exports plus imports) to GDP has increased steadily since 2009, reaching 66% of GDP in 2019 (Figure 1.3, Panel A). This ratio declined slightly in 2020-21 in Canada as in many other countries due to the global pandemic and resulting disruptions in companies' operations and global supply chains (GVCs) (OECD, 2021[13]). Canada's increased openness to FDI and international trade are strongly linked. Globally, foreign multinationals are the main drivers of global value chains and are responsible for the majority of international trade flows. Foreign companies also contribute significantly to Canada's trade and integration in GVCs. Statistics Canada indicators show that foreign multinationals are responsible for most Canadian exports and imports of goods and commercial services (Figure 1.3, Panel B).

Figure 1.3. Foreign firms are an important driver of Canada's trade

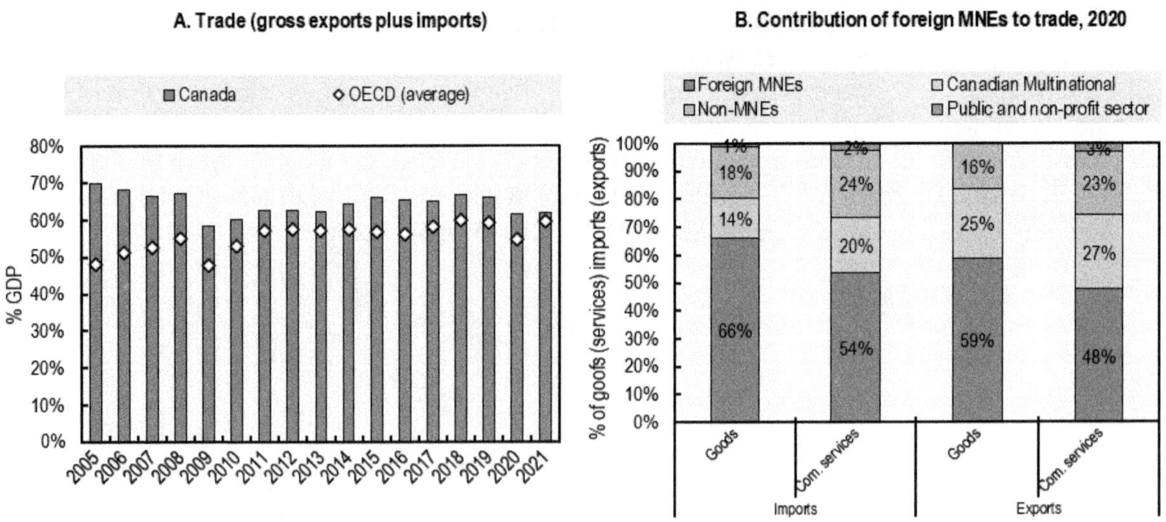

Source: OECD Trade in goods and services (2023[14]), https://stats.oecd.org/; Statistics Canada, Activities of MNE per type of multinational (2023[15]), https://www150.statcan.gc.ca/n1/en/type/data?MM=1

1.1.3. FDI is unevenly distributed across sectors…

A few sectors attract the majority of FDI in Canada. The FDI stock is mainly concentrated in services (70%), manufacturing (18%) and mining and oil and gas extraction (10%) (Figure 1.4). Within services, management of companies and enterprises holds the largest share (31% of total FDI), followed by finance (13% of total FDI) and trade (11% of total FDI). Over the past ten years, the share of investments classified in management of companies and enterprises has increased significantly, by about 14 percentage points. At the same time, investment shares in manufacturing and mining and oil and gas extraction have decreased by 11 and 8 percentage points respectively (although investment in absolute values increased in both sectors between 2012 and 2022). Management of companies and enterprises consists of head offices and special purpose entities (SPEs), such as holding companies. SPEs are set up to channel investments through an intermediary country and generally have no physical presence or activities in the host country. According to Statistics Canada, however, the role of SPEs in Canada is marginal and investments classified in this category are ultimately redistributed to corporate group companies associated with other sectors, such as mining, oil and gas extraction, and manufacturing (Government of Canada, 2022[16]). This implies that FDI shares for these sectors are likely to be underestimated.

Figure 1.4. The largest share of FDI stock is in services, particularly management of companies and enterprises

FDI positions by sector (NAICS)

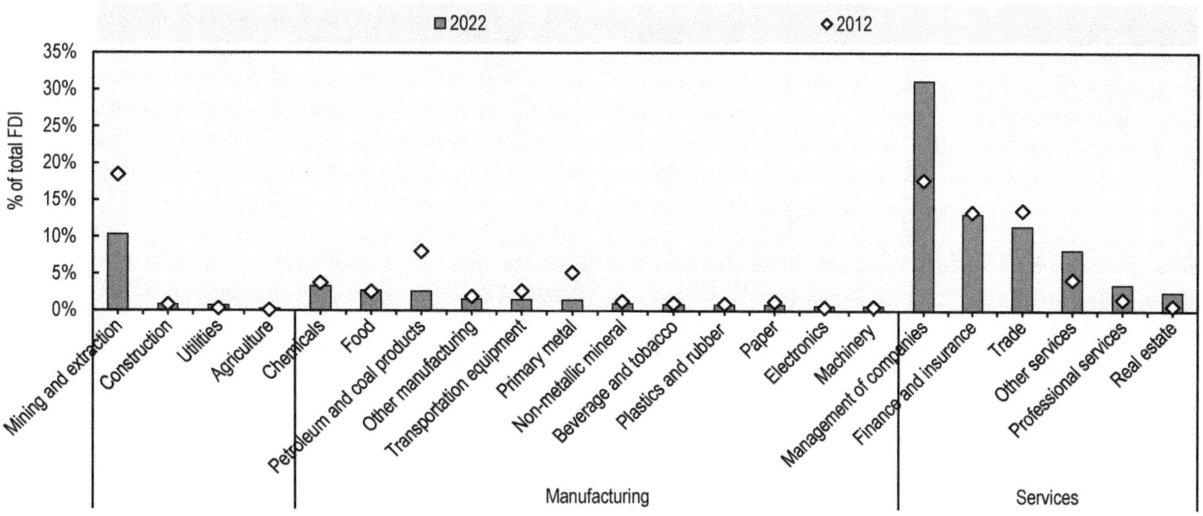

Note: Management of companies and enterprises includes head offices and special purpose entities (SPEs).
Source: OECD elaboration based on Statistics Canada, International investment position (2022[17]), https://doi.org/10.25318/3610000901-eng.

The contribution of FDI to economic activity (measured in terms of value added and jobs) also varies greatly among sectors. In 2020, foreign firms in Canada were responsible for approximately 15% of GDP and 13% of employment. The value added and jobs created by foreign firms mainly benefited services and manufacturing. Almost 60% percent of the value added and 70% of the jobs created by foreign firms were in the services sector, which is responsible for 71% of domestic economic activity (as measured by real domestic value added) (Figure 1.5, Panel B and C). 28% of the value added and 24% of the jobs created by foreign enterprises were generated in the manufacturing sector. This is a significant contribution considering that this sector is responsible for only 9% of economic activity in Canada (Figure 1.5, Panel A). About 10% of value added and 3% of jobs were created in the mining, and energy sector, while smaller contributions both in terms of value added and jobs were made in construction and agriculture.

The extent to which FDI influences the economic activity of the host economy also depends on the mode of entry of foreign investors. Greenfield investments (new establishment and expansions of foreign companies) are often associated with increased employment generation, particularly in manufacturing and services, and especially in the short term. According to data on greenfield FDI announcements from the Financial Times, the manufacturing sector (mainly transport equipment, electronics, food & beverages) received 33% of total announced greenfield FDI over 2003-22, and business support services received around 15% over the same period. These investments were responsible for 43% (manufacturing) and 33% (business support services) of total jobs associated with announced greenfield FDI in Canada (Figure 1.6).

Figure 1.5. Foreign MNEs created the largest shares of value added and employment in services and manufacturing

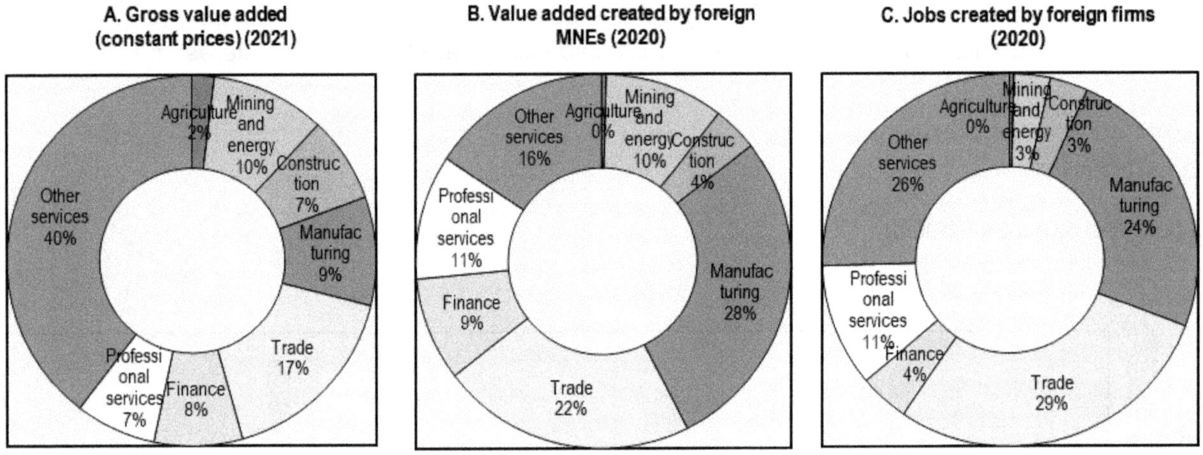

Source: OECD elaboration based on Statistics Canada, Activities of MNE per type of multinational (2023[15]), https://www150.statcan.gc.ca/n1/en/type/data?MM=1, OECD National Accounts (OECD, 2023[2])

Figure 1.6. Most jobs created by greenfield FDI between 2003 and 2022 were in manufacturing and business and other support services

Cumulative capital expenditure and jobs of greenfield FDI over the period 2003-22

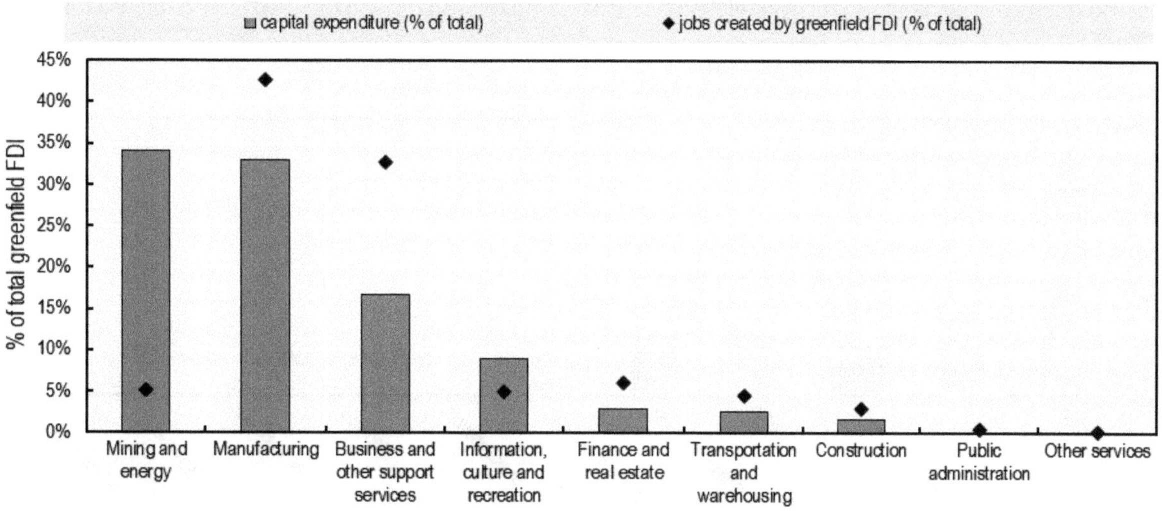

Source: OECD elaboration based on Financial Times (2023[18]), https://www.fdimarkets.com/

1.1.4. ...and provinces

According to Statistics Canada data, about 90% of value added generated by foreign multinational enterprises in Canada is concentrated in five provinces: Ontario (45%), Quebec (17%), New Brunswick (11%), Alberta (10%), and British Columbia (9%), (Figure 1.7). A similar distribution across provinces is found when looking at announced greenfield FDI data from the Financial Times. Significant geographical concentration of FDI is not unique to Canada and is observed in most OECD countries. FDI tends to concentrate near major economic centres (Toronto, Vancouver, Montreal, Edmonton, Calgary), which tend to have better infrastructure and services and where many suppliers and buyers are located. Moreover, Ontario, Alberta, British Columbia and Quebec also account for the largest share of population and economic activity in Canada.

The jobs created by foreign multinational enterprises are also concentrated in the same regions (except New Brunswick). 50% of the jobs are in Ontario, 17% in Quebec, 13% in British Columbia and 12% in Alberta. Only about 8% of jobs created by foreign firms are located in other regions. Looking at Financial Times data, however, greenfield FDI has created more jobs per US dollar invested in New Brunswick, Nova Scotia and Manitoba. This is due to several investment projects in business services (particularly companies providing costumer support services), software and IT services, and transport and logistics, which have created a significant number of jobs in these provinces as also revealed in the OECD business consultation for this study.

Figure 1.7. Activities of foreign multinational enterprises are concentrated in Ontario, Alberta, British Columbia and Quebec

Activities of foreign multinational enterprises by province (2020) Greenfield FDI expenditure and jobs (% of total greenfield FDI expenditure/jobs created by greenfield FDI)

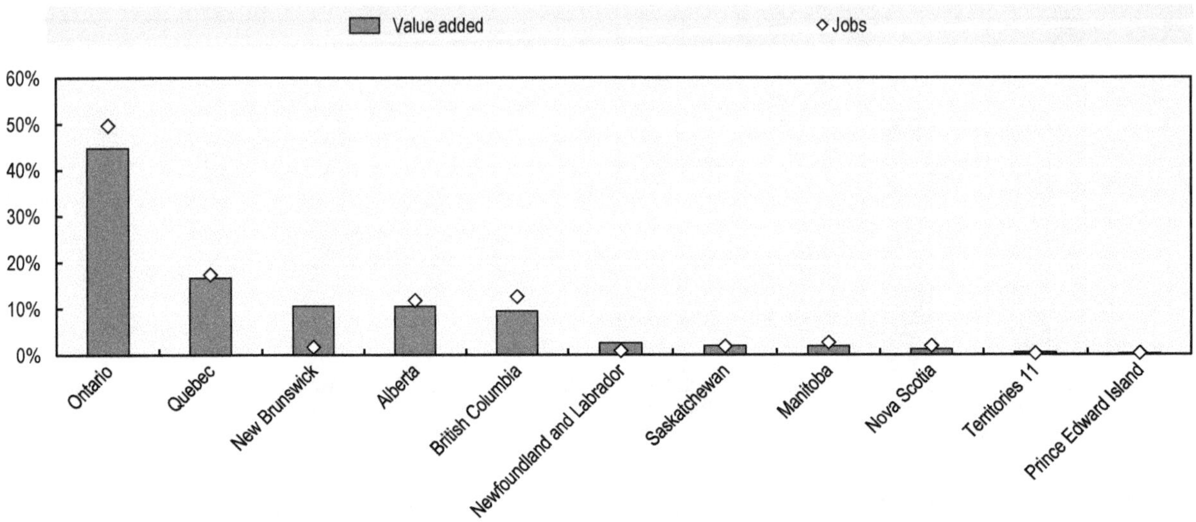

Source: OECD elaboration based Statistics Canada, Activities of MNE per type of multinational (2023[19]), https://www150.statcan.gc.ca/n1/en/type/data?MM=1 Financial Times (2023[18]),

Regional (or inter-provincial as in the case of Canada) disparities in FDI tend to be higher in Canada than in other OECD countries. The Gini coefficient calculated based on greenfield FDI per capita provides a useful measure of FDI disparities between regions or provinces in a country, which takes into account differences in population levels (OECD, 2022[19]). The coefficient ranges from 0 (perfect equality in the regional distribution of FDI per capita) to 1 (perfect inequality). The indicator shows that in Canada FDI per capita is more unevenly distributed than in most OECD countries (Figure 1.8, Panel A). Such disparities appear to be related to regional productivity differences, explained by the concentration of FDI in few places with high productivity but low population such as regions with natural resources (Figure 1.8, Panel B). As such, revealed regional disparities of FDI and productivity reflect differences in sectoral compositions among provinces. Moreover, Canada's extensive geographical size, combined with a relatively low population, further contributes to the uneven distribution of FDI across the country

Figure 1.8. Canada' high provincial disparities in FDI per capita are associated with regional productivity differences

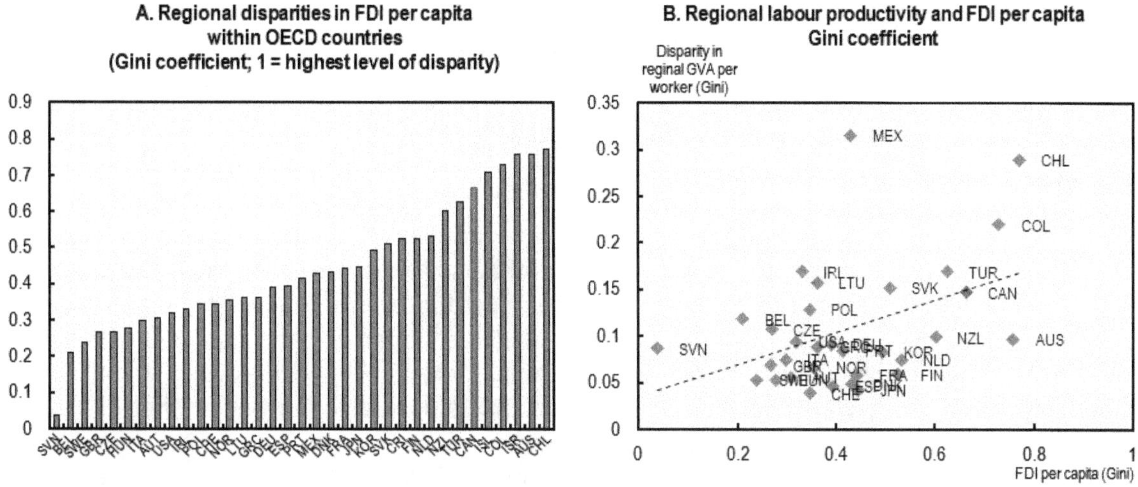

Note: For more details on the calculation of the Gini coefficient for FDI per capita, see OECD (2022[19]).
Source: OECD elaboration based on Financial Times (2023[18]), https://www.fdimarkets.com/; and OECD Regional Database (2023[20])

1.2. Impacts of FDI by areas of sustainable development

1.2.1. Foreign firms support trade, are on average more productive and innovative, and create extensive linkages with Canadian firms

FDI is an important driver of Canada's trade and integration into GVCs. A significant share of FDI in Canada, particularly greenfield FDI, is attracted to export oriented sectors such as mining and energy (including metals), ICT and electronics and transport equipment. Moreover, foreign multinational enterprises (MNEs) in Canada are responsible for a significant share of merchandise exports and commercial service exports (in 2020, about 60% of merchandise exports and close to 50% of commercial service exports). Foreign firms are also more involved in GVCs than domestic firms, especially in terms of backward linkages.

Overall, foreign firm activity in Canada is concentrated in sectors with lower labour productivity levels. However, affiliates of foreign MNEs (henceforth simply foreign firms or foreign companies) are on average more productive than domestic firms in most sectors of the economy. Productivity levels among domestic Canadian firms within sectors are likely to vary significantly, which is not analysed in this report. It is likely that larger domestic firms have productivity levels that are similar to those of foreign firms, while smaller firms have typically lower productivity levels. The foreign premium is especially large in finance and insurance, construction and utilities, where foreign MNEs are 50% more productive than domestic firms. Foreign companies are also an important catalyst for innovation in Canada. On average, foreign multinationals have a higher R&D intensity than Canadian firms. The results of an OECD business consultation conducted for this study (Box 1.1) show that foreign firms engage more often in innovative activities, particularly in product and process innovation and joint product development with other firms. This foreign premium in relation to R&D appears to be particularly high in the professional, scientific and technical sectors and in the information and culture industries. Moreover, over 2018--22, R&D investments made up the bulk of greenfield FDI in creative industries (91%), financial services (42%) and ICT and electronics (34%).

Value chain linkages between foreign MNEs and domestic firms, i.e. when foreign MNEs buy or sell goods and services from/to domestic firms, can be an important channel for knowledge and technology transfer and encourage positive productivity spillovers. Foreign firms established in Canada source a considerable share of their inputs from the domestic market, particularly from Canadian non-MNEs (about 40% of total inputs in 2016), similar to what has been observed for other large open economies such as the United States, the United Kingdom, France and Italy. In contrast, while over 60% of the output of foreign firms in Canada feeds back into domestic value chains, only 22% is used as input by domestic non-MNE firms, a lower share than observed in several large OECD economies (24% in the United States; 31% in Australia for example).

Canadian firms, particularly SMEs, appear to have the capabilities to become successful suppliers and partners to foreign MNEs and absorb the knowledge, skills and technologies that FDI brings to the host economy. Canadian SMEs appear to be more engaged in product and business process innovation than many peers in economies such as Australia, the United States, Japan and the European Union. Among Canadian firms, smaller ones have a higher R&D capacity (21% of R&D expenditure and 25% of R&D personnel). However, the digital capacities of Canadian SMEs appear to lag behind that of peer OECD economies, including with regard to the use of Artificial Intelligence and cloud computing services as well as the provision of ICT training to their employees, pointing towards potential weaknesses in fostering strategic partnerships with technology-intensive investors.

Policy efforts to diversify the type of FDI that Canada attracts towards high-productivity and R&D-intensive sectors and activities could continue and be scaled up further. Canada can play an important role in strengthening the contribution of FDI to productivity and innovation by developing investment promotion tools and processes to target and prioritise investments with higher technological intensity. Canada could also consider facilitating market access to FDI that may limit its positive impact on productivity growth, innovation, and integration in GVCs. Canada could collaborate with federal and provincial government agencies responsible for innovation and entrepreneurship development to help design supplier development programmes in line with investors' needs and strengthen the productive and innovative capacities of Canadian firms, in particular SMEs. Policy efforts could also focus on facilitating knowledge-intensive investments from already established foreign MNEs, by developing ties with universities, applied research institutions, science and technology parks; participating in entrepreneurial networks; and establishing open innovation infrastructures.

Box 1.1. The OECD consultation on the sustainability practices of foreign and domestic companies in Canada

The assessment of the impacts of FDI in Canada draws on the qualitative insights from an OECD business consultation on the corporate sustainability practices of a group of domestic and foreign companies. The consultation was conducted in 2022 in collaboration with Invest in Canada. It involved an online survey and telephone interviews of 23 Canadian companies and 33 foreign companies with operations in Canada, selected to be representative of a variety of industries, company sizes and countries of origin. The sample of Canadian firms include large firms and SMEs, but we have no information on whether or not these firms are MNEs themselves, i.e. whether or not they have investments abroad.

The survey contains questions related to four sustainability clusters, namely (i) trade, productivity and innovation; (ii) employment, job quality and skills; (iii) diversity and inclusion of vulnerable people (women, Indigenous peoples, people with disabilities, and foreign workers); (iv) and low-carbon transition. The questions are based on the conceptual framework and measurement methodology developed under the OECD FDI Qualities Initiative and build on the experience of other business consultations conducted by the OECD in similar studies.

It is important to keep in mind that the consultation is not based on a representative sample of companies and therefore does not allow for generalisation of the results to the entire population of companies operating in Canada. It offers original information on company practices in four areas of sustainability – including job quality, skills, diversity and inclusion, and the low-carbon transition – for which company-level information from official statistical sources is scarce or difficult to access. The findings of the consultation are used throughout the study to complement other statistical information and enrich the assessment with qualitative insights and examples of sustainable development practices by foreign companies in Canada. Annex 1.A provides further information on the methodology of the consultation and summary statistics on the group of companies that participated in the consultation.

Source: OECD (2019[21]), FDI Qualities Indicators: Measuring the sustainable development impacts of investment, https://www.oecd.org/fr/investissement/fdi-qualities-indicators.htm; OECD (2022[22]), FDI Qualities Policy Toolkit, https://doi.org/10.1787/7ba74100-en.; OECD (2021[23]), Investment Policy Reviews: Thailand, https://doi.org/10.1787/c4eeee1c-en.; OECD (2021[24]), The Impact of Regulation on International Investment in Finland, https://doi.org/10.1787/b1bf8bee-en.

1.2.2. Foreign firms create more quality jobs and contribute to upskilling, but persistent skill imbalances limit the benefits of these job opportunities

Foreign firms contribute importantly to job creation in Canada. They employed about 13% of the workforce in 2020, despite representing less than 1% of the total population of firms. Their contribution to job- creation differs across sectors, provinces and occupations. Most jobs are in manufacturing, wholesale and retail trade, and services related to IT and R&D. The bulk of jobs created by FDI is concentrated in the province of Ontario (see Sections 1.1.3 and 1.1.4). Many of these jobs are created in high-tech and knowledge-intensive activities and are likely to be well-paid – 25% of jobs created by greenfield FDI in the past 20 years were in software and IT ((Financial Times, 2023[18]).

Foreign firms in Canada have a mixed impact on job quality, such as wages, job security and employer-worker relations. The OECD business consultation conducted for this study provides anecdotal evidence that foreign firms may pay on average higher wages than domestic firms and have a lower proportion of workers with temporary and part-time jobs (Box 1.1). This finding would need to be confirmed with more representative data on job quality at the firm level. For example, the sector of activity of foreign and domestic firms matters: Foreign firms are key employers in the retail trade sector, where job tenures are relatively low. Job quality, particularly of vulnerable groups, is also affected by workers' voice arrangements and collective bargaining, for which coverage rates have been falling in sectors where large foreign firms operate. Furthermore, the sample of domestic firms includes large firms and SMEs but no information is available on whether or not they are MNEs themselves. It is likely that practices and conditions related to job quality vary depending on the type of domestic firms. The business consultation conducted for this report does not allow to make this distinction.

Canada has the most educated workforce in the OECD area, which is a major attractiveness factor for FDI that can itself support upskilling for the digital and green transitions. However, large foreign employers in Canada face significant skills imbalances – a combination of skills shortages and mismatches – in tech-related industries and in skilled tradespeople, potentially affecting Canada's attractiveness to FDI. Aligning the investment promotion, employment and skills development strategies will help ensure that labour demand generated by foreign firms in promoted sectors is met with available and adequately trained labour to realise the contribution of FDI and limit potential adverse impacts. This also requires improving data collection and integrating FDI, as a forward-looking indicator of future skill needs, into skill anticipation mechanisms.

Foreign MNEs in Canada are less severely affected by skill shortages than domestic firms as they rely on their larger size and global experience to deploy more sophisticated strategies to scout talent and train their workers. They can mobilise specialised talent from their headquarter or other subsidiaries to facilitate their establishment in markets facing severe skill shortages and can provide global networking and mentoring opportunities and classroom and curriculum-based training. They also often partner with Canadian colleges and universities to provide technical apprenticeships or work-integrated learning opportunities. Further facilitating partnerships between foreign firms and education providers and encouraging new investors to transfer specialised staff from other subsidiaries in early stages of their operations could contribute to lowering skill imbalances.

1.2.3. FDI is prevalent in sectors where vulnerable workers are less likely to work and foreign firms have a less diverse workforce than Canadian firms

A workforce that is representative of people of all genders, sexual orientations, ethnicities, races, religions and abilities is not only ethically desirable, but also offers a variety of talents and perspectives, which can positively impact business performance and productivity. Inclusion of vulnerable groups is a key value and an important policy priority for the Government of Canada (Government of Canada, 2022[25]). FDI in Canada is prevalent in sectors with less participation of vulnerable groups. These are the primary sectors, particularly mining and oil and gas extraction, business and support services (i.e. management of companies and enterprises), manufacturing, finance and trade. Less than a third of women and just over a third of Indigenous peoples, people with disabilities and immigrants work in these sectors. On the contrary, these categories of workers are over-represented in sectors –such as health and social care, educational services, wholesale and retail trade, and public administration – that benefit less from FDI. Improving the representation of these vulnerable groups where Canada attracts or wants to attract more investment (high-tech and R&D-intensive sectors, green sectors, etc.) is crucial to ensure that the job opportunities created by foreign investors benefit all segments of the population.

The OECD business consultation conducted for this study indicates that Canadian companies are more aware of the importance of having a diverse workforce. While foreign and domestic companies have on average a comparable share of vulnerable employees, domestic companies have a higher share of women, Indigenous peoples, and persons with disabilities. On the other hand, foreign companies have a higher share of foreign workers (i.e., foreign nationals with permanent resident status or study/work-visa status).[1] Canadian companies also have a higher proportion of women, Indigenous peoples and persons with disabilities among their managers and are more likely to use inclusive workplace practices (e.g. inclusive hiring strategies, diversity training) than foreign companies. However, the survey reveals that the foreign companies attach more importance to employee training. A higher proportion of foreign companies offer formal training and foreign companies have on average higher percentages of employees from vulnerable groups who have received training, compared to Canadian companies. In addition, a higher percentage of foreign companies have female representation in ownership, although further analysis indicates that this appears to be related to company size, sectors and origin of foreign companies.

Overall, the survey results show that values of diversity and inclusion of vulnerable people are more ingrained in the corporate culture of Canadian companies. Conveying the importance of these values to foreign companies, for example through information campaigns, initiatives, and events, is important to improve the contribution of foreign companies on diversity and inclusion. Another policy consideration involves giving priority to investments by foreign companies that exhibit a commitment to promoting inclusion among vulnerable workers. This can be achieved, for instance, by integrating diversity objectives into existing investment incentive programs.

1.2.4. FDI has the potential to accelerate the green transition in Canada

Canada has an ambitious plan to reduce the economy's net emissions to zero by 2050. As economic activity in Canada remains carbon- and energy-intensive, a plan to mitigate the impact of climate change on the most vulnerable population groups and to significantly reduce emissions will be necessary to honour international climate commitments. Foreign investors can play a key role in Canada's green transition by investing in low- and zero -emission technologies and transferring knowledge and technologies to domestic companies through supply chain relationships, market interactions and labour mobility.

In recent years, the country has made progress in phasing out coal-fired power while expanding renewable energy capacity, generating more than 80% of its electricity from non-emitting sources. However, the Canadian economy remains carbon-intensive due to oil and gas extraction, road transport and residential heating, which still account for 61% of Canada's greenhouse gas emissions. Electrification of key sectors such as transport, buildings and industry, and the upgrade of the electricity grid will be crucial for Canada to meet its environmental goals. Canada is a global leader in the development and deployment of new low- and zero emission technologies, with potential applications across a wide array of carbon-intensive industries that have been challenging to decarbonise, such as steel, cement, and heavy transport. Further advancement of these technologies will be critical in meeting the objectives of the Paris Agreement.

Foreign direct investment (FDI) can provide the financial and technological resources needed to accelerate Canada's green transition, but FDI in Canada remains concentrated in relatively more carbon-intensive activities compared to domestic investment, especially in mining, chemicals, and pharmaceuticals value chains. Moreover, the stock of FDI in green technology is low compared to other OECD countries and green FDI inflows have been very volatile over the past decade. At the same time, fossil fuels still account for a large share (about 84%) of FDI in the Canadian energy sector, and investments in green R&D are small compared to FDI in other forms of R&D. This indicates that there is still ample scope for improving the contribution of FDI to de-carbonisation in Canada. Nevertheless, the OECD business consultation reveals that foreign companies are more likely to invest in green technology training than domestic ones, contributing to the development of the skills needed for the green transition.

References

Crowe, D. et al. (2022), "Population ageing and government revenue: Expected trends and policy considerations to boost revenue", *OECD Economics Department Working Papers, OECD Publishing, Paris* 1737, https://doi.org/10.1787/9ce9e8e3-en. [5]

Financial Times (2023), *FDI Markets: the in-depth crossborder investment monitor from the Financial Time*, https://www.fdimarkets.com/. [18]

Government of Canada (2023), *Net-Zero Emissions by 2050*, https://www.canada.ca/en/services/environment/weather/climatechange/climate-plan/net-zero-emissions-2050.html. [8]

Government of Canada (2022), *Inclusion and respect for diversity*, https://www.international.gc.ca/world-monde/issues_development-enjeux_developpement/human_rights-droits_homme/inclusion_respect.aspx?lang=eng. [25]

Government of Canada (2022), *State of Trade 2021 - A Closer Look at Foreign Direct Investment (FDI)*, https://www.international.gc.ca/transparency-transparence/state-trade-commerce-international/2021.aspx?lang=eng. [16]

IEA (2022), *Canada 2022: Energy Policy Review*, https://www.iea.org/events/canada-2022-energy-policy-review. [9]

OECD (2023), *FDI in Figures. April 2023*, https://www.oecd.org/daf/inv/investment-policy/FDI-in-Figures-April-2023.pdf. [10]

OECD (2023), *FDI Statistics*, https://stats.oecd.org/. [12]

OECD (2023), *National Accounts*, https://stats.oecd.org/. [2]

OECD (2023), *OECD Economic Surveys: Canada 2023*, OECD Publishing, Paris, https://doi.org/10.1787/7eb16f83-en. [1]

OECD (2023), *OECD Regional Database*, https://www.oecd.org/regional/regional-policy/regionalstatisticsandindicators.htm. [20]

OECD (2023), *Trade in goods and services*, https://stats.oecd.org/. [14]

OECD (2022), *Business Consultation on Sustainability Practices in Canada*. [26]

OECD (2022), *FDI Qualities Policy Toolkit*, OECD Publishing, Paris, https://doi.org/10.1787/7ba74100-en. [22]

OECD (2022), "The geography of foreign investment in OECD member countries: How investment promotion agencies support regional development", *OECD Business and Finance Policy Papers, OECD Publishing, Paris* 20, https://doi.org/10.1787/1f293a25-en. [19]

OECD (2021), *Economic Policy Reforms 2021: Going for Growth: Shaping a Vibrant Recovery*, https://doi.org/10.1787/3c796721-en. [6]

OECD (2021), *Global Value Chains: Efficiency and Risks in the Context of COVID-19*, https://www.oecd.org/coronavirus/policy-responses/global-value-chains-efficiency-and-risks-in-the-context-of-covid-19-67c75fdc/. [13]

OECD (2021), *OECD Investment Policy Reviews: Thailand*, OECD Investment Policy Reviews, OECD Publishing, Paris, https://doi.org/10.1787/c4eeee1c-en. [23]

OECD (2021), *The Impact of Regulation on International Investment in Finland*, OECD Publishing, Paris, https://doi.org/10.1787/b1bf8bee-en. [24]

OECD (2020), *Preparing for the Future of Work in Canada*, OECD Reviews on Local Job Creation, OECD Publishing, Paris, https://doi.org/10.1787/05c1b185-en. [4]

OECD (2020), *Workforce Innovation to Foster Positive Learning Environments in Canada*, Getting Skills Right, OECD Publishing, Paris, https://doi.org/10.1787/a92cf94d-en. [3]

OECD (2019), *FDI Qualities Indicators: Measuring the sustainable development impacts of investment*, https://www.oecd.org/fr/investissement/fdi-qualities-indicators.htm. [21]

Statistics Canada (2023), *Activities of multinational enterprises in Canada, Canadian and foreign multinationals, by province, sector and industry, establishment level*, https://www150.statcan.gc.ca/t1/tbl1/en/tv.action?pid=3610062001&pickMembers%5B0%5D=2.3&pickMembers%5B1%5D=3.2&cubeTimeFrame.startYear=2014&cubeTimeFrame.endYear=2018&referencePeriods=20140101%2C20180101. [15]

Statistics Canada (2022), *Immigrants make up the largest share of the population in over 150 years and continue to shape who we are as Canadians*, https://www150.statcan.gc.ca/n1/daily-quotidien/221026/dq221026a-eng.htm. [7]

Statistics Canada (2022), *Table 36-10-0009-01 International investment position, Canadian direct investment abroad and foreign direct investment in Canada, by North American Industry Classification System (NAICS) and region, annual (x 1,000,000)*, https://doi.org/10.25318/3610000901-eng. [17]

UNCTAD (2007), *World Investment Report 2007*, https://unctad.org/system/files/official-document/wir2007_en.pdf. [11]

Annex 1.A. The OECD business consultation on sustainability practices: methodology and summary statistics

A consultation on the sustainable practices of Canadian and foreign companies operating in Canada was conducted by the OECD in collaboration with Invest in Canada from October to November 2022. The consultation consisted of an online questionnaire (30 questions) and a 30-minute telephone interview. 24 Canadian and 33 foreign companies participated in the consultation. A foreign company is a company resident in Canada of which an investor resident in another economy owns, directly or indirectly, 10% or more of the voting power.

Some companies were contacted from a list provided by Invest in Canada. Others were contacted through Business at OECD (BIAC), chambers of commerce, foreign embassies and consulates, trade and investment offices in Canada, as well as directly through companies' contact information available on their websites (via e-mail or telephone). The companies were selected taking into account various criteria, in particular a diverse selection of size, sector, geographical distribution within Canada and, in the case of foreign companies, their country of origin and date of entry into the Canadian market.

The questionnaire is structured in five sections:

1. **General information:** it includes questions on the company name, sector, location, ownership and total annual turnover;
2. **Employment, job quality and skills**: it includes questions on number of employees, cost of labour, type of contract (e.g. full time permanent, part-time), skills distribution and training practices; the skills distribution included three levels:
    a. High-skilled: employees whose tasks require extensive theoretical and technical knowledge. For example, engineers, lawyers, technicians.
    b. Mid-skilled: employees whose tasks require some level of skills and training. For example, clerical support workers, sales workers, machine operators and assemblers.
    c. Low-skilled: employees whose tasks require no specific skills and training. For example, agricultural forestry and fishery labourers, construction workers.
3. **Diversity and inclusion**: it includes questions on vulnerable employees (women, Indigenous peoples, immigrants and foreign workers/students, and people with disabilities), such as numbers of employees among these groups of workers, number of managers, number of employees who received training, and on the diversity and inclusive workplace practices of companies;
4. **Carbon footprint and energy transition**: it includes questions on sustainability staff, green training, environmental certifications, strategic objectives and targets, recent environmental audits, and recent adoptions of various environmental measures;
5. **Trade, GVC integration, productivity and innovation**: it includes questions on recent innovation activities, partnerships with domestic firms on joint product development and/or service provision (including on R&D partnerships, size of partner firm, and staff exchanges), and supplier training;

Companies were sent an e-mail invitation to participate in the consultation and a link to the online questionnaire. After completing the survey, companies were invited to participate in a 30-minute telephone interview whose objective was to gain a deeper perspective of their practices and activities in these areas of sustainable development. Interview participants included CEOs and general managers, as well as corporate heads of sustainability, communications, innovation, accounting and human resources.

Since the sample of companies surveyed is not representative of the entire population of Canadian and foreign companies operating in Canada, the analysis and indicators derived from the survey must be interpreted with care. Information is used in the report to add anecdotal evidence and to supplement the analysis of quantitative information from official statistical sources, especially in areas where statistical information tends to be scarce or difficult to access.

Most of the companies surveyed operate in the manufacturing and service sectors (Annex Figure 1.A.1, Panel A). Within manufacturing there are companies in the pharmaceutical, automotive, other transport, chemical, food and electronics sectors. Companies in services operate in professional and administrative services, retail trade, information and communication, and financial and insurance activities. In the mining and quarrying sector, there are companies involved in oil and gas and metal extraction. Companies in the energy sector deal with green energy and waste management, while the construction sector includes two companies that are involved in infrastructure and construction. Finally, the company in the agricultural sector is an agro-technical company.

Annex Figure 1.A.1. Distribution of firms by sector, province and origin

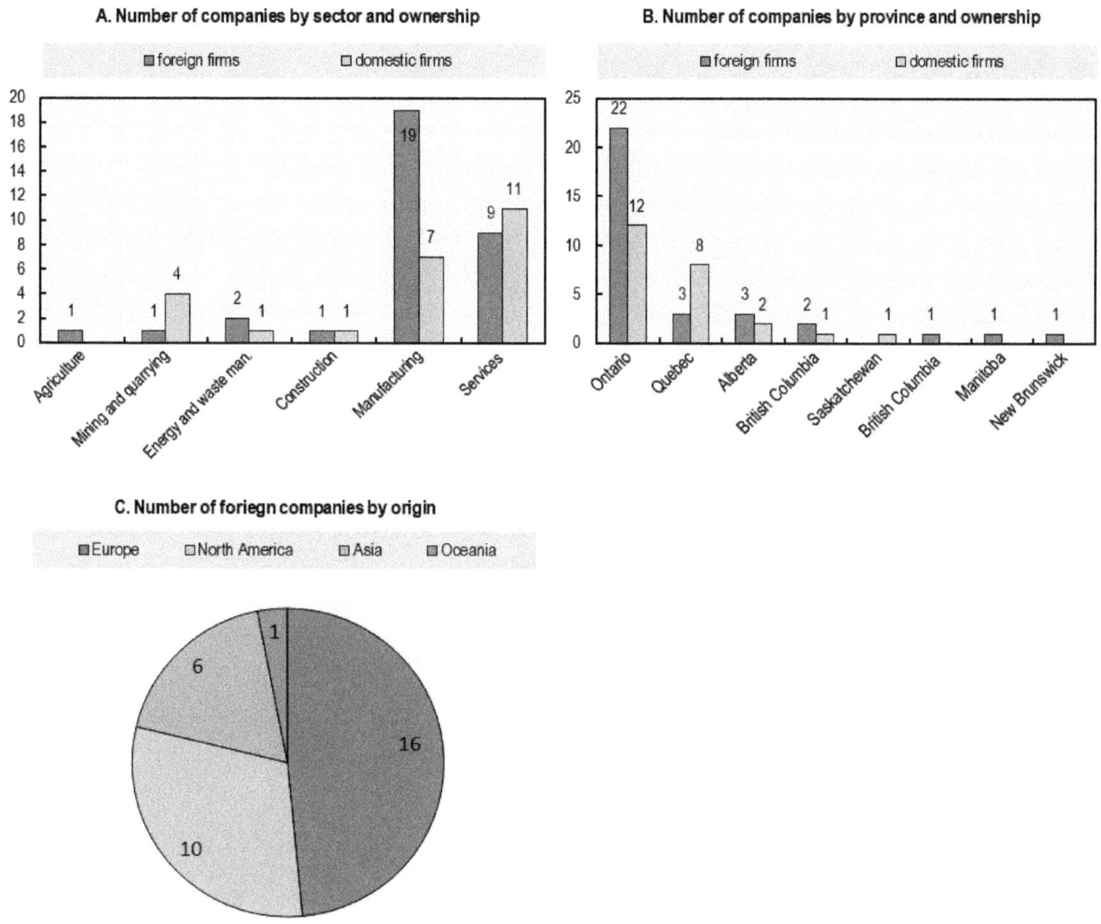

Source: OECD (2022[26])

Most of the firms which participated in the consultation are headquartered or have their Canadian subsidiary in Ontario (Annex Figure 1.A.1, Panel B). Quebec, Alberta and British Columbia, are the second, third and fourth more represented provinces, respectively. Only a minority of companies are located in Saskatchewan, Manitoba, and New Brunswick. Approximately half of foreign companies are headquartered in Europe (Austria, Denmark, Finland, France, Germany, Ireland, the Netherlands, Spain, and the UK). Ten companies come from north America, seven of which from Canada's largest FDI contributor, the US. A smaller number of companies are from Asia and Oceania, namely India, Japan, Korea, New Zealand, Taiwan, and the United Arab Emirates.

Notes

[1] Foreign workers include immigrants (i.e. people born outside Canada with permanent resident status), and temporary foreign workers (i.e. people on temporary work or study visas or who have applied for refugee status). Not all foreign workers can be considered 'vulnerable' workers and some of them may be highly educated and have well-paid jobs.

2 The contribution of FDI to productivity, innovation and integration in GVCs

This chapter examines the contribution of foreign direct investment to productivity, innovation and the integration of the Canadian economy into global value chains. It analyses productivity differences between foreign and domestic firms and the extent of value chain linkages between foreign multinationals and Canadian firms, an important channel of productivity spillovers. It also assesses the role of foreign firms in innovation and the local capacity of domestic firms, particularly small and medium-sized enterprises to benefit from the diffusion of knowledge and technology brought by FDI.

2.1. Summary of key findings

Foreign direct investment (FDI), particularly greenfield investment (i.e. new establishments by foreign companies), is an important driver of Canada's trade and integration into global value chains (GVCs). In Canada, greenfield FDI is concentrated in a small number of highly export-oriented sectors, including mining and energy, ICT and electronics and transport equipment. The integration of the Canadian economy in GVCs is limited, however. Since much of the FDI Canada attracts, particularly greenfield investment, is export-oriented, multinational enterprises (MNEs) account for a sizable share of Canada's trade and integration in GVCs. Foreign MNEs are responsible for 57% of export value and are more involved in GVCs than domestic firms, particularly in terms of backward linkages.

Canadian labour productivity has lagged behind that of a number of other OECD economies such as the United States, Australia, Switzerland and Germany. To some extent, low productivity growth over the past decades is attributed to lagging investments, poor innovation performance and constraints in the business environment. Affiliates of foreign MNEs established in Canada appear to be more productive than domestic players in most sectors of the economy. This foreign productivity premium is particularly higher in finance and insurance, construction, and utilities, where foreign firms are 50% more productive than domestic firms. The scale of foreign firms' productivity premium also varies depending on the capacities of domestic firms, with Canadian multinationals exhibiting narrower performance gaps than Canadian non-multinationals as a result of their greater access to trade networks, advanced technologies and innovation.

Affiliates of foreign MNEs in Canada are on average more R&D-intensive than domestic firms. The results of an OECD business consultation conducted for this study show that foreign firms are considerably more engaged in innovative business activities, including product and process innovations as well as joint product development with other firms. Differences in R&D intensity between foreign MNEs and domestic firms are particularly large in professional, scientific and technical sectors and in information and cultural industries. In the past five years, R&D investments made up a large part of greenfield FDI in creative industries (91%), financial services (42%), and ICT and electronics (34%).

Sell and buy linkages between affiliates of foreign MNEs and domestic firms can strengthen the potential for productivity spillovers, by facilitating domestic firms' participation in GVCs and the transfer of knowledge and technology. Domestic buy linkages exist if foreign MNEs source intermediate inputs and services from domestic firms, while sell linkages emerge when foreign MNEs supply intermediates that are further processed by domestic firms or sell final products. Foreign affiliates established in Canada source a sizeable share of their inputs from the domestic market, in particular from domestic non-MNEs, which account for approximately 40% of total inputs. Similar results hold for other large open economies such as the United States, France, and Italy, with large domestic markets for intermediate inputs. Moreover, more than 60% of the production of foreign affiliates in Canada feeds back into domestic value chains, of which 22% is used as an input by domestic non-MNEs.

For productivity and innovation spillovers to materialise, domestic firms, particularly small and medium-sized enterprises (SMEs), should have the necessary capacities to become successful suppliers and partners of foreign MNEs and absorb the knowledge, skills and technologies that FDI brings to the host economy. Canadian SMEs are on average more engaged in product and business process innovation than many other peer economies such as Australia, the United States, Japan and the European Union as a whole. Among Canadian firms, more R&D capacity is also found in smaller enterprises, which represent 21% of R&D expenditures and 25% of R&D personnel. However, the digital capacities of Canadian SMEs appear to lag behind that of peer OECD economies, including with regard to the use of Artificial Intelligence (AI) and cloud computing services as well as the provision of ICT training to their employees, pointing towards potential weaknesses in fostering strategic partnerships with technology-intensive investors.

Policy considerations

- **Policy efforts to diversify the type of FDI that Canada attracts towards high-productivity and R&D-intensive sectors and activities could continue and be scaled up further.** In Canada, only a few sectors are reported to attract the majority of FDI, which is concentrated in the management of companies and enterprises (where investments may be ultimately redistributed to other sectors), finance, trade and mining and oil and gas extraction.
- **Beyond targeting and prioritising new R&D-intensive investments, Canada's government agencies responsible for investment and innovation promotion could enhance collaboration to facilitate knowledge-intensive investments from established foreign multinational enterprises (MNEs).** Encouraging expansion by existing investors is a prevalent entry mode for R&D-focused FDI. These foreign MNEs could benefit from developing partnerships with local universities and applied research institutions, collaborating with science and technology parks, accessing qualified R&D talent, and engaging in entrepreneurial networks and open innovation programs, including innovation testing and piloting infrastructures/platforms.
- **Canada could consider revising market access restrictions to FDI where these limits the positive impacts of international investment on productivity growth, innovation, and integration in GVCs.** Currently, Canada is ranked the fourth most restrictive economy in the OECD according to the 2020 OECD FDI Regulatory Restrictiveness Index. Fewer restrictions for investments in more productive, innovative, and knowledge-intensive sectors can increase the direct impact that foreign firms have through their own activities on sectoral and aggregate productivity growth. Openness to FDI may not only improve productivity in industries that get market access, but also those in downstream sectors that benefit from potentially better access to high quality inputs and services domestically.
- **Comprehensive supplier development programmes in line with investors' needs could be designed to strengthen the productive and innovative capacities of Canadian firms, in particular SMEs.** Although supplier linkages between foreign and domestic firms in Canada are common, Canadian SMEs exhibit a low adoption of advanced technologies as well as digital tools and processes, which may limit the extent of collaboration with foreign investors, and therefore the potential for knowledge and technology spillovers.

2.2. The contribution of FDI to trade and integration in GVCs

While exports are important for the Canadian economy, its focus on the early production stages of the supply chain and closer to raw materials, has constrained its deeper integration into global value chains (GVCs). The spread of production across multiple countries through GVCs can include more firms in international trade, leading to productivity enhancements and access to knowledge, technology and skills. FDI, in turn, has the potential to drive improvements in exporting and GVC participation. Foreign multinationals are often more intensive exporters that have positive impacts on other firms' exporting though their business connections and spillover effects on domestic firm competitiveness. The presence of multinational firms can strengthen the host economy's international connections and market linkages. Domestic firm exporting can also be supported through foreign investments bringing enhanced productivity, innovations and new technologies, and improved access to finance (Kastratović, 2020[1]).

2.2.1. International trade and investment have shaped the Canadian economy, but integration in GVCs remains limited

Natural resources and proximity to the US market make Canada an attractive destination for foreign investment. However, relative to GDP, inward and outward stocks of FDI both declined following the global financial crisis, recovering only gradually in the late 2010s and with greater recent growth in outward net FDI stocks (Figure 2.1). Relative to GDP, Canada's inward net FDI stocks are the 11th largest in the OECD area and are greater than those of several other large economies. This is despite the comparative restrictiveness of FDI policies; Canada was ranked the fourth most restrictive economy in the OECD in the 2020 FDI Regulatory Restrictiveness Index (Figure 2.2)

Under the Investment Canada Act, investments in certain sectors of strategic importance for national security are screened to ensure that they do not have a negative impact on critical infrastructure. While screening mechanisms are increasingly common among OECD economies and serve legitimate policy objectives related to national security, other market access barriers such as foreign ownership restrictions may hamper Canada's investment performance. Such restrictions are relatively highest in network sectors (e.g. media and telecommunications) and air transport. For instance, in telecommunications both ownership and board composition must be at least 80% Canadian in operators with more than 10% of market share (OECD, 2023[2]). Access to public procurement contracts is also limited to regional trade agreement partners and signatories to the WTO's Government Procurement Agreement (OECD, 2022[3]). The need for such restrictions should be evaluated with a view to removing those that have large economic costs and limit the Canadian economy's potential to attract productivity-enhancing investment.

Figure 2.1. Inward net FDI stocks as a share of GDP in selected economies, 2005-2021

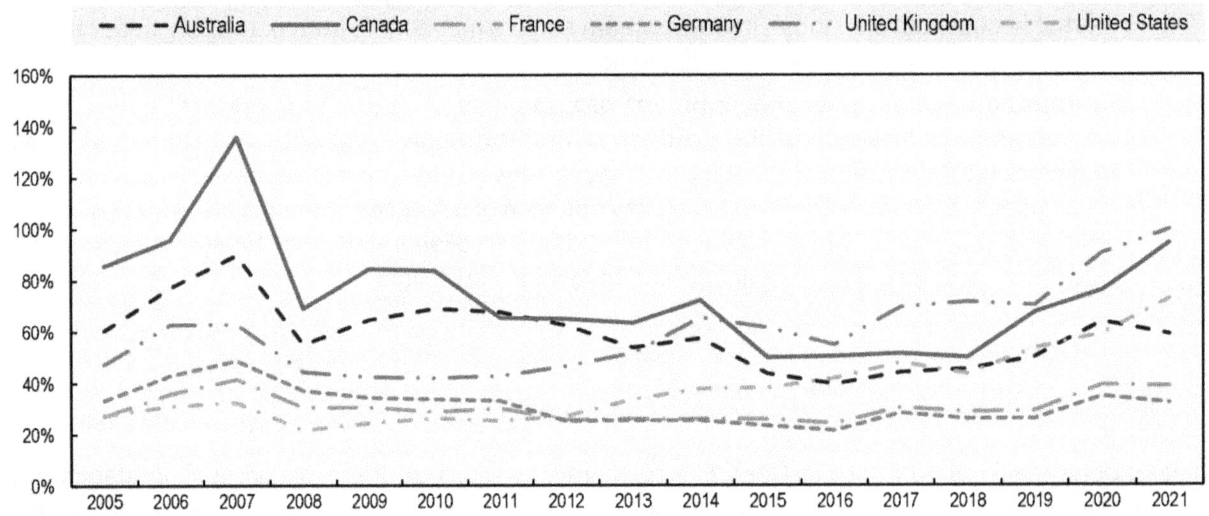

Source: OECD FDI Statistics (2023[4]), https://stats.oecd.org/

Figure 2.2. FDI Regulatory Restrictiveness Index, 2020

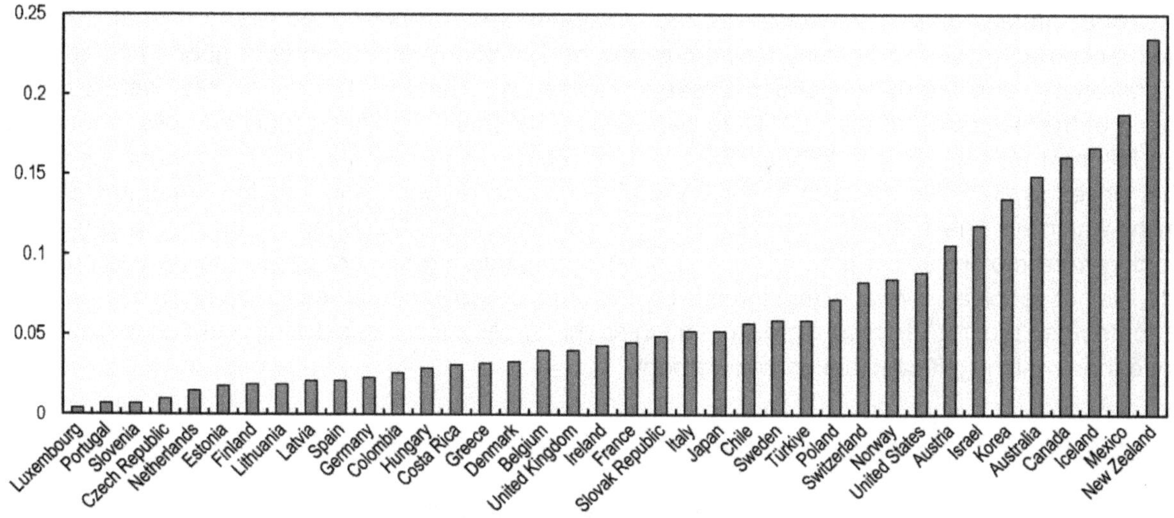

Note: The FDI Regulatory Restrictiveness Index measures statutory restrictions on foreign direct investment on a scale from 0 (open) to 1 (closed).
Source: OECD FDI Regulatory Restrictiveness Index (2023), https://stats.oecd.org/Index.aspx?datasetcode=FDIINDEX

Investment inflows and trade performance are closely connected; Greenfield FDI, i.e. new establishments by foreign companies, are relatively concentrated in a small number of highly export-oriented sectors, with much of it originating in the United States. Over 2003-22, most greenfield FDI came from the United States (45%), followed by the Netherlands (14%) and France (6%) and was directed towards projects in mining and energy (34%), ICT and electronics (17%) and transport equipment (10%) (Financial Times, 2023[5]). These sectors were among the more important contributors to the rapid expansion of Canadian exporting in the 1990s, on the back of deepening trade with the United States under new trade agreements. The US accounts for three quarters of exports and Canada's exports are among the least diversified by market in the OECD. At 0.57, its export destination Hirschman-Herfindahl Index has been quite consistent over the past decade and is not surprisingly exceeded only by Mexico's (0.61) (Figure 2.3.).

Figure 2.3. Hirschman-Herfindahl Index by goods export destination for OECD countries, 2021

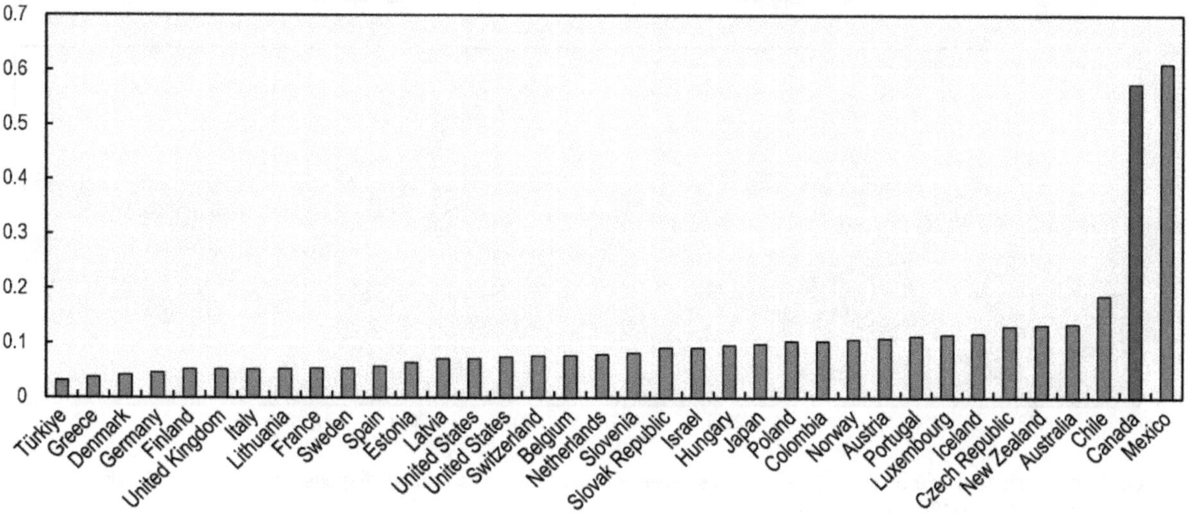

Note: The index varies from 0 to 1, with higher values indicating less export diversification.
Source: Authors' calculation based on the OECD Bilateral Trade in Goods database (2023[6]), https://stats.oecd.org/

Exports as a share of GDP have since declined from the peak of 44% in 2000 and are below that of most other OECD economies, but above the export share in some of the larger advanced economies – including the United States, Japan, Australia, United Kingdom and France (Figure 2.4., Panel A). Export performance has proven to be fairly resilient to recent disruptions with exports of goods and services in 2022 gradually returning to pre-pandemic levels (Figure 2.4., Panel B). Energy exports were particularly affected at the beginning of the COVID-19 pandemic. The share of mineral fuels and oils in total export value fell from 22% in 2019 to 18% in 2020, before rebounding to 24% in 2021. Stronger demand and higher prices in 2022, an effect of post-COVID19 economic rebound and inflation pressures stemming from the war in Ukraine, further boosted exporting through much of 2022. Supply chain disruptions affecting exporting from motor vehicle production and other manufacturing sectors appear to be easing as well. While it is not yet clear to what extent foreign-owned firms directly contributed to this recovery, the sectors that contributed most to the recent growth – such as motor vehicle manufacturing and the energy sector – include those with significant foreign involvement.

Figure 2.4. Export performance and trends

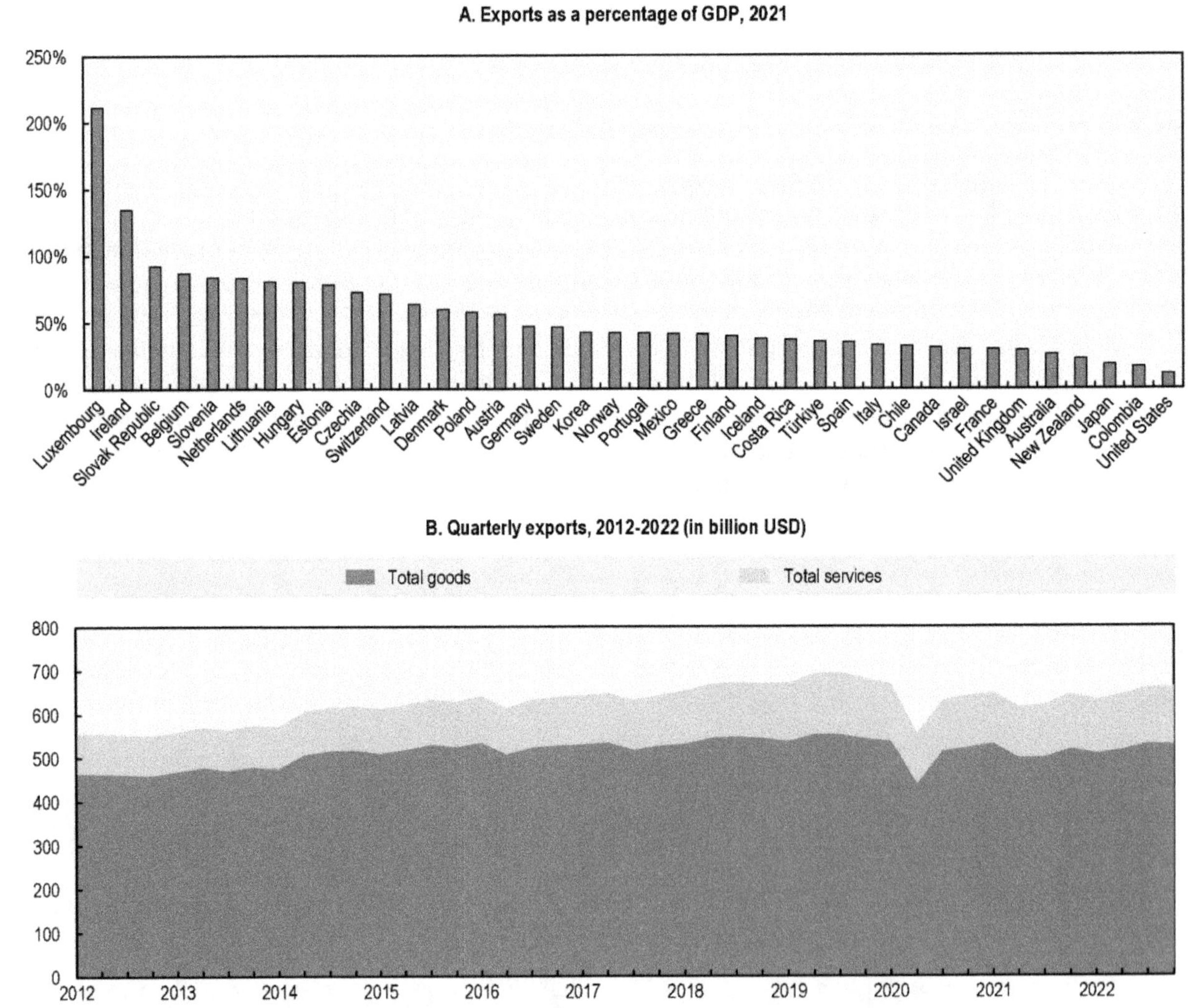

Source: OECD International Trade Statistics (2023[7]), https://stats.oecd.org/; Statistics Canada, Exports and Imports of Goods and Services, (2023[8]), https://doi.org/10.25318/1210013401-eng

While goods are by far the most important element of exports, manufacturing is a less important source of exports than in much of the OECD. Goods account for 82% of total export value. Canadian exports are thus somewhat more service-oriented than Australia's (89% goods exports), but much less service-oriented than the exports of the United States and United Kingdom, where goods represent only 69% and 49%, respectively, of total exports. Most goods exports are from the manufacturing sector (65%), followed by mining and quarrying (23%) and agriculture, forestry and fishing (6%). Canada is thus among the OECD countries whose exports are least reliant on manufacturing. Measured across five major sectors, Canadian goods exports are relatively diversified in their composition; the Hirschman-Herfindahl Index in 2021 was 0.54. Only Colombia (0.38), Turkey (0.39), Chile (0.45), Mexico (0.49) and Australia (0.53) had more diversified exports by sector.

Canada's participation in GVCs has been restrained as a result of its limited manufacturing exporting and reliance on the early production stages of the supply chain. The Canadian economy makes moderate use of imported inputs in producing goods and services for export (backwards participation) and exports few goods and services that are later used in destination countries' exports (forward participation) (Figure 2.5.). In 2018, foreign value added contributed to the 25% total value of Canadian gross exports. This was close to the median of OECD member countries. Domestic value added accounted for just 15% of re-exported goods, however; one of the lowest rates among OECD members. A large share of Canadian exports is ultimately destined for the United States's domestic market, limiting the scale of forward GVC linkages through the export of intermediate products. To the extent that this form of GVC participation has deepened in the past decade, it has mostly been driven by sector change and the growing importance of the mining sector in providing materials for value chains' early stages. Meanwhile, the fragmentation of automotive supply chains has increased Canada's backward linkages in GVCs (de Backer and Miroudot, 2016[9]).

The limited integration in GVCs means that Canada may miss out opportunities for productivity growth and innovation. Productivity spillovers may occur from both backward and forward participation in GVCs, by enabling countries to use inputs that are not available in the domestic economy or that have an advantage in terms of price or quality; but also by accessing technology and knowledge brought from export destinations (Criscuolo and Timmis, 2017[10]). Further GVC integration could be particularly important for Canada's export performance by developing comparative advantages in selected stages of the production process rather than having to master the production of entire products.

Figure 2.5. Backward and forward participation in global value chains by OECD economies, 2018

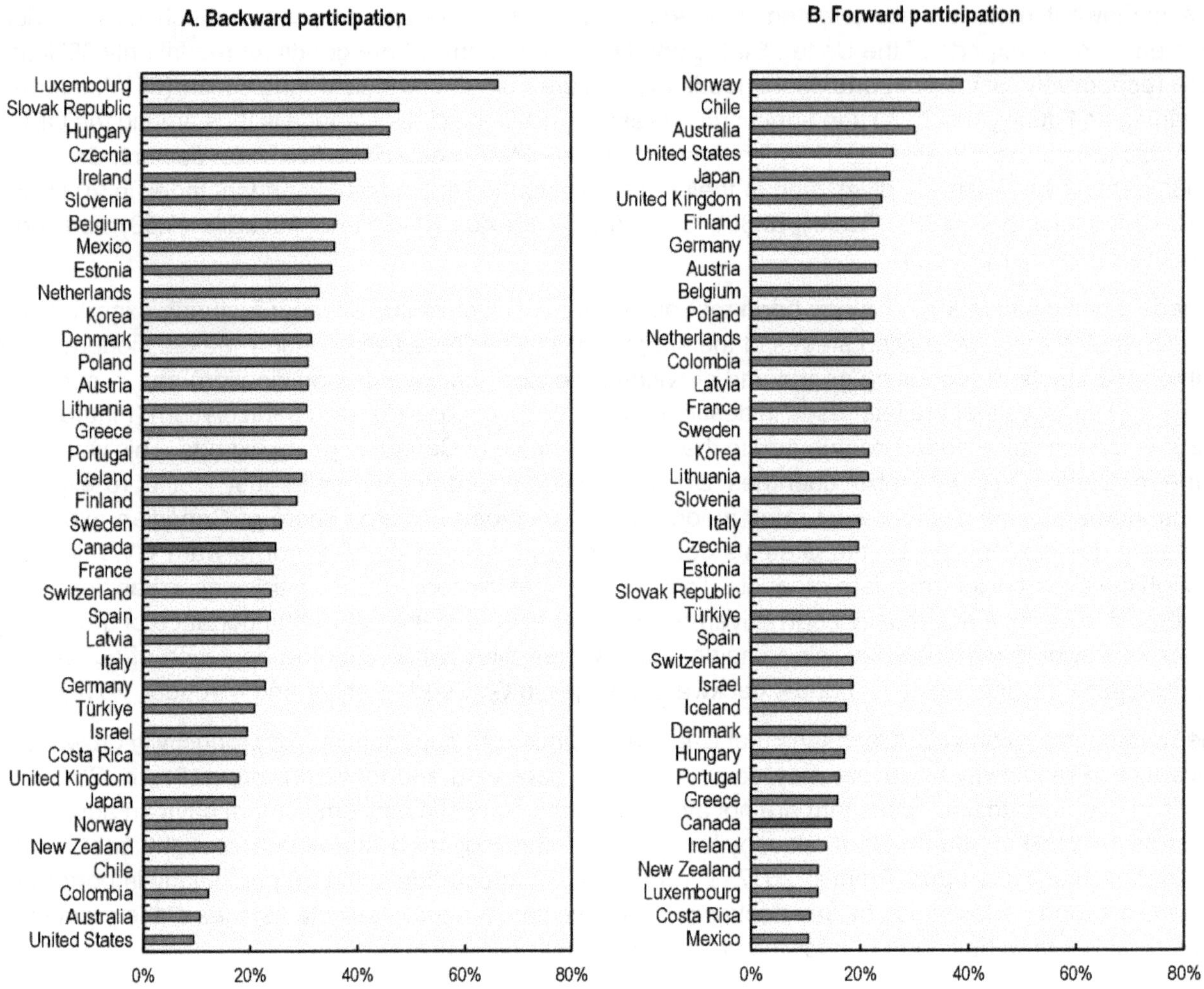

Note: Backward participation in GVCs is defined as the foreign value added share of gross exports. Forward participation in GVCs is defined as the domestic foreign value added share of foreign gross exports.
Source: OECD Trade in Value Added (TiVA) Database (2023[11]), https://stats.oecd.org/

2.2.2. Foreign firms play a major role in driving Canada's export performance

FDI strengthens Canada's export capacities. Foreign firms are highly involved in trade, directly boosting Canadian exporting. They also indirectly contribute to exporting by domestic firms by strengthening their international connections and enhancing competitiveness. Foreign multinationals are responsible for 57% of Canadian export value, including 59% of merchandise exports and 48% of commercial service exports, despite accounting for just 30% of operating revenues in the corporate sector (which includes foreign and Canadian multinational enterprises, as well as non-multinational enterprises). Not surprisingly, much of this comes from subsidiaries of US firms, which accounted for 48% of the value of merchandise and commercial service exports by foreign MNEs in 2020.

Relatedly, exports are also relatively more important to foreign firms. In 2020, merchandise and commercial service exports represented 25% of the operating revenue of foreign MNEs, compared with just 12% and 4% for Canadian multinational and non-multinational enterprises, respectively (Figure 2.6.). All three firm categories increased their export orientation over the previous decade; this share increased by 1.5 percentage points for foreign multinationals, by 1.0 percentage points for Canadian multinationals and by 0.7% for non-multinationals. Goods exports are the largest component of total exports across all three firm categories, but are relatively more important for foreign MNEs, for which they represent 85% of exports. In comparison, merchandise exports account for 82% of the total of Canadian multinationals and 77% of non-multinationals.

Foreign multinationals do not appear to contribute much to export sector diversification. Export values by sector are similar to those of the Canadian economy as a whole, led by manufacturing (67% of foreign firms' exports and 62% of Canadian merchandise exports); mining, quarrying, and oil and gas extraction (19% and 17%, respectively); and wholesale trade (12% and 15%, respectively) (Figure 2.7.).

Figure 2.6. Merchandise and commercial service exports as a share of operating revenue

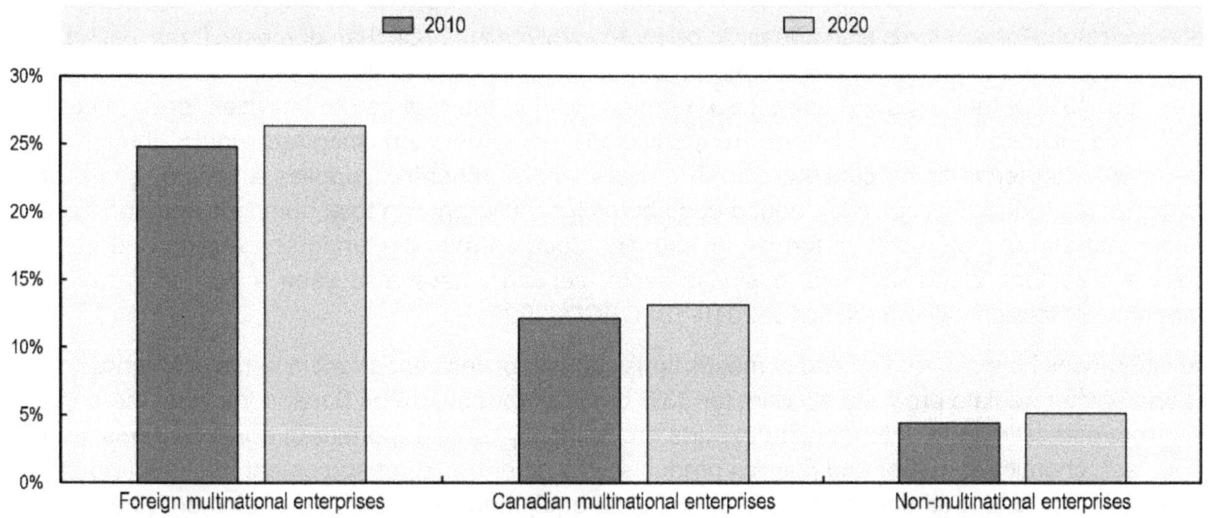

Source: Statistics Canada (2023[12]), Activities of Multinational Enterprises in Canada, https://doi.org/10.25318/3610060401-eng

Figure 2.7. Exports as a share of operating revenue in selected sectors, 2020

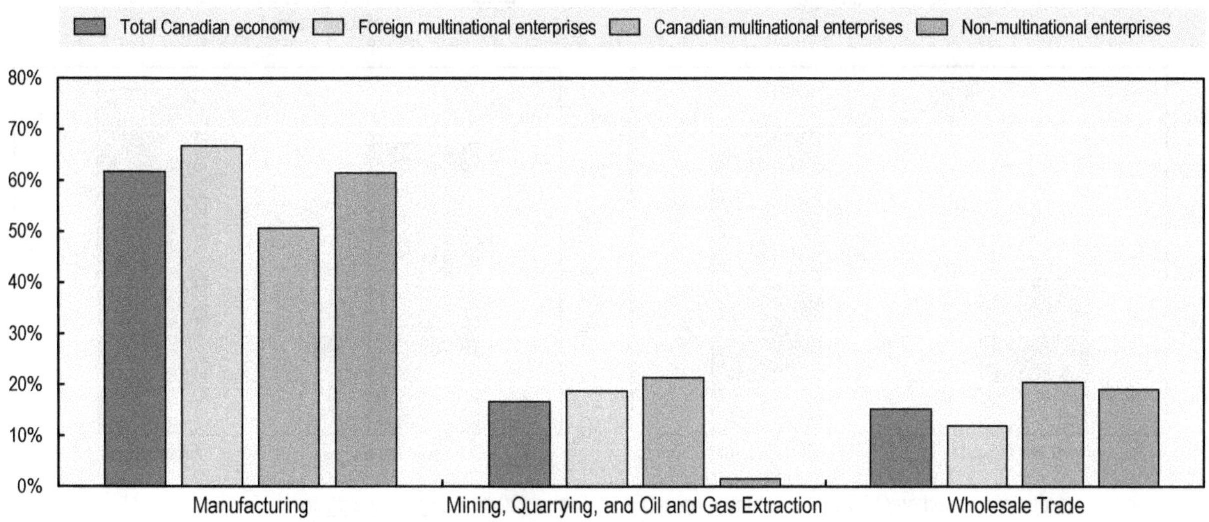

Source: Statistics Canada (2023[12]), Activities of Multinational Enterprises in Canada, https://doi.org/10.25318/3610060401-eng

While foreign firms have a particularly strong presence in a number of export-intensive sectors such as manufacturing, these businesses are more trade-oriented than domestic firms across much of the economy. Foreign firms are the most active exporters in most sectors. Only in wholesale trade, retail trade, real estate and rental and leasing, health care and social assistance, and other (non-public administration) services are Canadian multinationals more export-oriented. Non-multinational enterprises are the most export-oriented in finance and insurance, though foreign-owned firms account for just 1.2% of total exports from this sector. The export performance of foreign firms also does not appear to be just a result of size differences. Larger businesses are responsible for most exports. Firms with 250 and more employees were responsible for 66% of exports in 2021, despite their accounting for less than half of value added. Foreign firms are not particularly large, however. Foreign multinationals, on average, employed 18% fewer workers than Canadian multinationals in 2020, though this gap has narrowed somewhat from the 23% difference in 2010 (Statistics Canada, 2023[12]).

Not surprisingly, foreign firms also appear to be more involved in GVCs than domestic firms, particularly in terms of backward linkages. Foreign firms in Canada import 29% of their inputs, while domestic firms import just 15% of their inputs (Figure 2.8.). Foreign firms in the real estate activities, basic metals, and rubber and plastics products sectors are particularly dependent on imported inputs, though foreign investment also tends to be concentrated in sectors where importing supplies a greater share of final demand in Canada.[1] Foreign value added contributes less to supplying total domestic demand in several sectors that attract high levels of foreign investment, such as manufacturing and mining and quarrying. These two sectors, along with total business sector services, have also seen a decline in the relative importance of foreign value added over 2010-18 (OECD, 2023[11]).

The differences between foreign and domestic firms seem to be less important in terms of forward linkages. Exports of intermediate products account for 33% of the output of foreign firms; somewhat more than the 28% from domestic firms. Intermediate exports are relatively more important to domestic firms in utilities industries[2], chemicals, rubber and plastics products; and other transport equipment and to foreign firms in accommodation and food service activities; electrical equipment; and arts, entertainment and recreation and other service activities.

Figure 2.8. Imported inputs and exports of intermediate goods by firm ownership, 2016

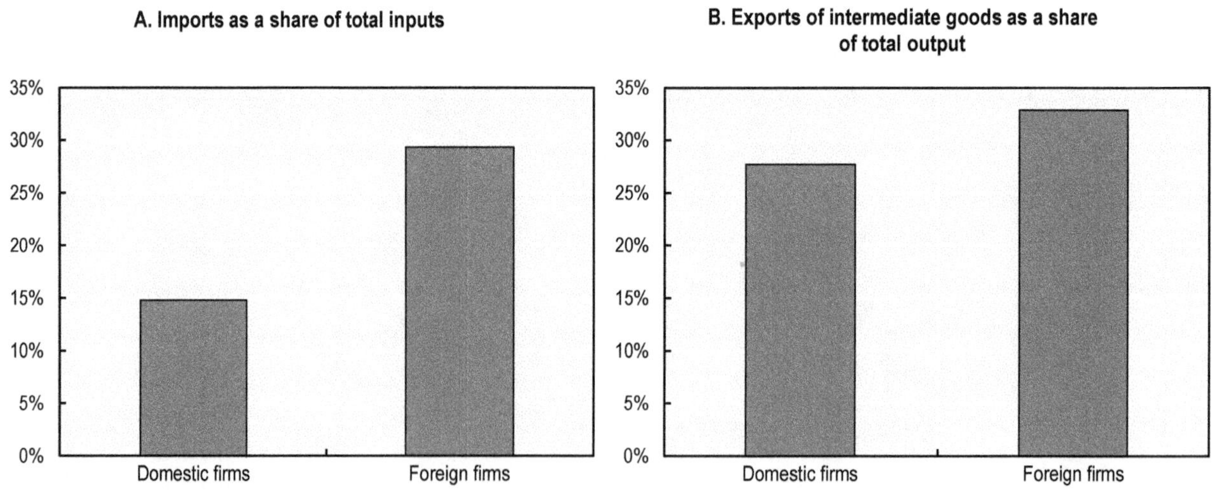

Source: Authors' calculations based on OECD Inter-Country Input-Output Tables (2023[13]), http://oe.cd/icio

2.3. Productivity trends and FDI spillovers

FDI inflows can be associated with improved productivity, which is needed to boost Canada's growth prospects. Not only are foreign firms typically more efficient than average in host countries, and thus direct contributors to productivity growth, their presence can indirectly boost productivity among domestic firms where knowledge and technology spillovers are fostered (OECD, 2019[14]). Domestic firms that supply foreign entrants can see productivity gains through their improved access to product and service quality standards, knowledge, technology and finance. Other firms may benefit from imitating more productive peers or by hiring workers that have gained new knowledge and skills through their work with foreign and internationally-oriented firms (OECD, 2022[15]). Realising this potential in Canada depends in large part on the establishment of stronger linkages between firms. The type, motives, origin and sector of the investment, as well as the scale and structure of the investing firm all affect the local embeddedness of foreign firms and the extent to which the host economy can benefit from productivity spillovers (OECD, 2022[15]).

2.3.1. Canada's labour productivity growth continues to underperform relative to leading OECD economies

Although Canada's labour productivity has trailed behind that of the United States and several other advanced economies like Australia, the United Kingdom, France, and Germany, there is significant potential for improvement through strategic investments and collaborations. According to OECD (2023[2]), productivity growth has been restrained by insufficient capital deepening and investment by firms. Despite these challenges, Canada's labour productivity, at USD 62 per hour worked in 2021, is close to the median among OECD countries (Figure 2.9). While this level is lower than that of the United States and most European countries, and notably below the G7 average of USD 74, it underscores the opportunity for Canada to leverage foreign direct investment (FDI) to enhance productivity.

Canada's recent labour productivity growth has been relatively modest, averaging just 1.0% over 2012-2021, ranking 21st among 37 OECD member countries with comparable data. Factors such as depressed oil prices and limited investment in the sector during 2014-2022 have contributed to this trend. However, Canada has the potential to overcome these challenges with targeted FDI that fosters innovation, improves market efficiency, and addresses barriers such as inter-provincial trade differences in technical standards and regulations, along with limitations on labour mobility. By strategically leveraging FDI to enhance innovation, address regulatory barriers, and stimulate investment, Canada can unlock its economic potential and strengthen its competitiveness on the global stage.

The 2023 OECD Economic Survey of Canada highlights the need to accelerate reduction in internal barriers to trade and investment, which may have large economic costs and limit the efficiency and scope of labour markets (OECD, 2023[2]). A wide range of policy actions can potentially increase business sector productivity, including improvements in infrastructure, reforms to improve vocational education and skills development, cutting red tape in setting up businesses and strengthening competition law and regulation. As seen in Section 2.2.1, fewer restrictions for investments in more productive, innovative and knowledge-intensive sectors (e.g. telecommunications, information technology, professional and technical services) can increase the direct impact that foreign firms have through their own activities on sectoral and aggregate productivity growth (OECD, 2022[15]). Openness to FDI may not only affect productivity in industries that get market access, but also those in downstream sectors that benefit from potentially better access to high quality inputs and services domestically.

Figure 2.9. Labour productivity in OECD countries

GDP per hour worked in 2021 and average annual productivity growth in 2012-2021

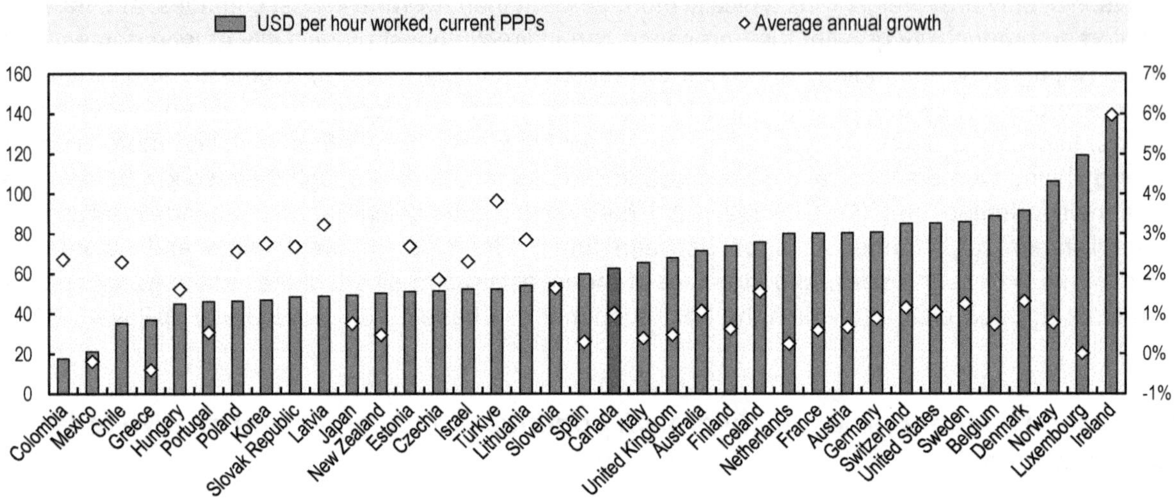

Source: OECD Productivity Statistics Database (2023[16]), https://doi.org/10.1787/pdtvy-data-en

2.3.2. Foreign firms are more productive than domestic firms in most sectors

Overall, foreign firm activity in Canada appears to be concentrated in less productive sectors (Figure 2.10). The two sectors where foreign firms account for the highest shares of value added – other services (except public administration) and accommodation and food services – have the lowest productivity levels. Similarly, professional, scientific and technical services as well as agriculture and manufacturing, which exhibit relatively high foreign firm activity, are found among the lower productivity sectors. By contrast, utilities and mining, oil and gas extraction, information and cultural industries and financial services exhibit lower shares of foreign firm value added but are significantly more productive than the rest of the economy. This concentration of foreign firm activity in low-productivity sectors contributes to foreign firms having, on average, 23% lower value added per worker than their domestic counterparts.

Although additional analysis is required to fully understand the impact of foreign firm activity on sectoral and overall labour productivity, the concentration of foreign firms in sectors with lower labour productivity levels can be attributed to combination of market entry strategies, sector characteristics and potentially the regulatory landscape. For instance, in certain sectors, foreign firms might focus on activities that don't necessarily leverage high technology or automation, which are typically associated with higher productivity, while in other sectors productivity spillovers from FDI might not be fully realised due to barriers related to workforce skill gaps or incompatible infrastructure. Regulatory environments, trade policies and local competition may also shape the strategic decisions of foreign firms, impacting where and how they invest, and consequently affecting their productivity levels.

Figure 2.10. Foreign firms' share of value added and sector productivity

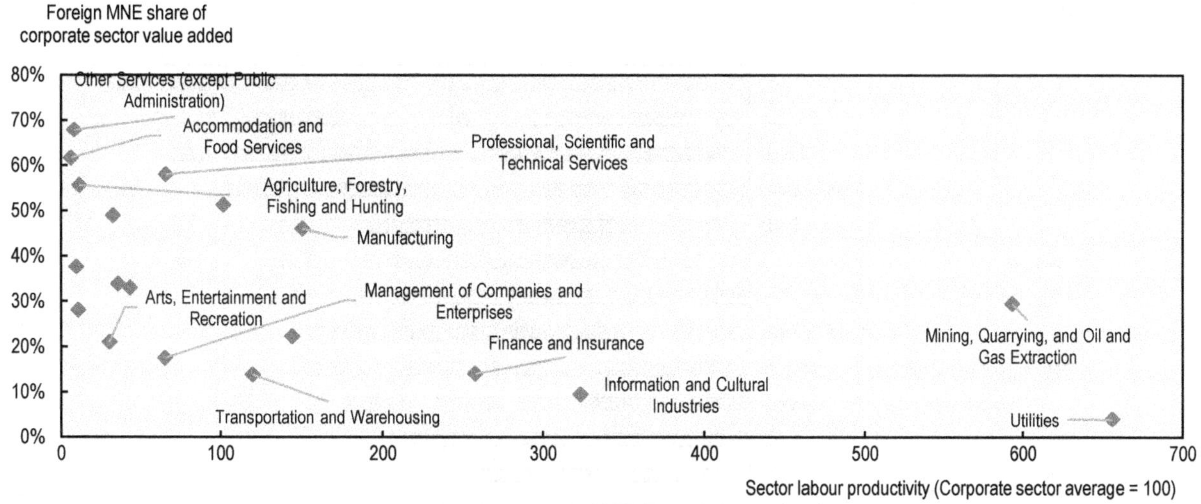

Note: The corporate sector includes foreign multinational enterprises, Canadian multinational enterprises and non-multinational enterprises.
Source: Authors' calculations based on Statistics Canada (2023[12]), Activities of Multinational Enterprises in Canada, https://doi.org/10.25318/3610060401-eng

Analysing productivity gaps at sector level shows that foreign firms are more productive than domestic ones in most sectors (the indicator in Figure 2.11. is above 1 in 11 out of 19 sectors). The foreign premium is highest in the financial and insurance, construction and utilities sectors, where foreign firms are more than 50% more productive than domestic firms. On the other hand, foreign firms are relatively less productive than domestic firms in healthcare and social assistance, real estate, rental and leasing services as well as in the management of companies and enterprises, possibly due to the presence of few highly productive domestic players.

The productivity premium that foreign firms exhibit in most sectors in Canada suggests that knowledge and technology spillovers from FDI could be leveraged on to close productivity gaps in these sectors. These findings reflect evidence from other OECD economies where foreign firms tend to be larger and more technology- and export-intensive, both features associated with higher productivity levels. However, the ability to do so also depends on the capacities of domestic firms to absorb knowledge spillovers, which are assessed in Section 2.4.3.

Figure 2.11. Relative labour productivity of foreign multinational enterprises, 2020

>1 = foreign firms are more productive than domestic firms

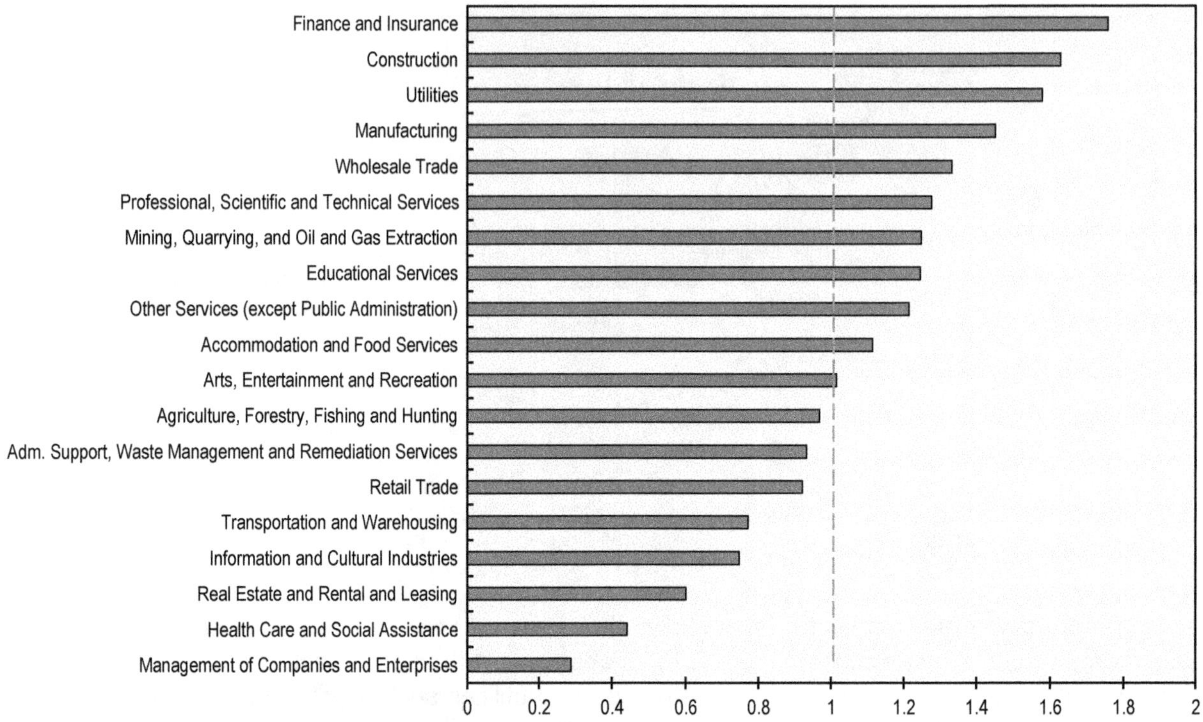

Source: Authors' calculations based on Statistics Canada (2023[12]), Activities of Multinational Enterprises in Canada, https://doi.org/10.25318/3610060401-eng

2.3.3. Foreign firms have built strong linkages with some domestic producers

Since more productive foreign firms may seek to limit potential knowledge and technology spillovers benefitting their competitors, positive effects on domestic firms' productivity are more often found among upstream suppliers (OECD, 2023[17]). Foreign investors usually require better quality inputs from local suppliers and are, therefore, willing to share knowledge and technology with them to encourage the adoption of more efficient business processes (OECD, 2023[17]). The training and on-the-job learning opportunities offered by foreign investors may also be extended to the workforce of domestic firms with which they develop buyer-supplier linkages to ensure efficiency and product quality. Moderate productivity gaps between firms tend to suggest similar levels of technological sophistication and the potential for positive spillovers between them (OECD, 2022[15]). However, foreign firms can also generate negative spillovers through unsustainable or irresponsible practices of their supply chains. If local companies are not quick to adapt, competition from foreign-owned companies may also result in the exit of some domestically-owned firms. Increased competition for talent may also make it more difficult for local companies to recruit skilled workers, particularly in more remote areas where the labour pool is smaller.

In comparison with peer OECD economies, foreign firms in Canada focus primarily on the domestic market for their sourcing of inputs (buy linkages) and the use of their outputs (sell linkages). In 2016, foreign affiliates purchased 19% of their intermediate inputs from other foreign affiliates in the country (Figure 2.12). This is the 5th-highest rate among OECD member countries and nearly double that of the United States (10.7%). Domestic firms still account for a considerable share of supply (about 62%), however, as international sourcing is relatively low. These linkages may provide a channel for knowledge and technology spillovers benefitting smaller Canadian businesses. Non-multinationals are particularly important suppliers. They provide approximately 40% of foreign affiliates' inputs. The extent of domestic buy linkages is on the whole similar to that of other large economies such as the United States, the United Kingdom, France and Italy, and is explained by the relatively larger markets for intermediate goods in these countries. In terms of foreign affiliates' sell linkages, 69% of the output of foreign affiliates is sold to the domestic market. About 22% is bought by domestic non-MNEs, 6% by domestic MNEs and 12% by other foreign firms established locally (Figure 2.13). As with the Canadian economy as a whole, which has limited forward participation in GVCs, relatively little output from foreign affiliates is used in international intermediate consumption.

Figure 2.12. Sourcing structure of foreign affiliates by country, 2016

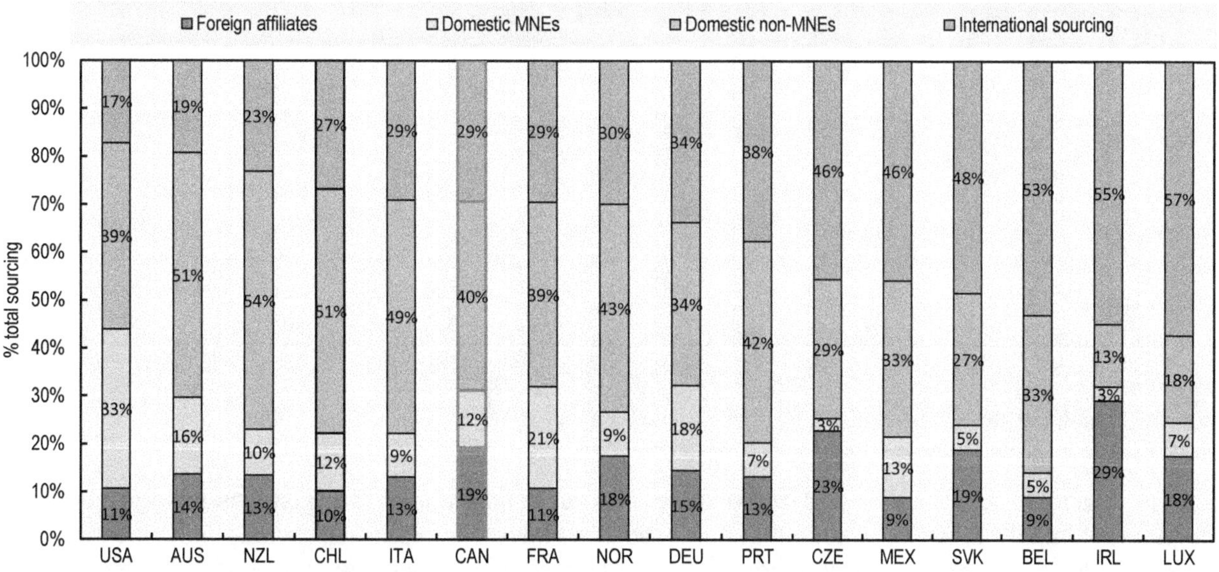

Source: OECD Analytical AMNE Database, (2016[18]), https://www.oecd.org/sti/ind/analytical-amne-database.htm

To some extent, the realisation of productivity spillovers from foreign firms is constrained by the limited supply of intermediate products by domestic firms. Foreign firms are more heavily dependent on imported inputs than their domestic counterparts. Merchandise and commercial services imports by foreign multinational enterprises were worth CAD 395 billion in 2020. This represented 43% of their operating expenses, a considerably higher share than among Canadian multinational enterprises (19.6% of operating expenses) and non-multinational enterprises (16%) (Statistics Canada, 2023[12]). This difference does not appear to be the result of the sectoral composition of foreign investment. In fact, merchandise and service imports as a share of operating expenses are highest in foreign multinationals in all sectors but finance and insurance, where these are highest in non-multinational enterprises.

While foreign firms import a greater share of their inputs than do domestic firms, both groups make similar use of inputs from the Canadian operations of foreign and domestic businesses. Among foreign firms, 73% of non-imported inputs originate in domestic firms, while this share among domestic firms is slightly higher (76%). Domestic firms make up a relatively large share of non-imported inputs in a number of manufacturing sectors, including wood and cork product; food products, beverages and tobacco; and fabricated metal products, as well as services sectors including human health and social work activities and public administration, defence and compulsory social security (OECD, 2023[13]).[3]

Figure 2.13. Output use of foreign affiliates, 2016

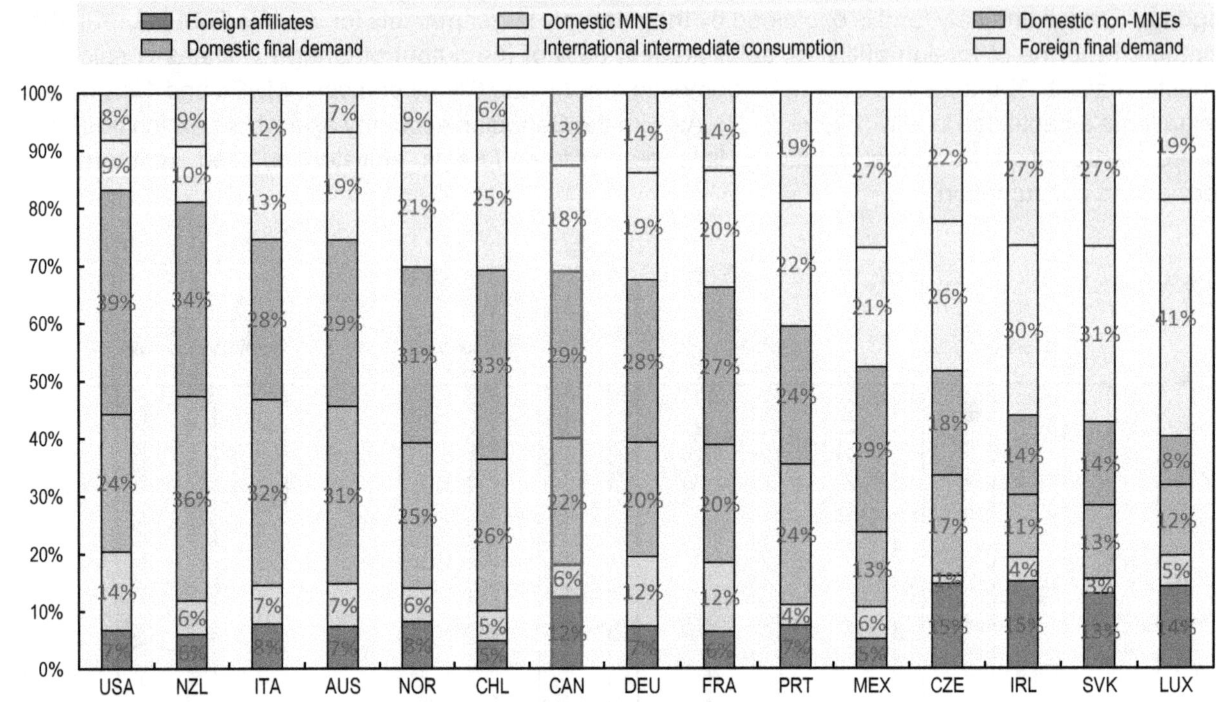

Source: OECD Analytical AMNE Database (2016[18]), https://www.oecd.org/sti/ind/analytical-amne-database.htm

Seizing the additional spillovers that could result from strengthening these business linkages between foreign and domestic firms will require that domestic firms have the capacities to adopt new technologies, improve quality and make production more efficient. This should be achievable for many businesses. As illustrated above, overall Canadian productivity is around the middle of OECD member countries and productivity gaps by firm ownership are moderate in most sectors of the economy. These challenges may be more significant for lower-productivity SMEs. Non-multinational firms, although they represent a substantial 41% of total Canadian employment and contribute 29.9% to the overall value added are typically quite small, with an average of only 2.6 employees per enterprise in 2020 (Statistics Canada, 2023[12]).

2.3.4. Acquisitions may involve productivity spillovers from FDI on domestic firms

More direct involvement of foreign firms that have acquired SMEs and other domestic firms may lead to new opportunities for SME growth and upgrading. As part of scaling up their innovation activities, Canadian SMEs frequently look for foreign investors or outright buyers. This also can allow these emerging businesses to expand their export capacity and presence to international markets. Canadian SME entrepreneurs who choose to be acquired are twice as likely to experience sales growth above their industry average, and as a result 13% of Canadian entrepreneurs (as many as 170,000 SMEs) plan to be acquired over the next five years, as of 2021 (Business Development Canada, 2021[19]). A significant share of this is being driven by venture capital (VC) investment, amount to 8 billion CAD in 2022 across Canada. Foreign investors made up 67% of the VC flows to Canadian companies, with US VC firms at 49% and non-US foreign firms at 18%, respectively (Consulting.ca, 2023[20]). Foreign VCs make relatively larger investments than domestic VCs, provide a higher chance of a successful exit for Canadian entrepreneurs and are likelier to provide pathways to access foreign markets (Kong, Nitani and Riding, 2015[21]). Although foreign VCs are more risk-averse on the Canadian market than domestic ones, opting to choose beneficiaries that are likelier to succeed in the market, the dominance of the Canadian VC space by foreign firms and their relative success, provides a significant added benefit to the innovation and productivity of Canadian SMEs.

Started in 2013, a Canadian SME that manufactures and supplies network communication products and solutions for critical infrastructure scaled up significantly following a funding round in 2018 from a large multinational German automation products manufacturer. The latter supported the launch of its RAPTOR Series Platform, an industrial IoT communications networking platform that enables secure and reliable communications between devices, equipment, and the people managing critical infrastructure. After a significant slowing of innovation due to the COVID-19 pandemic, the German manufacturer fully acquired the Canadian SME in January 2023. A New Zealand-founded cloud accounting software company, expanded to Canada in 2018 and has since acquired two Canadian businesses in Calgary and in Toronto. The acquisition has led to increased automation and efficiency in customer services and increased the company's presence in Calgary's rapidly growing tech community. Similarly, a Montreal-based SME that provides an AI-driven data simulation and predictive analysis platform conducted a first round of institutional financing in 2020 led by the Canadian venture capital arm of foreign bank subsidiary. Thanks to its financing, the SME continues to expand its client base, specifically in HR and finance, with plans to grow internationally. The company has also bolstered its AI with new features specific to key issues such as ensuring compliance with the EU's General Data Protection Regulation (GDPR) and ISO 27001 standards.

2.4. FDI and the potential for innovation diffusion

Enhancing innovation will play a key role in driving deeper involvement in GVCs and boosting productivity growth in Canada (Box 2.1). Multinationals are often highly active in R&D and innovation. Their investments can help grow sectors that are more R&D intensive. The wider economy may also benefit from the new knowledge and technologies brought into the host economy through FDI. Like productivity improvements, positive spillovers on innovation can be transmitted through supply chain linkages and other types of strategic partnerships (e.g. R&D collaboration, joint ventures, technology licensing agreements). Domestic firms may also engage in joint projects with foreign firms to produce new products, improve processes and develop new innovations (OECD, 2022[15]; OECD, 2019[14]). Large multinational firms have increasingly taken part in the open innovation transformation by developing partnerships with smaller enterprises or by setting up innovation labs and accelerators where start-ups and other small firms can nurture new business ideas and business models.

2.4.1. Relatively low R&D expenditure constrains Canada's innovation performance

In addition to factors such as the tax structure and competition regulations (OECD, 2023[2]), several structural aspects play a role in shaping innovation in Canada. These include Canada's position within global value chains, its relatively small and geographically dispersed population, and the significance of natural resource sectors, which are generally less innovation-intensive (Council of Canadian Academies, 2009[22]). Encouraging more innovation is essential for the development of new products, services and production technologies that can enhance efficiency within Canadian businesses (OECD, 2022[15]). Moreover, Canada's investment in research and development (R&D) has not kept pace with growth seen in other OECD countries. While gross expenditure on R&D (GERD) increased across OECD member nations from 2.1% of GDP in 2000 to 2.7% in 2020, Canada's investments in this area remained relatively stable during the same period, moving from 1.9% to 1.8% (Figure 2.14).

With this growing gap in R&D intensity, Canada's share of patents filed across OECD member countries fell from a recent peak of 2.1% in 2010 to 1.9% in 2019. Higher education and government play important roles in research and development in Canada. While most (51.6%) of gross expenditure on R&D is performed by the business enterprise sector, this is much less than the sector's average share across the OECD (72%) (Figure 2.15). The higher education sector, on the other hand, is responsible for 39% of GERD, more than double the OECD average of 16%.

Figure 2.14. Gross expenditure on research and development, 2020

As a percentage of GDP

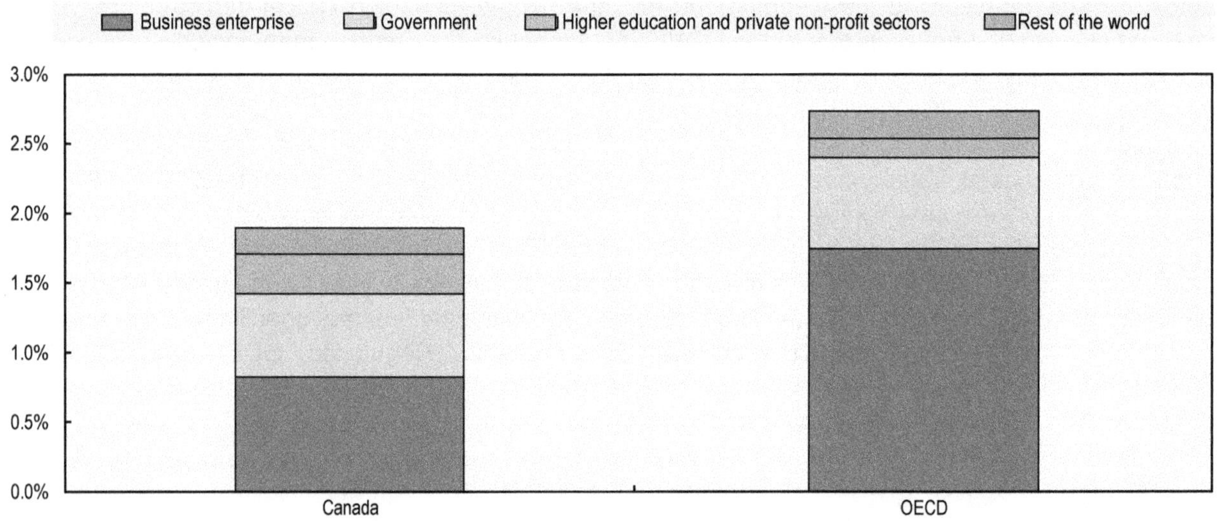

Source: OECD Main Science and Technology Indicators (2023[23]), https://stats.oecd.org/Index.aspx?DataSetCode=MSTI_PUB

Box 2.1. Intangible capital and GVC participation

Intangible capital includes knowledge-based assets such as datasets and other computerised information, innovative property, and economic competencies such as firm organisation and business strategies that is often of particular importance to multinational enterprises (OECD, 2021[24]). Indeed, the total intellectual property of foreign multinational enterprises was CAD 13 billion in 2019, which represented 29% of the total in the Canadian corporate sector. Foreign firms accounted for the greatest share of corporate sector intellectual property in wholesale trade (57.3%); manufacturing (42.9%); and professional, scientific and technical services.

Intangible capital tends to play an important role at both the early and final stages of global value chains – through, for example, the activities of firms responsible for research and development and branding – where significant value addition takes place. Not surprisingly for a country with limited involvement in GVCs, Canadian intangible capital is responsible for a moderate share of global production and trade. A study of intangible trade balances in OECD countries in 2015 shows that Canada accounts for a slightly smaller share than Mexico of shares to intangible capital embodied in global production of final goods and services (Alsamawi et al., 2020[25]).

Although it does not capture the returns to intangible capital embodied in trade, it is notable that Canada's net international technological receipts are typically negative, despite an increase in recent years. The United States is the closest partner for these transactions, accounting for 61% of receipts and 52% of payments. Foreign firms are responsible for most international transactions involving innovation and technology. International technology receipts and payments of foreign multinational enterprises represented 73% and 72% of all international technology receipts and payments, across the Canadian economy (Statistics Canada, 2023[12]).

Constraints on foreign investment and the need for further development in innovation systems may be influencing Canadian engagement in global value chains. This can impact a firm's ability to fully utilise and capitalise on intangible assets (Statistics Canada, 2023[12]). International comparisons indicate that the benefits of intangible capital are closely tied to openness and support for innovation. Trade and investment policies can play a pivotal role in enhancing the returns on intangible capital. Additionally, innovation policies, including public funding for R&D, are shown to support increased returns on intangible capital (Alsamawi et al., 2020[25]). It's worth noting that trade policies should consider the effects of barriers in key industries on innovation. Although Canada's overall trade restrictions are not particularly severe, certain sectors, such as telecommunications, exhibit high levels of restrictiveness.

Source: OECD (2021[24]), Multinational enterprises and intangible capital, https://www.oecd-ilibrary.org/science-and-technology/multinational-enterprises-and-intangible-capital_6827b3c9-en; Alsamawi et al., (2020[25]), Returns to intangible capital in global value chains: New evidence on trends and policy determinants, https://doi.org/10.1787/4cd06f19-en; Statistics Canada (2023[12]), Activities of Multinational Enterprises in Canada, https://doi.org/10.25318/3610060401-eng

Figure 2.15. Gross expenditure on research and development by sector, 2020

As a percentage of gross expenditure on R&D

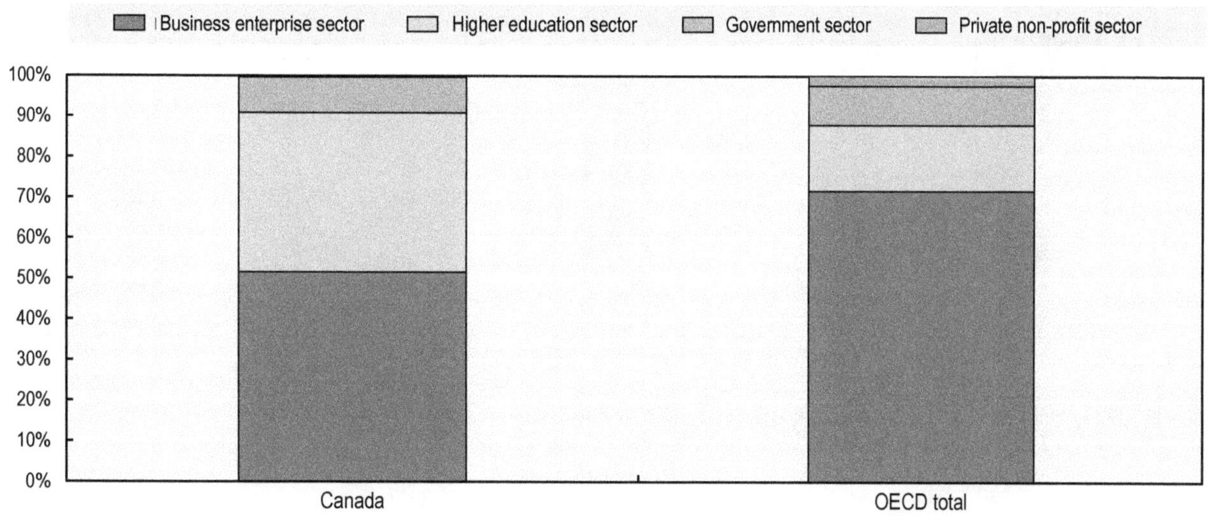

Source: OECD Main Science and Technology Indicators (2023[23]), https://stats.oecd.org/Index.aspx?DataSetCode=MSTI_PUB

2.4.2. Foreign firms make significant contributions to innovation in Canada

FDI plays a major role in supporting innovation directly, as foreign affiliates invest in knowledge-intensive sectors and activities. Indeed, these businesses are often more innovative than average, both because of firm-level differences and because economic sectors with higher levels of R&D expenditure per unit of value added often attract larger shares of FDI (OECD, 2019[14]; OECD, 2022[15]). Large multinational enterprises typically depend on firm-specific knowledge, technologies or brands that make them competitive operating at a large scale and in multiple markets. Across OECD economies, foreign affiliates generate a greater share of their revenues through intangible assets than do domestic firms (OECD, 2021[24]).

Foreign firms are much more R&D-intensive than Canadian businesses and are considerably more engaged in business activities related to innovation. They amounted for the greatest share of intramural R&D expenditures in the corporate sector in 2020 (42%), while Canadian multinationals and non-multinationals were each responsible for 32% and 26%, respectively. Foreign firms are highly engaged in all kinds of innovative activities. According to the results of an OECD business consultation conducted for this study (Annex 1.A), which involved 24 domestic and 33 foreign businesses, foreign firms were more likely than their domestic counterparts to have been engaged in a wide array of innovative activities – including product innovation, process innovation, joint product development, organizational innovation and market innovation (Figure 2.16).

Although there is significant foreign investment in more innovative sectors of the Canadian economy, sectoral differences do not fully explain foreign firms' greater investment in R&D. Foreign multinational enterprises spend more on intramural R&D than domestic businesses in many sectors. This difference is especially clear in more R&D-intensive sectors, such as professional, scientific and technical sectors and in information and cultural industries (Figure 2.17).

Figure 2.16. Shares of surveyed firms engaged in innovative activities during the past three years

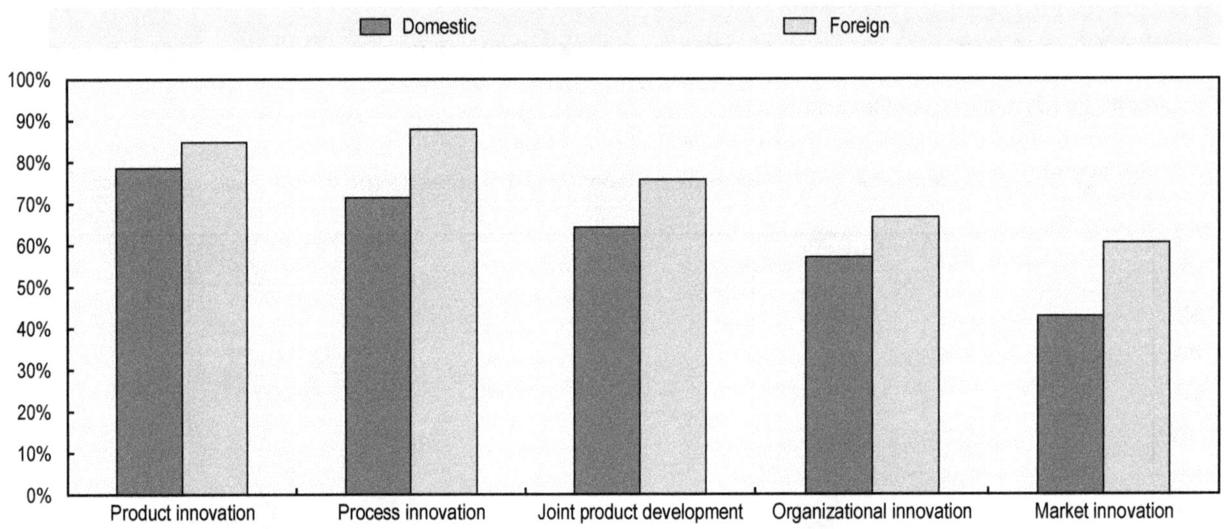

Notes: In total, 33 affiliates of foreign firms and 24 domestic firms were surveyed in 2022.
Source: OECD (2022[26]), Business Consultation on Sustainability Practices in Canada.

Figure 2.17. Intramural R&D expenditure as a percentage of value added by ownership and sector, 2020

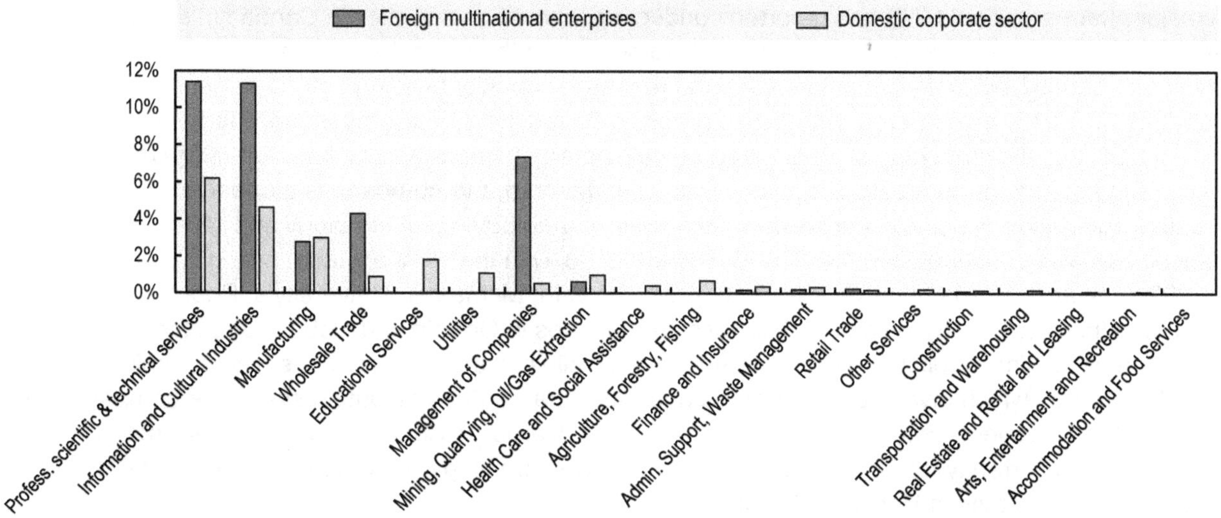

Source: Statistics Canada (2023[12]), Activities of Multinational Enterprises in Canada, https://doi.org/10.25318/3610060401-eng

Data on greenfield FDI projects tell a similar story about the sectors in which FDI is driving innovation. Across all sectors over 2018-22, 21% of capital invested in greenfield FDI projects was in projects mainly for research and development activities. This share was particularly high in creative industries (91%), financial services (42%), and ICT and electronics (34%) (Figure 2.18). In the R&D-intensive pharmaceuticals sector, for example, large foreign firms are responsible for much of the investment made in innovation (Box 2.2).

Figure 2.18. Share of greenfield FDI in R&D activities by sector, 2018-2022

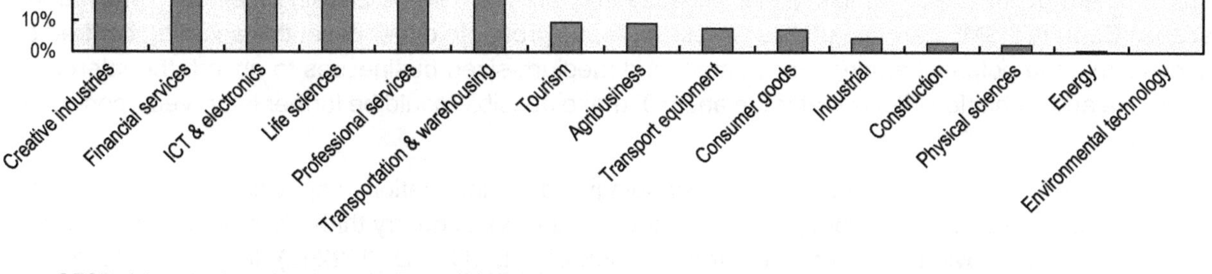

Source: OECD elaboration based on Financial Times (2023[5]), https://www.fdimarkets.com/

Box 2.2. Foreign MNEs as a driver of R&D in Canada: life sciences and pharmaceuticals

A major pharmaceutical MNE has reported conducting innovation activities in Canada in six therapeutic areas including pulmonology, cardiology, and women's health. Over the past ten years, the MNE has invested about $1 billion in Canadian R&D and research capacity building activities. As a part of these activities, in 2016, it partnered with San Francisco-based healthcare investment firm to invest 225 million USD into the launching of an engineered cell therapy company that it later fully acquired in 2019. With R&D housed at the MaRS Discovery District in Toronto, the company is pioneering methods for creating authentic cell types in the areas of neurology, cardiology, ophthalmology and immunology. This support has also continued into the COVID-19 pandemic, with the company committing 1.8 million CAD in 2020 towards its partnership research program with McMaster University's Population Health Research Institute (PHRI), on research across partner sites in Ontario and globally on potential COVID-19 treatments. Their collaboration involved several clinical trials in previous years, including the COMPASS trial, which involved 33 countries and more than 600 participating sites. The company has also made investments into activities at the Princess Margaret Cancer Centre, the Montreal Heart Institute and is currently funding the Chair for Clinical Epidemiology Research and Bleeding Disorders at McMaster University in Hamilton, Ontario.

Another leading global healthcare company has conducted R&D in multiple Canadian research centres and local labs. Between 2016 and 2022, the company conducted 55 clinical trials in 3019 patients in Canada, part of their 63.8 million CAD in R&D investment from 2016 to 2021. In April 2023, the company made their largest investment in Canada yet, announcing a collaboration with a British Columbia-based biotechnology company to develop bio-printed tissue therapeutics, which has the potential to significantly improve treatments for diabetes and obesity. The joint research and product development leverage the two companies' expertise in bioprinting technology as well asstem cell differentiation and cell therapy development and manufacturing. The company has also been supporting R&D in academic institutions, such as at the University of Toronto, through donations to establish a research network that will support healthier urban populations, especially in addressing root causes diabetes and other serious chronic diseases.

Source: OECD (2022[26]), Business Consultation on Sustainability Practices in Canada.

2.4.3. Canadian SMEs are well-positioned to collaborate with foreign investors on innovative and R&D projects, but are lagging in digital capacities

On average, Canadian SMEs tend to be quite innovative but less technologically-intensive than the smaller firms in other advanced economies, either because they are not commercialising their own innovations or because Canada's SMEs are a particularly heterogenous group. In either case, this seeming contradiction suggests that the potential among many small- and medium-sized businesses to absorb the international knowledge and technology flows that trade and FDI make possible could be further improved upon (OECD, 2023[17]).

Like productivity spillovers, knowledge, technology, and innovation capacities can spread from technologically more advanced foreign firms to others in the host country through information sharing with suppliers, workers moving between firms and imitation effects (OECD, 2022[15]). In addition, foreign and domestic firms may collaborate on joint projects to develop new goods and services or improved production processes. The OECD business consultation conducted for this study revealed that most of the recent partnerships of foreign multinational enterprises in Canada with domestic firms for joint product development or service provision have included innovative, R&D and technology-intensive activities (Figure 2.19).

In the area of innovation and R&D, a number of sources reveal that Canadian SMEs are relatively more innovative and knowledge-intensive than those in many other OECD economies, even if are often acquired or transfer their patents to larger foreign firms rather than commercialising these themselves (Gallini and Hollis, 2019[27]). Among domestic firms, more of R&D capacity is found in smaller enterprises; 21% of in-house R&D expenditure and 25.6% of in-house R&D personnel are found in firms with 5 to 9 employees. Among foreign firms, 22% of in-house R&D expenditure and 20% of in-house R&D personnel are found in firms with 500 to 999 employees, the largest shares by size category (Statistics Canada, 2022[28]). Many SMEs introduce innovations in terms of new products or novel processes, marketing or forms of organization. In 2022, 72% of these firms had engaged in business process innovation, while 52% had engaged in product innovation, higher than in several other OECD economies (Figure 2.20.).

Figure 2.19. Shares of surveyed firms partnering with domestic firms for joint product development or service provision during the past three years

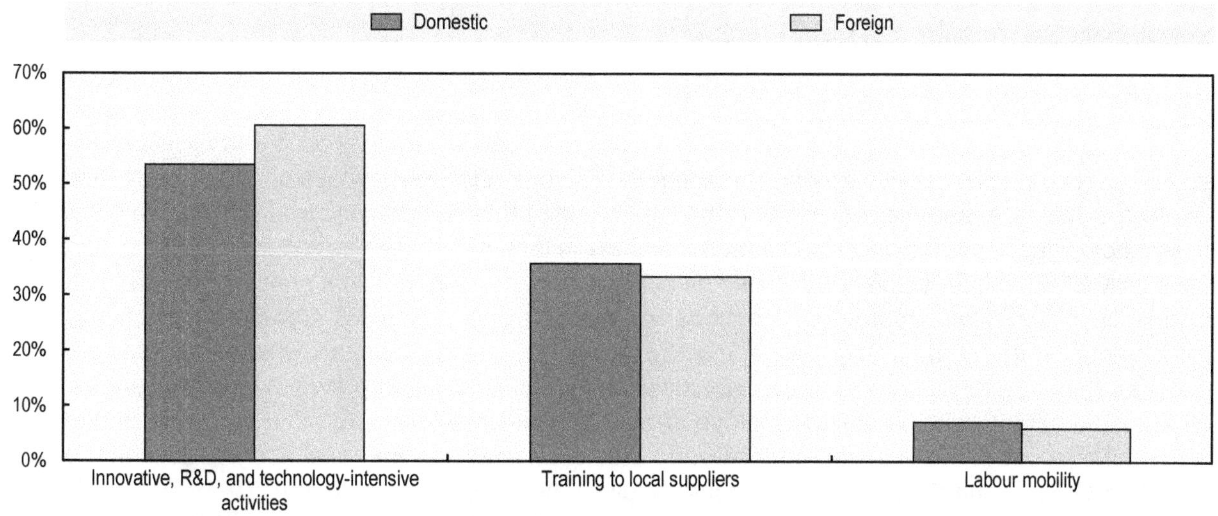

Note: In total, 33 foreign affiliates and 24 domestic firms were surveyed in 2022.
Source: OECD (2022[26]), Business Consultation on Sustainability Practices in Canada.

Figure 2.20. Share of SMEs introducing innovations, 2022

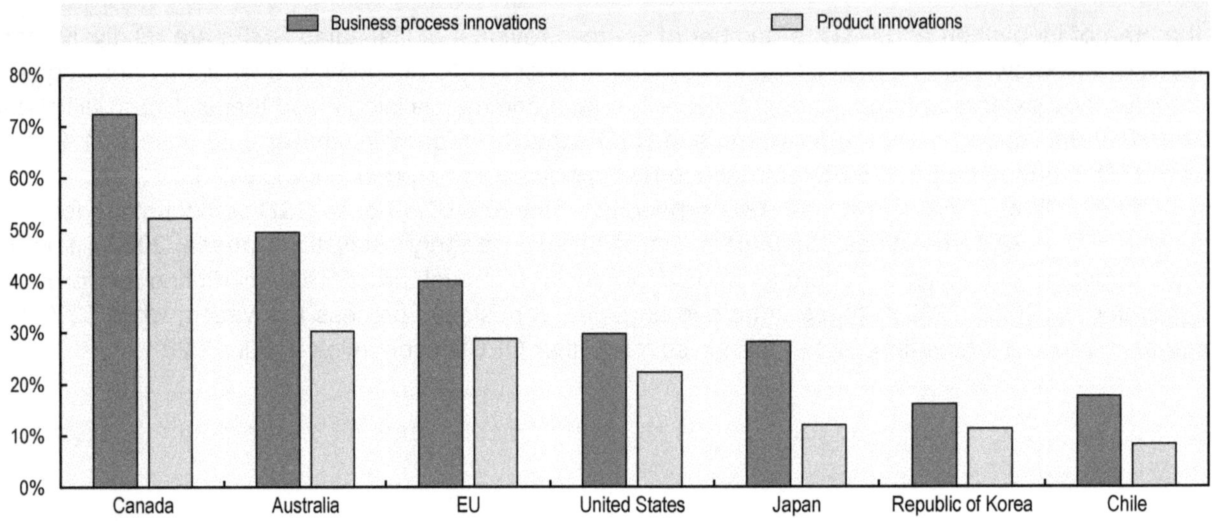

Note: Notes: SMEs include firms with 10 to 249 employees.
Source: European Commission (2022[29]), European Innovation Scorecard,https://research-and-innovation.ec.europa.eu/statistics/performance-indicators/european-innovation-scoreboard_en#eis-interactive-tool

Despite this record of innovation among Canadian SMEs, their relatively low use of advanced technologies as well as digital tools and processes may limit the impact of their innovations and potential to collaborate with technologically advanced foreign firms. Emerging digital technologies have the potential to help firms – especially SMEs – offer tailored products and services, create more efficient supply chains and increase participation in GVCs, and improve connections with markets and customers. Compared with a number of EU countries, the use of artificial intelligence by Canadian businesses is quite low, across all business size categories (Figure 2.21). Just 4% of small businesses (with 10 to 49 employees) use AI, well below the 11% of medium firms (with 50 to 249 employees) and 27% of large firms (with 250 and more employees). At 18%, businesses in the finance and insurance activities sector are the most likely to use AI and, as in many other OECD countries, AI use is particularly low in the construction sector (0.7% of firms). Similarly, the share of Canadian small businesses using Internet of things (9%) ranked 24th out of 28 OECD member countries with available data in 2021, while they also lag behind other OECD economies in terms of use of cloud computing services (e.g. finance and accounting software, customer relationship management systems, digital storage of files, etc.) and the provision of ICT training to their employees. Digital tools and processes at the workplace are key assets for technology and innovation absorption, managing organisational changes or enabling integration in GVCs through exports or linkages with foreign affiliates at home.

These findings suggest that Canadian SMEs could be further supported to become suppliers and partners of technology-intensive foreign investors. Policies targeting the absorptive capacity of local SMEs can take many forms (e.g. subsidies, grants, loans, tax relief, infrastructures, training programmes), target various aspects of SME performance (e.g. access to innovation assets, access to skills, access to finance), and be aligned with the scope and priorities of facilitation and aftercare services offered to foreign investors. Such a comprehensive approach could help align domestic supplier capabilities with the needs of foreign investors and further strengthen the spillover potential of FDI.

Figure 2.21. Share of SMEs with digital and R&D-intensive capacities

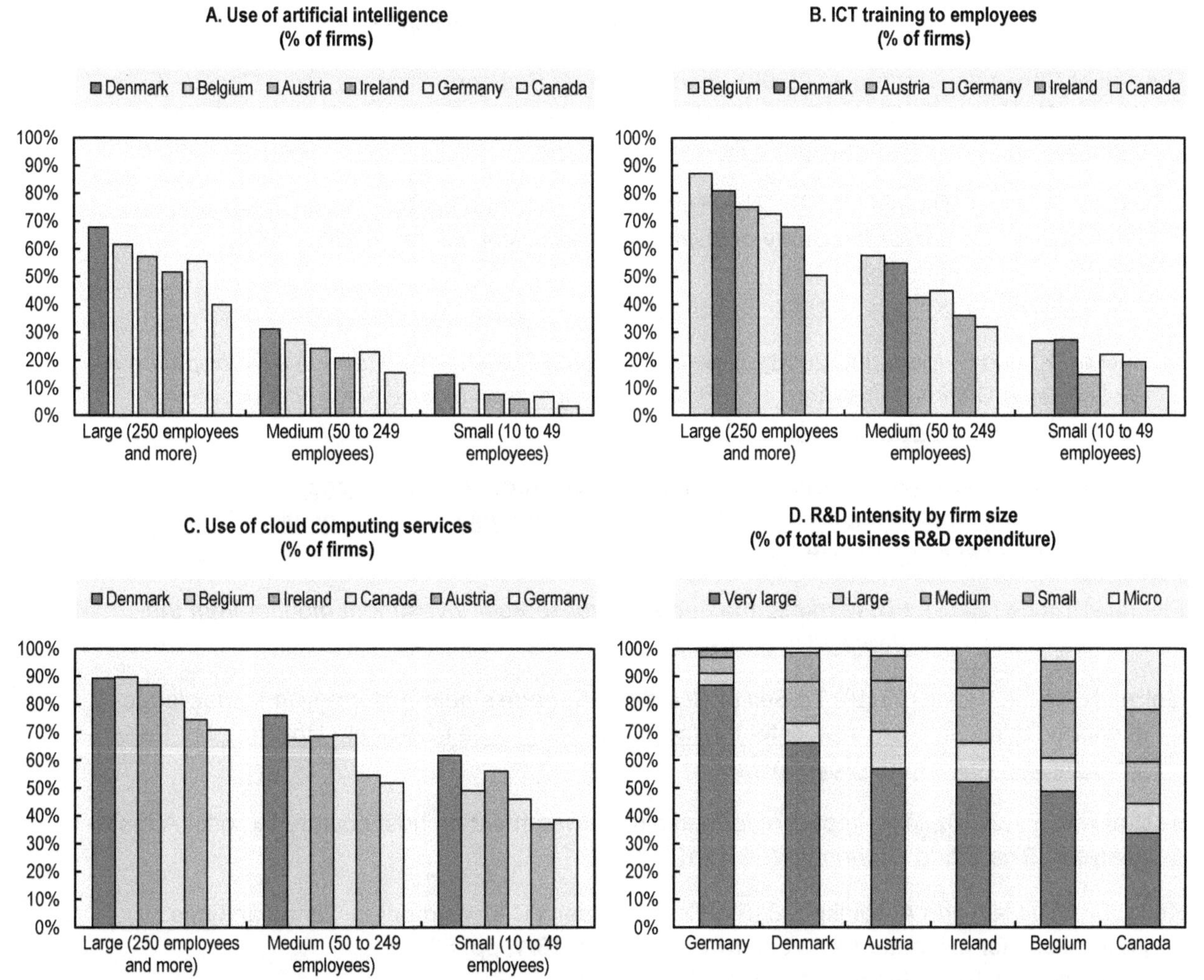

Notes: For R&D intensity, the following firm size categories are presented: i) very large firms: 500 employees or more; ii) large firms: from 250 to 499 employees; iii) medium firms: from 50 to 249 employees; iv) small firms: from 10 to 49 employees; v) micro firms: from 1 to 9 employees.
Source: OECD (2023[30]), ITC Access and Usage by Business Database, https://stats.oecd.org/Index.aspx?DataSetCode=ICT_BUS; OECD (2023[23]), Main Science and Technology Indicators, https://stats.oecd.org/Index.aspx?DataSetCode=MSTI_PUB

References

Alsamawi, A. et al. (2020), "Returns to intangible capital in global value chains: New evidence on trends and policy determinants", *OECD Trade Policy Papers*, No. 240, OECD Publishing, Paris, https://doi.org/10.1787/4cd06f19-en. [25]

Becker, B. et al. (2020), "FDI in hot labour markets: The implications of the war for talent", *Journal of International Business Policy*, Vol. 3/2, pp. 107-133, https://doi.org/10.1057/s42214-020-00052-y. [31]

Brosseau, L. (2020), *Recognition of the Foreign Qualifications of Immigrants*, Library of Parliament Background Papers, https://lop.parl.ca/staticfiles/PublicWebsite/Home/ResearchPublications/BackgroundPapers/PDF/2020-86-e.pdf. [33]

Business Development Canada (2021), *Business Acquisitions: A Strategy That Drives Growth.* [19]

Consulting.ca (2023), *Canadian VC investment drops to $8.19 billion in 2022.* [20]

Council of Canadian Academies (2009), *Innovation and Business Strategy: Why Canada Falls Short – Report of the Expert Panel on Business Innovation*, Council of Canadian Academies, https://cca-reports.ca/wp-content/uploads/2018/10/2009-06-11-innovation-report-1.pdf. [22]

Criscuolo, C. and J. Timmis (2017), "The Relationship Between Global Value Chains and Productivity", *Centre for the Study of Living Standards*, Vol. 32, pp. 61-83, https://www.oecd.org/global-forum-productivity/events/Relashionship_btween_GVCs_and_productivity_6_09_2016.pdf. [10]

de Backer, K. and S. Miroudot (2016), *New International Evidence on Canada's Participation in Global Value Chains*, https://irpp.org/research-studies/new-international-evidence-on-canadas-participation-in-global-value-chains/. [9]

European Commission (2022), *European Innovation Scorecard*, https://research-and-innovation.ec.europa.eu/statistics/performance-indicators/european-innovation-scoreboard_en#eis-interactive-tool. [29]

Financial Times (2023), *FDI Markets: the in-depth crossborder investment monitor from the Financial Time*, https://www.fdimarkets.com/. [5]

Gallini, N. and A. Hollis (2019), *To Sell or Scale Up: Canada's patent strategy in a knowledge economy*, https://irpp.org/wp-content/uploads/2019/08/To-Sell-Or-Scale-Up-Canadas-Patent-Strategy-in-a-Knowledge-Economy.pdf. [27]

Kastratović, R. (2020), "The impact of foreign direct investment on host country exports: A meta-analysis", *The World Economy*, Vol. 43/12. [1]

Kong, S., M. Nitani and A. Riding (2015), "Cross-border VC investment in Canadian firms: implications for exit patterns", *Venture Capital*, Vol. 18/1, pp. 63-93, https://doi.org/10.1080/13691066.2015.1078566. [21]

OECD (2023), *Bilateral Trade in Goods by Industry and End-use (BTDIxE),*, https://stats.oecd.org/. [6]

OECD (2023), *FDI Statistics*, https://stats.oecd.org/. [4]

OECD (2023), *Inter-Country Input-Output (ICIO) Tables*, http://oe.cd/icio. [13]

OECD (2023), *International Trade Statistics*, https://stats.oecd.org/. [7]

OECD (2023), *ITC Access and Usage by Business Database*, https://stats.oecd.org/Index.aspx?DataSetCode=ICT_BUS. [30]

OECD (2023), *Main Science and Technology Indicators*, https://stats.oecd.org/Index.aspx?DataSetCode=MSTI_PUB. [23]

OECD (2023), *OECD Economic Surveys: Canada 2023*, OECD Publishing, Paris, https://doi.org/10.1787/7eb16f83-en. [2]

OECD (2023), *Policy Toolkit for Strengthening FDI and SME Linkages*, OECD Publishing, Paris, https://doi.org/10.1787/688bde9a-en. [17]

OECD (2023), *Productivity Statistics Database*, https://doi.org/10.1787/pdtvy-data-en. [16]

OECD (2023), *Trade in Value Added (TiVA) Database*, https://stats.oecd.org/. [11]

OECD (2022), *Business Consultation on Sustainability Practices in Canada*. [26]

OECD (2022), *Disability, Work and Inclusion: Mainstreaming in All Policies and Practices*, OECD Publishing, Paris, https://doi.org/10.1787/1eaa5e9c-en. [32]

OECD (2022), *FDI Qualities Policy Toolkit*, OECD Publishing, Paris, https://doi.org/10.1787/7ba74100-en. [15]

OECD (2022), *OECD Services Trade Restrictiveness Index (STRI): Canada*, http://www.oecd.org/trade/topics/services-trade/documents/oecd-stri-country-note-can.pdf. [3]

OECD (2021), *Multinational enterprises and intangible capital*, https://www.oecd-ilibrary.org/science-and-technology/multinational-enterprises-and-intangible-capital_6827b3c9-en. [24]

OECD (2019), *FDI Qualities Indicators: Measuring the sustainable development impacts of investment*, OECD Publishing, http://www.oecd.org/investment/investment-policy/FDI-Qualities-Indicators-Measuring-Sustainable-Development-Impacts.pdf. [14]

OECD (2016), *Analytical AMNE Database*, http://www.oecd.org/sti/ind/analytical-amne-database.htm. [18]

Statistics Canada (2023), *Activities of Multinational Enterprises in Canada*, https://doi.org/10.25318/3610060401-eng. [12]

Statistics Canada (2023), *Exports and Imports of Goods and Services*, https://doi.org/10.25318/1210013401-eng. [8]

Statistics Canada (2022), *Business Enterprise in-House Research and Development Expenditures*, https://www150.statcan.gc.ca/t1/tbl1/en/cv.action?pid=2710033501. [28]

Notes

[1] For example, utilities, information industries and construction are among the sectors with the least foreign direct investment and some of the highest shares of foreign value added embodied in domestic demand.

[2] Utilities industries include electricity, gas, steam and air condition supply and water supply, sewerage, waste management and remediation activities.

[3] Data refers to 2016.

3 The contribution of FDI to employment, job quality and skills

This chapter examines the contribution of FDI to labour market outcomes in Canada. It assesses the impact of FDI on employment creation and job quality, considering both wage and non-wage working conditions. It also examines how FDI influences skills development and how foreign MNEs address potential skills imbalances, including through their training practices.

3.1. Summary of key findings

Foreign investment creates many quality jobs in the Canadian economy, but not to the same extent across sectors, provinces, occupations and workers (see also Chapter 4). Foreign MNEs employed 13% of the workforce in 2020 while they represented only 0.6% of the total number of firms. Their contribution to employment is particularly important in manufacturing, wholesale and retail trade and professional, scientific and technical services related to IT and R&D, in contrast with Canadian MNEs that employ many workers in finance and insurance. The contribution of FDI to employment strongly varies across Canadian provinces and employment by foreign MNEs is geographically more concentrated than employment by domestic firms – Ontario hosted nearly half of all jobs created by greenfield FDI between 2003 and 2022.

The job creation intensity of FDI in Canada is lower than in most OECD countries but jobs are often in high-tech occupations – a quarter of jobs created by greenfield FDI were in software and IT. Since 2005, Canada received nearly one third of its greenfield FDI in capital-intensive sectors like mining. Overall, one million USD of greenfield investment in Canada created 1.3 jobs - half the OECD average. The job creation intensity of FDI in Canada is lower than in the OECD even in labour-intensive sectors such as software and IT. However, jobs created in those sectors are often in R&D activities that require highly specialised engineers, in contrast with the United States, for instance, where FDI in the IT sector goes to a larger extent to less skill-intensive services that need more human resources.

Beyond job creation, foreign firms in Canada have a mixed impact on several dimensions of job quality such as wages, job security and employer-worker relations. The OECD Business Consultation on Corporate Sustainability Practices suggests that foreign firms pay, on average, wages that are higher than private domestic firms, mostly when they are large manufacturing exporters. Canadian MNEs may be paying equally high wages – it is to a large extent international operations of firms that generates the foreign wage premium. A lower proportion of foreign firms' employees are in non-standard forms of employment – workers with temporary and part-time job contracts – than domestic firms. This difference is likely to be driven by the smaller share of low-skilled workers in foreign MNEs that tend to have limited bargaining power. However, a non-negligible share of workers of foreign firms in Canada are in the retail trade industry, a sector with relatively low job tenure and moderately high proportion of temporary workers.

The effects of foreign firms on improving job quality are also contingent on whether they operate in sectors covered by collective bargaining agreements or established effective workers' voice arrangements. Collective bargaining coverage rate has been falling in Canada over the past few decades, particularly in sectors where foreign MNEs operate such as manufacturing and wholesale and retail trade. In non-unionised settings, foreign firms in Canada rely on their HR bodies to oversee labour relations. These are set or largely shaped by the MNE headquarters and the source country labour practices. All firms must comply with local labour rules, but there are no laws that facilitate board-level employee representation that are present in many OECD countries.

Canada has the most educated workforce in the OECD area, which is a major attractiveness factor for FDI that can itself support the development of skills needed for the digital and green transitions (see also Chapter 5). Skill needs of foreign MNEs in Canada are large in high-skilled digital and STEM jobs and in mid-skilled jobs requiring skilled trades. Canada's tight labour market and large skill imbalances affect all sectors, but are more acute in manufacturing, wholesale and retail trade and scientific services where foreign MNEs are key employers. Large foreign MNEs relying on skilled trades in manufacturing and wholesale and retail trade are at particular risk of facing skill mismatches, i.e., workers do not possess the right skills to perform their jobs. Skills shortages – when employers cannot fill a vacancy due to a lack of adequate candidates – are widespread and affect more than half of foreign MNEs in manufacturing, utilities, management of companies and enterprises, transportation, and waste management. Foreign MNEs report the greatest shortages for skilled trades in waste management and manufacturing sectors and for computer and data science skills in tech-related services, partly driven by competition for talent from the United States.

Despite the prevailing skills shortage, foreign MNEs in Canada are less severely affected by the lack of available talent than domestic firms. To address skills imbalances and remain globally competitive, MNEs often have broader horizons and more elaborated strategies than non-MNEs in terms of where they can draw their talent, what training they provide and how they retain workers. The OECD consultation conducted for this study shows that foreign firms tend to have more effective recruitment strategies, partly due to their larger size and international experience, rely on international talent mobility of workers from other subsidiaries and leverage their global training practices. They also often partner with Canadian colleges and universities to provide technical apprenticeships or work-integrated learning opportunities, providing a pipeline of skills development for students and potential path to employment after graduation.

Policy considerations

- **Ensure that the investment promotion strategy is aligned with strategies on employment and skills development**. Adopt a balanced approach towards job creation in the investment promotion strategy by targeting activities that create quality jobs in both mid- and high-skilled occupations, particularly those needed for Canada's digital and green transitions. Ensure that labour demand generated by foreign firms' entry in sectors or provinces targeted by the Government of Canada can be met with available, mobile and adequately trained labour to realise the contribution of FDI and limit potential adverse impacts in a context of tight labour markets.
- **Strengthen cooperation between foreign firms and relevant government authorities to promote quality jobs and protect the most vulnerable.** This includes raising awareness on labour standards, incentivise foreign firms and their suppliers to disclose compliance with them and ensure that firms-workers relations are adapted to a rapidly changing world of work accelerated by foreign investment, particularly in sectors with low collective bargaining coverage and job security and high share of less-skilled workers.
- **Explore ways for Canadian IPAs to support potential and existing foreign investors that face severe skills shortages, particularly in skilled trades and advanced digital skills**. This includes developing training programmes, in partnership with relevant authorities, that respond to increased labour demand in sectors targeted by Invest in Canada and that provide transferable, certifiable skills to facilitate labour mobility. Invest in Canada could also further facilitate training partnerships between foreign firms and Canadian colleges and universities and encourage foreign entrants to transfer specialised staff from other subsidiaries to support their early establishment in Canada, providing an opportunity to transfer knowledge in shortage.
- **Strengthen cooperation between Canadian IPAs, Statistics Canada and Employment and Social Development Canada to improve data availability, analysis and evaluation of policies related to FDI impact on the future of work.** Existing databases and surveys could provide further statistics by ownership type on skills needs and imbalances, measures taken by firms to address these imbalances (e.g., amount spent on training), wage levels and unionisation rates. Furthermore, consider involving Canadian IPAs in labour market information and skill needs and anticipation exercises to design and implement active labour and skills development programmes that target the skills needs of foreign firms as well.

3.2. The impact of FDI on employment and job quality

3.2.1. The contribution of foreign MNEs to employment is important but uneven across sectors and provinces

Foreign firms in Canada are responsible for a significant share of employment. Foreign firms – as compared to domestic ones – contribute more than proportionally to various metrics of Canada's economic performance and hold important employment opportunities. Although foreign firms represented merely 0.6% of the total number of active firms in Canada in 2020, they accounted for almost 25% of gross fixed capital formation and employed 13% of the workforce in the economy (Figure 3.1, Panel A). Compared to other OECD countries, the contribution of foreign MNEs to employment in Canada is greater than in other large economies like Germany or France, partly reflecting a significantly higher FDI stock to GDP ratio, but less than in small open economies like Luxembourg, Ireland, or Czechia (Figure 3.1, Panel B). As the largest foreign investor, the United States accounted for 62% of foreign firms' employment in Canada (OECD calculations based on Statistics Canada (2023[1])).

The contribution of foreign firms to job creation in Canada has increased over the past decade, reflecting a steady growth of the FDI stock, and MNEs – both foreign and Canadian – have proven more resilient than non-MNEs to the disruptions caused by the COVID-19 pandemic. Since 2010, the contribution of foreign and domestic MNEs to job creation has increased by about one percentage point each while that of Canadian non-MNEs has decreased by two percentage points (Figure 3.1, Panel A). As in other OECD countries, foreign companies in Canada were able to provide greater job security following the outbreak of the COVID-19 pandemic, and the number of jobs in foreign companies declined by only 6% year-on-year in 2020, while the number of jobs in Canadian MNEs and non-MNEs fell by 7% and 10% respectively.

Few sectors in Canada host most of the employment by foreign MNEs, reflecting the uneven distribution of FDI across sectors with different sizes and labour-intensities. Employment in foreign MNEs is largest in wholesale trade (35% of employment in the sector), manufacturing (33%), and mining (33%) followed by retail trade (22%), scientific and technical services (21%), and waste management (20%) (Figure 3.1, Panel C). Foreign firms in wholesale and retail trade and manufacturing each account for about 2-3% of jobs in the Canadian economy while mining, a less labour-intensive sector, accounts for only 0.4% of jobs in the overall economy. In some sectors that also have a high public sector share, such as education and healthcare, the share of both foreign and domestic MNE employment is low, while, for example, in finance and insurance the employment share of foreign firms is 50 percentage points lower than that of Canadian MNEs. Between 2010 and 2020, foreign MNEs created the most jobs in scientific, and technical services – comprising software engineering - as well as wholesale trade. They also outpaced job creation by Canadian MNEs in these two sectors.

Figure 3.1. Foreign MNEs contribute importantly to employment and labour market resilience

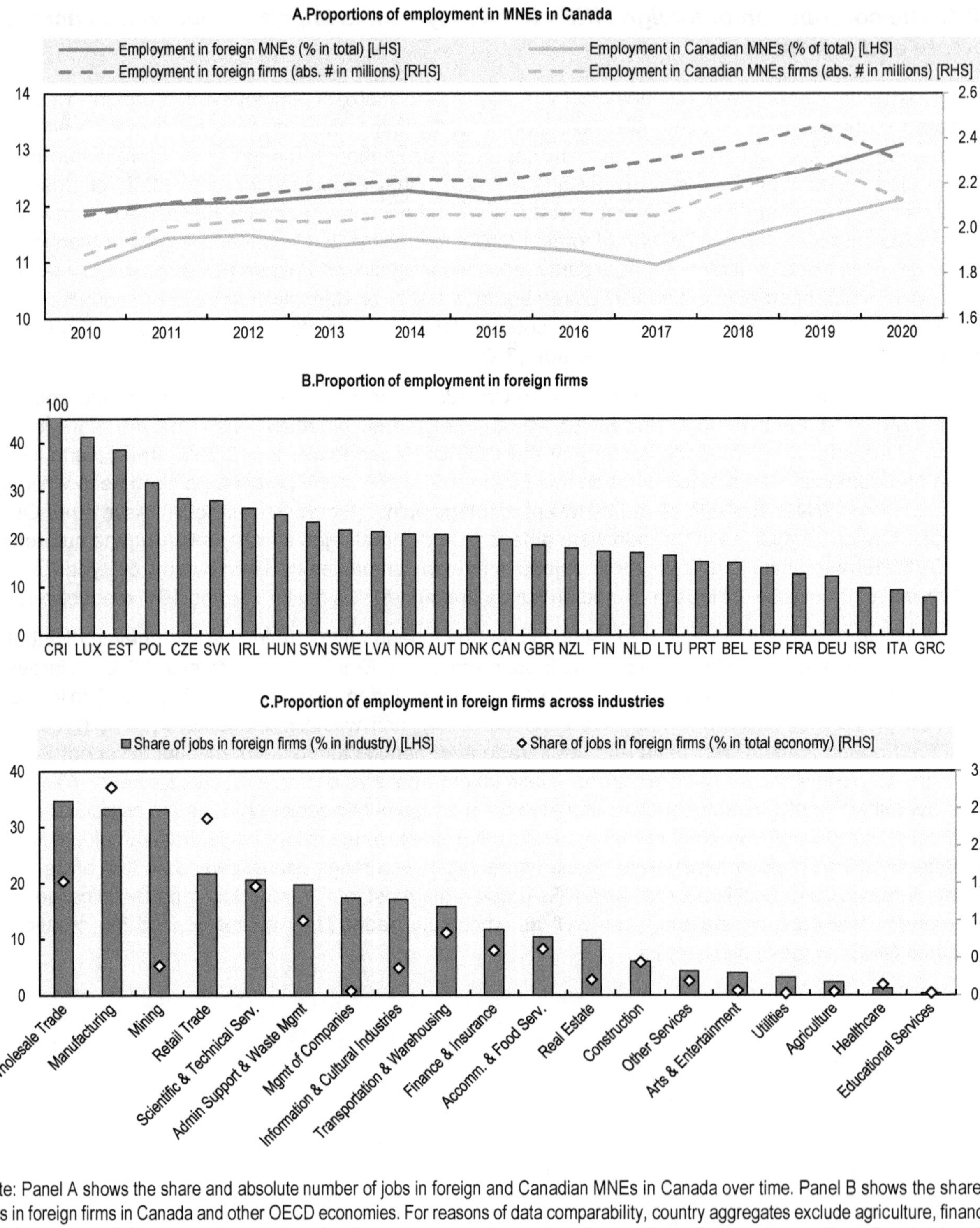

Note: Panel A shows the share and absolute number of jobs in foreign and Canadian MNEs in Canada over time. Panel B shows the share of jobs in foreign firms in Canada and other OECD economies. For reasons of data comparability, country aggregates exclude agriculture, financial and insurance activities, education services, healthcare, arts, entertainment and recreation, other services, and public administration (corresponding to ISIC rev. 4 sectors B-N, excluding K). The chart is based on the latest available data. Panel C shows the share of jobs in foreign firms in Canada for different industries (relative to the total of the respective industry as well as to the total Canadian economy).
Source: OECD elaboration based on Statistics Canada (2023[2]), https://www150.statcan.gc.ca/t1/tbl1/en/tv.action?pid=3610062001 and OECD (2023[3]), https://stats.oecd.org/Index.aspx?DataSetCode=AMNE_IN.

Foreign MNEs employ a significant share of workers in most Canadian provinces, but their contribution varies depending on their weight and characteristics across provinces. Differences in access to the littoral and proximity to large agglomerations, including integrated transborder areas with the United States such as the Detroit-Windsor region, also contribute to these varying levels of FDI and thus employment in foreign firms across provinces. In 2020, foreign MNEs employed 17% of workers in Ontario, followed by Alberta (13%), British Columbia (12%), New Brunswick (10%) and Quebec (10%) (Figure 3.2, Panel A). Together, the five provinces hosted 92% of total employment by foreign MNEs in Canada. Ontario, Alberta, British Columbia, and Quebec concentrate most of the FDI in Canada and a considerable share of foreign activity in these provinces is in manufacturing and service that are labour-intensive (Figure 3.2, Panel B). Other provinces receive much less FDI or, as in the case of Newfoundland and Labrador and Saskatchewan, have a higher share of foreign activity in sectors that are less labour-intensive, such as mining.

Figure 3.2. The number of jobs in foreign firms varies substantially across Canadian provinces

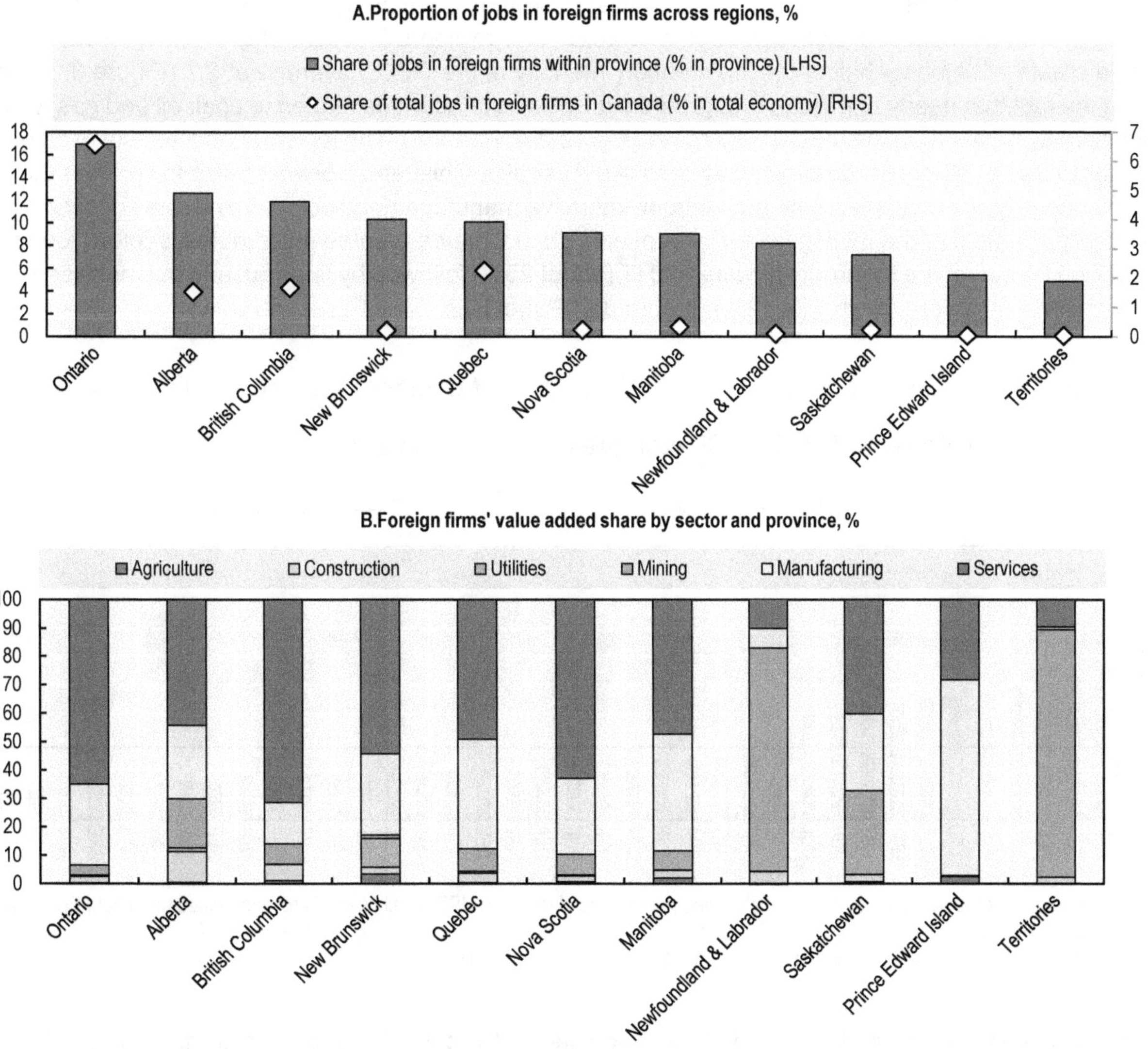

Note: Panel A shows the share of jobs in foreign firms across regions measured as share within provinces and as share in the total economy. Panel B shows the share of GDP (value added) by foreign firms in different sectors across provinces. 100% describe the total GDP by foreign firms in each province. Both charts are based on data from 2020.
Source: OECD elaboration based on Statistics Canada (2023[2]), https://www150.statcan.gc.ca/t1/tbl1/en/tv.action?pid=3610062001

3.2.2. Greenfield FDI creates less jobs in Canada than in most OECD countries, but many are in high-tech occupations

The important contribution of foreign MNEs to employment in Canada reflects the large stock of FDI that Canada hosts compared with other OECD economies. To understand how FDI may shape the future of work in Canada, it is equally important to identify what is the job creation potential of foreign investment projects. Especially greenfield FDI, i.e., the establishment of new foreign companies, is expected to have a significant direct and indirect impact on employment (OECD, 2019[4]). Apart from the type of FDI attracted (e.g., greenfield FDI or mergers & acquisitions), the economic structure of the host economy and its integration into global value chains (GVCs) are important determinants in this context. Countries with a comparative advantage in low- and medium-technology activities and competitive labour costs tend to attract more labour-intensive FDI than countries with a comparative advantage in high-technology, knowledge-intensive sectors, higher labour costs or with a large stock of natural resources.

Consequently, countries with high shares of FDI both in mining of natural resources and in knowledge intensive sectors such as Canada have comparatively lower job creation per invested dollar, but many jobs are in high-tech occupations. Between 2005 and 2022, one million US dollars of greenfield investment in Canada created 1.3 jobs – half of the job creation intensity of the OECD average at 2.7 (Figure 3.3). This reflects the fact that nearly one-quarter of greenfield FDI was in activities related to coal, oil and gas, which is significantly higher than the OECD aggregate (Figure 3.4, Panel A). The job creation intensity of Canada is similar to that of other resource-rich countries like Australia, Chile and Norway, but is lower than the job creation intensity of economies with large labour-intensive manufacturing sectors like Costa Rica, Czechia and Poland. Outside of the mining sector, greenfield FDI in Canada created most jobs in sectors requiring high-skilled labour, at the forefront software and IT (about 25%) followed by financial and business services and transport equipment (each with 12%) (Figure 3.4, Panel B).

Figure 3.3. Canada's job creation intensity is similar to that of other resource rich OECD countries

Job creation intensity of greenfield FDI in OECD economies, total over 2005-2022

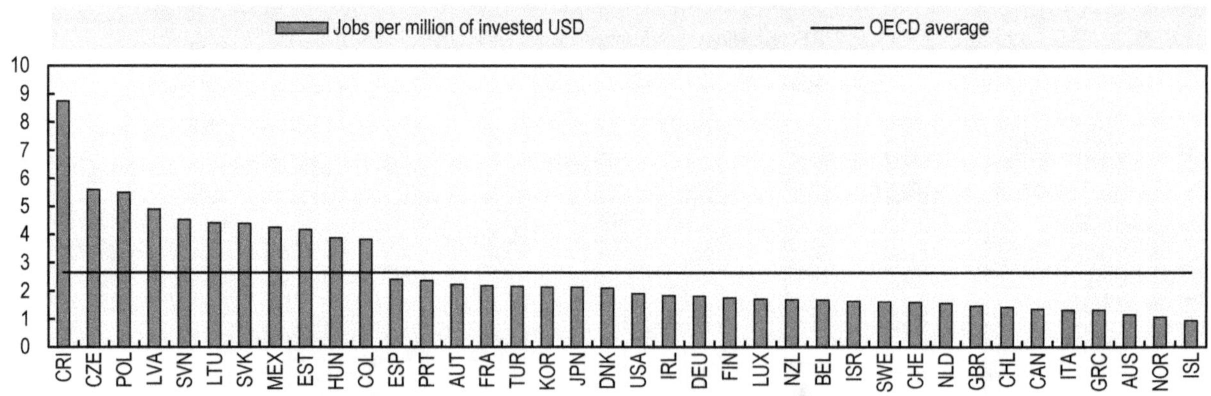

Note: This figure shows the average number of jobs created per millions of invested USD by all opened and announced greenfield FDI projects across OECD countries.
Source: OECD elaboration based on Financial Times (2023[5]), https://www.fdimarkets.com/

Transport equipment and software and IT, two sectors that receive large shares of greenfield FDI and account for significant shares of jobs created by investment, have lower job creation potential in Canada than in other OECD economies. While one million US dollars invested in the Canadian transport equipment and software and IT industry created between 1.4 and 2 jobs, one million US dollars invested in these sectors of other OECD countries created between 4 to 5 jobs (Figure 3.4, Panel C). These differences suggest that the split across value chain activities within a sector plays an important role in determining the job creation of FDI. Value chain activities range from research and development (R&D) at the beginning of a product lifecycle to manufacturing, marketing, logistics or maintenance and servicing. As these activities differ in their labour intensity, investments within a sector have a different job creation potential depending on the activities targeted. Greenfield FDI in service activities creates on average of about 4 jobs per million dollars invested in OECD countries, followed by R&D and manufacturing activities with job creation intensities of 3 and 2, respectively (OECD calculation based on Financial Times (2023[5])).

Figure 3.4. A large share of jobs created by greenfield FDI in Canada are in high-tech occupations

Proportions of created jobs and FDI across sectors in Canada and other OECD economies, total over 2005-2022

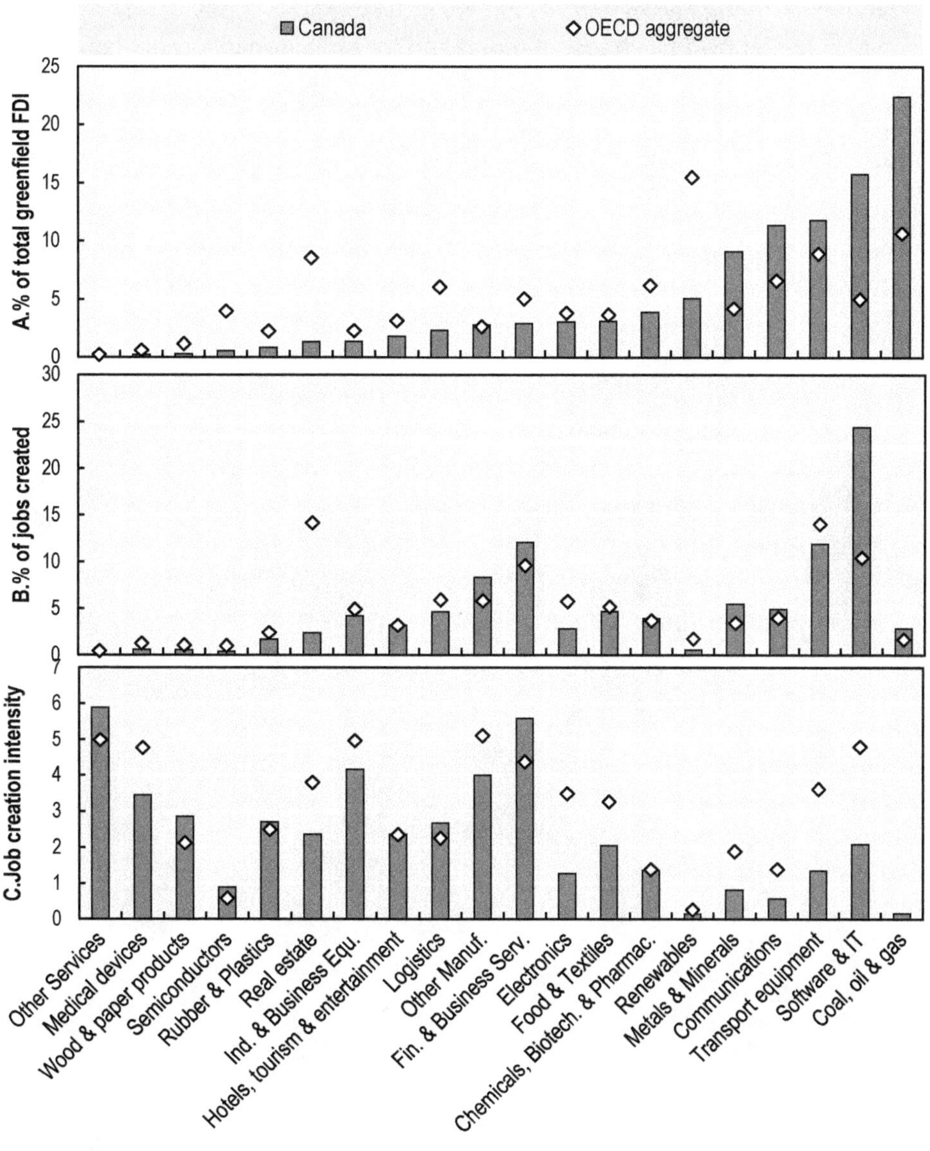

Note: This figure shows the distribution of greenfield FDI (Panel A), created jobs (Panel B) and job intensity (Panel C) across sectors in Canada and other OECD economies as total over 2005-2022 for all opened and announced projects. "OECD aggregate" includes all OECD members apart from Canada as simple aggregation. Due to data availability the definition of sectors follows the data source (Financial Times, 2023[5]) and does not follow the official NAICS sector classification.
Source: OECD elaboration based on Financial Markets (2023[5]), https://www.fdimarkets.com/

For example, both in Canada and in the United States about 85% of greenfield FDI in transport equipment is directed to manufacturing activities. However, while in the United States the remaining 15% is mainly directed to labour intensive services activities (logistics, headquarters as well as maintenance and servicing), in Canada it primarily went to R&D activities in the aerospace industry (Figure 3.5, Panel A). This shows that although the job creation through FDI in the Canadian transport equipment sector has been low, a relatively large number of high-skilled jobs has been created.

In case of the software and IT sector, the difference in the distribution of greenfield FDI across activities is even more pronounced. In the United States about two thirds of greenfield FDI in the software and IT sector is concentrated in labour-intensive services such as sales, marketing, and support whereas greenfield FDI in the Canadian software and IT sector was mostly concentrated in R&D activities especially for video games and software publishers (Figure 3.5, Panel B). From 2005 until 2022, opened and announced greenfield FDI projects in the software and IT industry are estimated to have created nearly 50,000 jobs in R&D activities, highlighting how FDI shapes the demand for skills and different occupations.

Figure 3.5. FDI in Transport Equipment and Software & IT industry is concentrated in R&D activities

FDI within Transport Equipment and Software & IT by activity, % in total sector greenfield FDI over 2005-2022

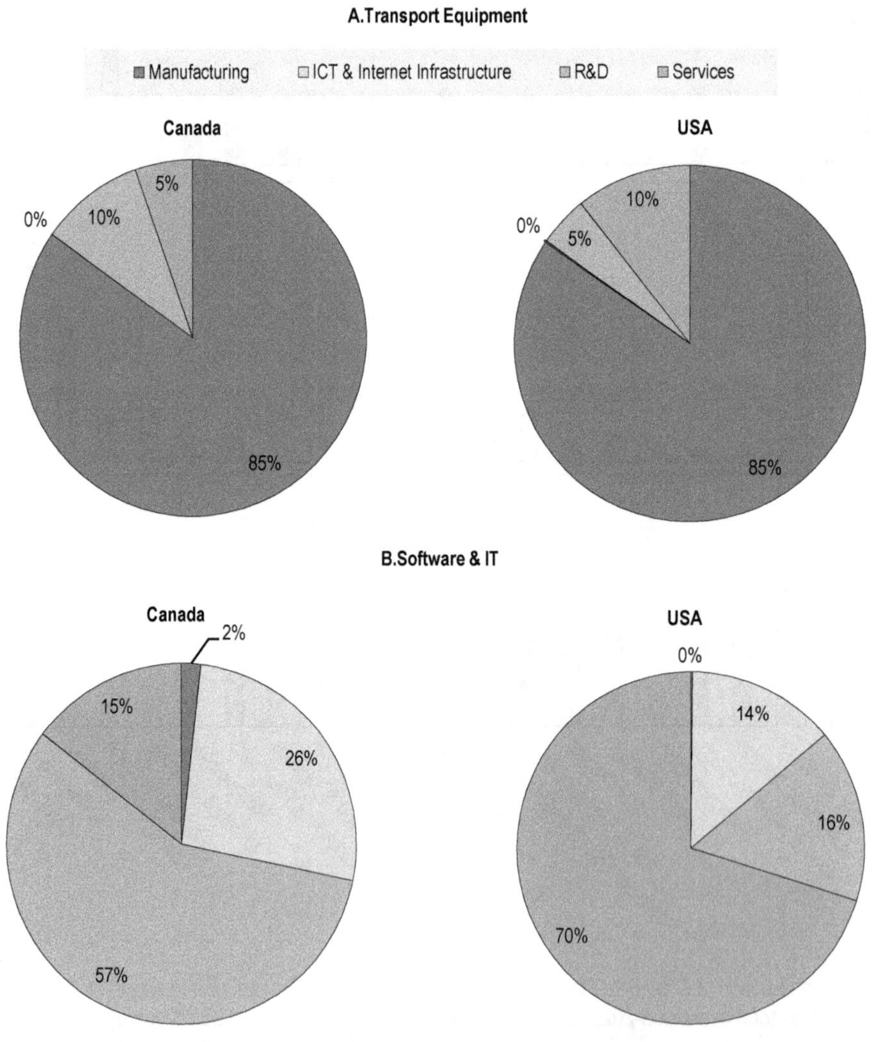

Note: This figure shows the share of greenfield FDI in the Transport equipment (Panel A) and Software and IT industry (Panel B) across different activities. *Service* activities include Business Services, Headquarters, Technical Support Centre, Education & Training, Shared Services Centre, Logistics, Distribution & Transportation, Customer Contact Centre, Maintenance & Servicing, as well as Sales, Marketing & Support.
Source: OECD elaboration based on Financial Markets (2023[5]), https://www.fdimarkets.com/

3.2.3. Foreign firms in Canada have a mixed impact on job quality

Foreign investment in Canada can contribute to improved labour market outcomes and better living standards. There is no available data on wages paid by foreign MNEs, Canadian MNEs and non-MNEs. The OECD business consultation on corporate sustainability practices, although not representative of firms' characteristics in Canada, suggests that foreign ownership is associated with higher wages. According to the business consultation, foreign firms pay, on average, wages that are about 27% higher than domestic firms, but not necessarily in all sectors and firm sizes (Figure 3.6). In general, the foreign wage premium is largely the result of foreign firms' higher productivity levels, company size, share of skilled workers, and exports (OECD, 2022[6])The gap between the foreign and domestic firms surveyed in Canada seems to be greatest among large companies and in the manufacturing sector – the size of the sample of the business consultation does not allow to examine wage differences in other specific sectors.

Figure 3.6. Foreign ownership is associated with higher wages but not in all sectors or firm sizes

Average annual cost of labour (including wages, salaries, bonuses, social security payments) per employee

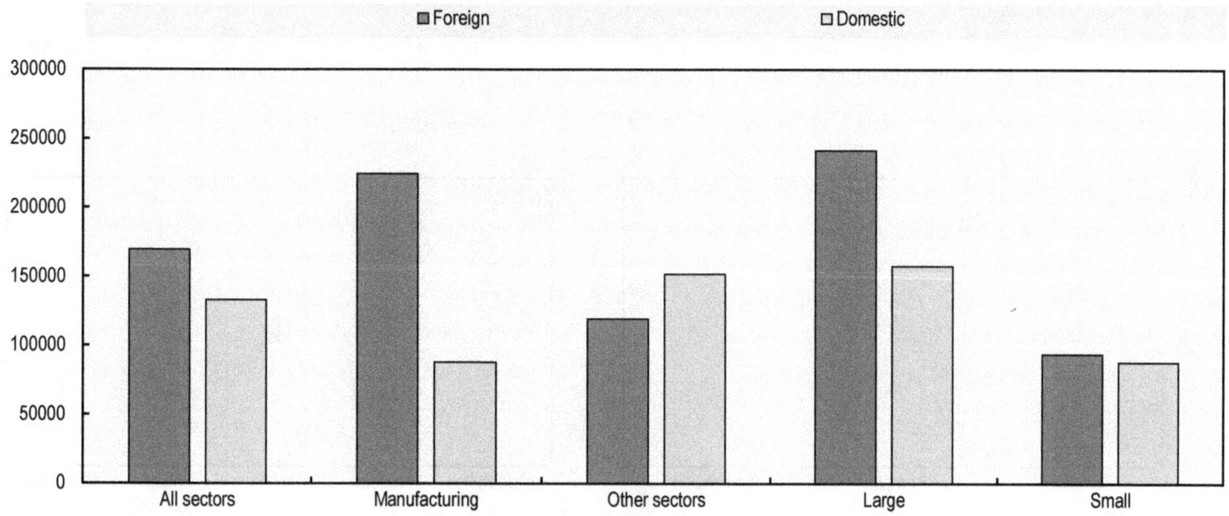

Source: OECD Business Consultation on Sustainability Practices in Canada (2022[7]).

The high foreign wage premium in Canadian manufacturing may be driven by the small and non-representative sample. It may also reflect the activity of export-oriented large foreign firms operating in highly competitive global markets where better wages help attract and retain skilled workers (Huang, 2016[8]). Foreign firms are responsible for 57% of Canadian export value, including 59% of merchandise exports (see Chapter 2). The difference in wages paid by the surveyed foreign and domestic firms is less pronounced or non-existent outside of the manufacturing sector. However, evidence shows that the foreign wage premium in Canada exists and is widespread across all sectors (Huang, 2016[8]; Sébastien and Brown, 2011[9]; Baldwin and Gu, 2005[10]). Earlier, albeit dated, evidence reveals that Canadian and foreign MNEs pay similar wages to their workers, but there is a large difference with non-MNEs, particularly for production workers (Baldwin and Gu, 2005[10]). Overall, it is membership in a multinational production network – and not foreign ownership *per se* – that generates the foreign wage premium (Setzler and Tintelnot, 2021[11]).

Foreign firms in Canada have a mixed impact on dimensions of job quality other than wages, including job security, occupational health and safety at work and such collective bargaining coverage. These differentiated impacts are mostly driven by differences in foreign and domestic investment concentration across sectors with distinct labour market features. Moreover, they depend on whether MNEs export their home country's labour practices and pass them on to domestic firms, or whether they adapt to host country standards (OECD, 2022[6]). Evidence suggests that foreign MNEs in Canada have brought aspects of their own HRM practices to Canadian subsidiaries, while also relying strongly on domestic practices and standards in place.

The OECD business consultation on corporate sustainability practices shows that foreign firms in Canada have lower proportions of employees in non-standard forms of employment – workers with temporary and part-time job contracts – than domestic firms (Figure 3.7, Panel A). This category of workers has lower earnings than employees on permanent contracts and a higher risk of having unstable lifetime employment. Job insecurity also affects firms' investment in training and, in turn, their productivity growth (OECD, 2019[12]). However, it is likely that this difference is driven by the smaller share of low-skilled workers among the foreign MNEs surveyed rather than the inherent labour practices of employers who aim for more stable employment contracts. Low-skilled workers are usually the most disadvantaged in terms of labour market security in OECD countries, including Canada (Figure 3.7, Panel B). Overall, the proportion of workers in non-standard forms of employment in Canada is higher than the OECD average.

Figure 3.7. Non-standard employment in Canada is lower among foreign firms

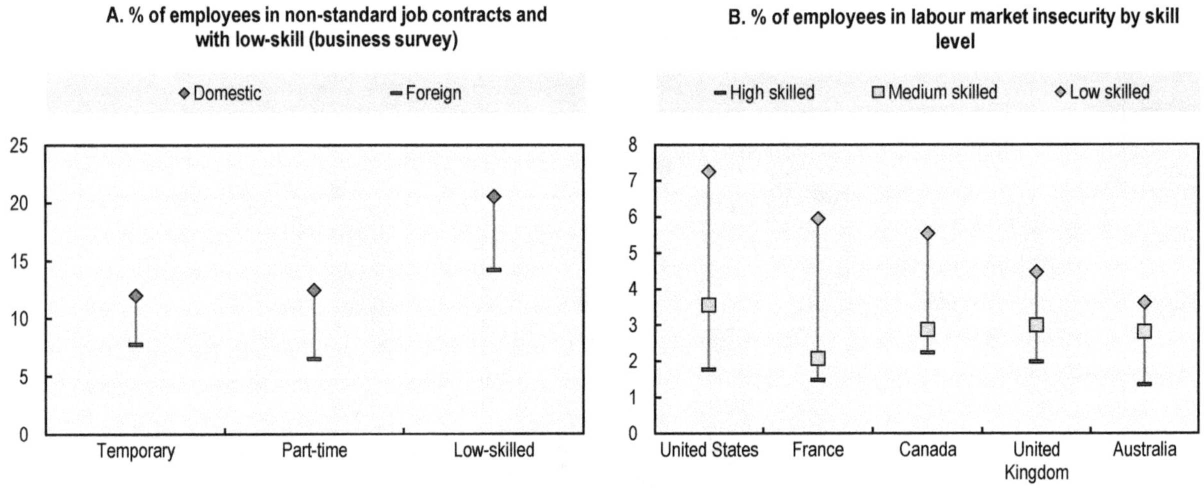

Note: Panel B: Data represents observations for 2016. The skill level B corresponds to the education level.
Source: Panel A: OECD Business Consultation on Sustainability Practices in Canada (2022[7]). Panel B: OECD Job Quality Database (2023[13]), https://www.oecd.org/statistics/job-quality.htm

The greater demand for skilled workers by foreign MNEs could, in principle, contribute to reduce job insecurity in Canada, but not necessarily to a greater extent than Canadian MNEs. Canadian MNEs are more present in high-skill intensive services such as finance and insurance, while foreign firms focus more on the production (manufacturing) and the sale of goods (wholesale and retail trade).These sectors comprised half of all jobs held by foreign firms in Canada in 2017, compared to one-third of all jobs held by Canadian MNEs (Statistics Canada, 2019[14]). The proportion of temporary workers in these different sectors is small, except retail trade, a sector with also relatively low average job tenure. Multinationals – foreign and domestic – can rapidly move their operations or activities across borders and affiliates in response to wage movements, changes in regulations or trade fluctuations. This can reduce job security – particularly for low-skilled workers – in the trading sector where profit margins are narrow. It is costlier to separate from the higher-skilled staff that are typically harder to find in periods of growth (OECD, 2022[6]).

The quality of the jobs created by foreign firms in Canada also depends on whether they operate in sectors covered by collective bargaining agreements and have effective workers' voice arrangements. Foreign investment is a catalyser of megatrends such as the digital and green transition that are transforming the world of work and creating uncertainty about labour market gains and losses. Collective bargaining systems and workers' voice arrangements help ensure that all workers benefit from these transformations, supporting solutions to emerging issues, integrating policies to anticipate skills needs, and supporting displaced workers in new forms of work (OECD, 2019[15]). Collective bargaining can also support a fairer sharing of productivity gains by influencing the wage formation process. This is relevant in the context of foreign firms that may poorly translate productivity related rents into wage benefits, particularly for less skilled workers with lower bargaining power (Criscuolo et al., 2020[16]; OECD, 2022[6]).

The rate of collective bargaining coverage has been falling in Canada over the past few decades, particularly in sectors where foreign MNEs operate. There is no publicly available data on the proportion of workers in foreign MNEs covered by a union agreement. However, applying sector-specific union coverage rates to employment trends in foreign and domestic firms, approximate measures by ownership type can be obtained. These measures suggest that the coverage rate within foreign MNEs is significantly lower than in Canadian MNEs and non-MNE firms (Figure 3.8, Panel A). The gap also considerably widened over the last decade. This has been driven mainly by a significant fall of union coverage in FDI-intensive sectors such as manufacturing and wholesale and retail trade (Figure 3.8, Panel B). Sectors where Canadian MNEs operate more significantly such as in finance and business services witnessed a lower decline. The decline in union coverage is not specific to Canada. Most OECD countries have experienced a similar trend (OECD, 2019[17]).

Figure 3.8. Change in union coverage in foreign and domestic firms based on industry coverage

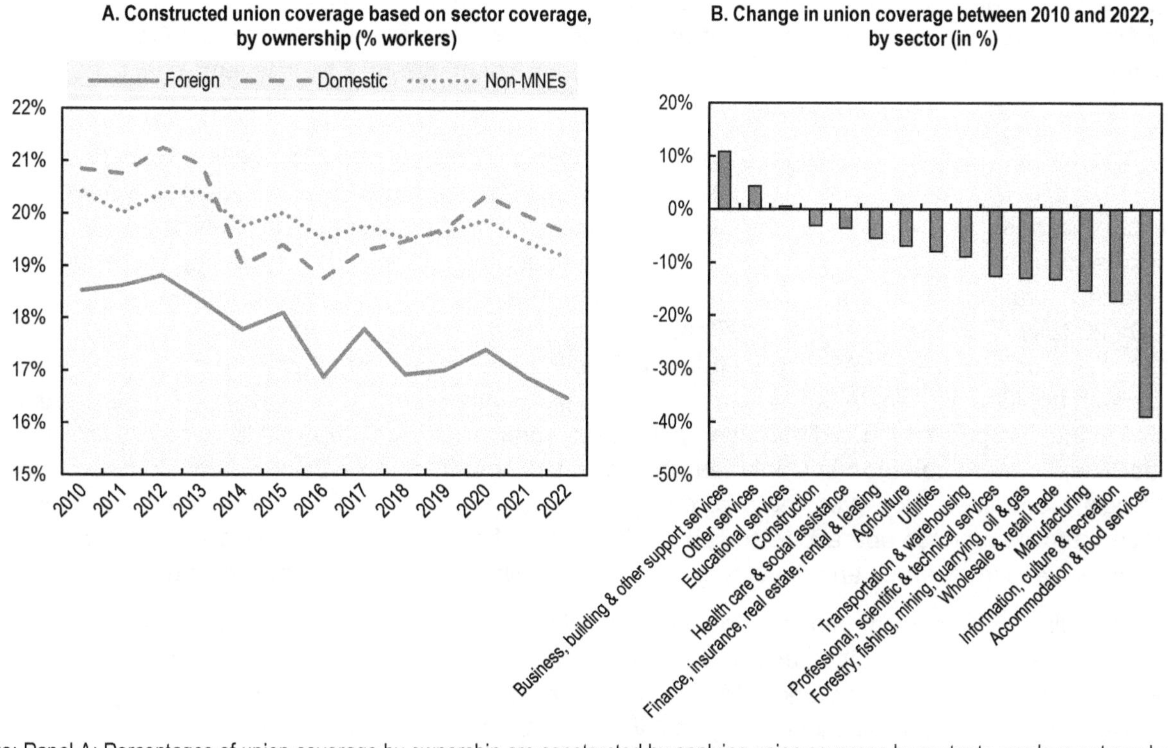

Note: Panel A: Percentages of union coverage by ownership are constructed by applying union coverage by sector to employment numbers by ownership type and by sector. Data for 2021 and 2022 is an estimate based on employment numbers for 2020.
Source: OECD elaboration based on Statistics Canada (2023[2]) and Statistics Canada (2023[18]), https://doi.org/10.25318/1410007001-eng

Engagement with unions could help ensure that the impact of foreign MNEs on job quality in Canada is based on domestic practices and not merely contingent on labour practices exported from the home country. Evidence from Ontario, largely within the manufacturing sector, suggests that foreign MNEs are more likely to comply with provincial employment laws when operations are unionised. Their country of origin affects the likelihood of compliance mostly in non-unionised workplaces – likelihood is higher among Western European or Scandinavian MNEs than in firms from countries with greater labour right violations (Pohler and Riddell, 2018[19]). Unionisation does not necessarily lead to stronger employer-employee relations, however, such as in the case of the mining sector, where some foreign MNEs have mimicked the limited engagement of Canadian firms with unions (Levesque et al., 2015[20]). The high concentration of FDI in some sectors may also allow foreign MNEs to lobby for their preferred HRM approach given sectoral dependence on FDI (Aguzzoli and Geary, 2014[21]).

Differences in skill-intensity can also influence the strength of engagement of foreign MNEs with labour unions. Despite the mixed engagement that foreign MNEs have had with workers and unions in Canada, evidence comparing Canada to Argentina and Mexico shows that workers of foreign MNEs in Canada have greater bargaining power, given their higher skill levels. This is also compounded by the greater autonomy of managers of foreign MNEs in Canada vis-à-vis their corporate headquarters, which contributes to their stronger engagement with labour unions. This differs from Argentina or Mexico, where subsidiary managers being more tied to their international HRM, combined with lower worker skill levels, leads the foreign MNEs to engage less with unions (Levesque et al., 2015[20]).

As sectors with lower union coverage rates attract the bulk of FDI in Canada, it is also crucial to examine firm-labour relations practices outside of the union context. Canada is among only ten OECD member states where unions are the only official worker-led representative voice in the workplace, with an absence of works councils and non-unionised worker representatives (OECD, 2019[17]). It is important to note that in Canada there are no laws facilitating employee representation at board level, which are present in twenty OECD member states (OECD, 2017[22]). There are some mandatory representative voice institutions in larger firms in Canada, such as health and safety committees (mandatory under most Canadian labour legislation), but these are less effective in non-union environments due to less employers' buy-in and employees' engagement (OECD, 2019[17]).

In Canada, in non-unionised settings, domestic and foreign firms rely on their HRM bodies to oversee labour relations. This can limit the impact of FDI on job quality, given the lower effectiveness of employee voice approaches, compared to unionisation and direct worker representation. Nevertheless, working conditions can be influenced by foreign firms' intrinsic characteristics, such as more advanced management practices than domestic firms, and good management can lead to higher job satisfaction (OECD, 2022[6]). For example, one of Canada's few non-unionised automakers, has team member relations function within its HRM. The staff in this function are former manufacturing employees who are familiar with frontline workers in the industry, which helps to understand their concerns. One subsidiary of an MNE in the energy sector has different employee relations practices compared to its parent firm in Asia, with activities that are common in Canadian corporate settings, such as a Joint Safety Committee and a Joint Social Committee. However, the differences in practices also stem from the fact that operations in headquarter focus more on operations and production, while those in Canada are largely made up of highly skilled employees in research and development functions, which makes different demands on employees.

Notwithstanding the nature of industrial relations of MNEs in Canada – whether in a unionised or non-unionised context, in practice, the bargaining power of MNEs vis-à-vis workers may still differ from that of domestic firms, perhaps due to workers' fears that wage demands (or negative shocks) may lead to the relocation of production. Their higher propensity to go abroad could adversely affect rent-sharing with workers and may also weaken MNEs' compliance with labour standards. The OECD Guidelines for MNEs indicate that, in the context of negotiations with workers' representatives, or while workers are exercising a right to organise, MNEs should not threaten to relocate activity to other countries to unfairly influence negotiations or to hinder the exercise of a right to organise (OECD, 2011[23]; OECD, 2022[6]).

Whether in Canada or elsewhere, one consequence of the bargaining imbalance in foreign MNEs at the national level has been the development of transnational workers' representations to better co-ordinate workers' bargaining policies. Global Framework Agreements (GFAs) have emerged as an innovative cross-border mechanism among MNEs to better co-ordinate workers' bargaining policies across national subsidiaries, providing workers with the right to unionise and bargain collectively. In Canada, there are dozens of foreign and domestic MNEs that have entered GFAs, in sectors such as manufacturing and construction. Although there are no analyses of their impacts for Canadian workers, global evidence suggests that GFAs have the capacity to improve workers' fundamental rights and bargaining power at work, but this also depends on the labour practices of the country of origin of the MNE (OECD, 2022[6]).

3.3. FDI impacts on skills development and imbalances

Canada's highly-educated workforce is an important pull factor for FDI that can itself, as part of a virtuous cycle, contribute to upskilling. Foreign investment can accelerate megatrends such as the digital and green transitions that, together with population ageing, change the supply and demand of skills on the labour market (OECD, 2020[24]). These trends may lead to changes in tasks, the elimination of some jobs and the creation of new jobs that require different skills. Economic growth and employment in Canada have gone back-to pre-COVID-19 pandemic levels, and the number of unemployed people to job vacancies went down to 1.2 in the second quarter of 2022 - the lowest level since 2015 (Statistics Canada, 2022[25]). Under these conditions skills imbalances can arise, making labour market adjustments to meet skills in demand by firms lengthy and costly, potentially limiting the benefits of FDI on workers and skills.

3.3.1. Foreign MNEs contribute to increased shares of skilled labour in Canada

Foreign firms draw heavily on the highly skilled Canadian labour force, which has the highest level of education among OECD countries. In 2021, 62% of the 25–64-year-old population had a tertiary education compared to 40% for the OECD average (OECD, 2023[26]). There is no data on skill intensity of foreign firms based on the National Occupational Classification (NOC) skill level, which identifies occupations by the education and training that is generally required. Among the companies surveyed in the OECD Business Consultation on Sustainability Practices in Canada, although not representative of firms' characteristics in Canada, the share of high-skilled employment was 64% in foreign firms compared to 58% in domestic firms, as reported (Figure 3.9, Panel A). This suggests that FDI in Canada could be raising the demand for skilled labour and, conditional on labour availability and mobility, potentially contribute to a growing share of high-skilled jobs in the workforce.

Despite the ongoing polarisation of the Canadian labour market away from mid-skilled and towards high-skilled jobs, foreign firms operate in sectors that also intensively rely on mid-skilled workers. Between 1998 and 2018, the share of high-skilled jobs in Canada increased by 4.4 percentage points whereas the share of mid- and low-skilled jobs declined by 4.1 and 0.3 percentage points respectively (OECD, 2020[24]). In sectors where foreign companies account for about one third of the labour force (e.g. manufacturing, mining and wholesale trade), more than 50% of firms report requiring management, business, basic digital and IT skills, but also depend on skilled trades like machinists or electricians (Figure 3.9, Panel B). However, these skills are in demand by employers in most other sectors of the Canadian economy.

Figure 3.9. Foreign firms in Canada raise the demand for both high and mid-skilled labour

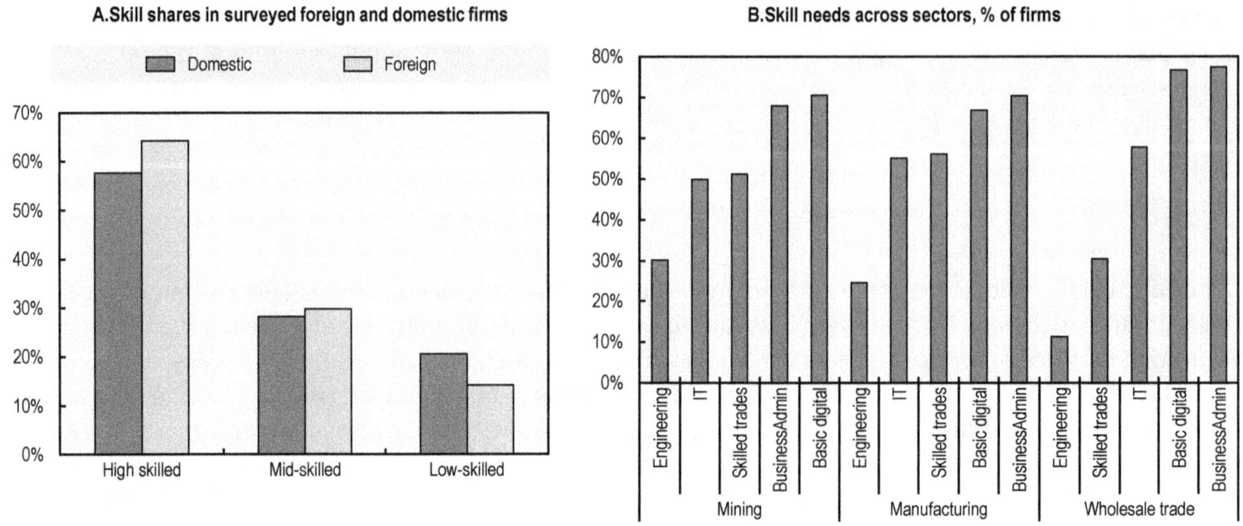

Note: Panel A: Skills shares in foreign and domestic firms based on the OECD Business Consultation on Sustainability Practices in Canada (OECD, 2022[7]). Panel B: Shares of corporate firms reporting skill needs across different sectors. Mining, Manufacturing and Wholesale trade are sectors in which foreign firms account for about one third of jobs. Panel B is based on survey data from 2019.
Source: OECD elaboration based on OECD (2022[7]) and Statistics Canada (2023[27]), https://www150.statcan.gc.ca/t1/tbl1/en/tv.action?pid=3310029901

3.3.2. Foreign firms in Canada face skills imbalances but they can also help reduce them

In Canada, as in other OECD countries, employers increasingly face skills imbalances that misalign the demand and supply of skills. As a result, employers cannot fill vacancies due to a lack of adequately qualified candidates, i.e., skills shortages, or employees do not possess the right set of skills to perform their tasks, i.e., skills mismatches (or skills gaps), leading to productivity losses and lower innovation. Foreign firms affect skills imbalances through their impact on both the supply and the demand of skilled labour (OECD, 2019[4]). On the one hand, the presence of foreign firms can exacerbate existing skills imbalances by raising the relative demand for skilled labour in the host economy, while, on the other hand, foreign firms may contribute to reduce skills imbalances by expanding the supply of skills in the host country, for example, by training their employees (Becker et al., 2020[28]; OECD, 2022[6]).

Skills mismatches in Canada may affect foreign business relying on mid-skilled workers

The Canadian labour market is increasingly experiencing skills mismatches. About 38% of workers have qualifications, i.e. levels of education, that are mismatched to their jobs, compared to 34% across the OECD (OECD (2022[29]), Figure 3.10). Underqualified workers, i.e., workers who possess lower qualifications than those required by their job, make up a greater share (23%) compared to those who are overqualified and thus unable to realise their full potential (16%). Qualifications – or the level of educational attainment – are a partial measure of actual skills, however. Some skills acquired in education may be lost over time and new skills are acquired through labour market experience. Skills mismatches can negatively impact productivity, with estimates suggesting that productivity in Canada could increase by over 2% if mismatches were lowered to best practice levels (Adalet McGowan and Andrews, 2017[30]).

Figure 3.10. Canada's labour market face skills mismatches more than in other OECD countries

Qualification mismatches of workers in Canada and other OECD countries, 2019

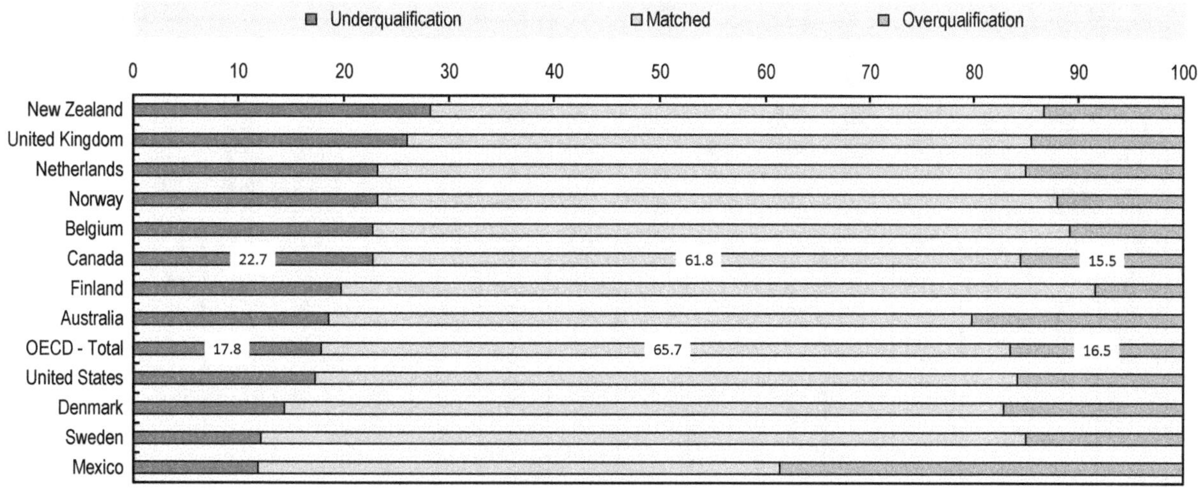

Note: This chart shows the average percentage of workers that have a qualification that does not match their job's requirements. The data refer to 2019, except for Australia (2016). A worker is over-qualified (under-qualified) when his/her highest educational attainment is above (below) the requirement of his/her job.
Source: OECD elaboration based on OECD (2022[29]), https://stats.oecd.org/Index.aspx?DataSetCode=S4J2022_MISMATCH

In an environment with rapid changes in skills requirements, population aging and a lack of lifelong training of employees may be key to explaining skill mismatches in the Canadian workforce. For example, workers aged 55 to 64, which represent a growing part of the workforce (18% of all working-age employees in 2023, an increase from 13% in 2007 (Statistics Canada, 2023[31])), are 1.8 times more likely to be under-skilled than those aged 45 to 54 (Parisa Mahboubi, 2019[32]).[1] Immigrants, despite being on average more educated than non-immigrants, are also likelier to be under-skilled for their jobs. This is driven by significantly lower literacy skills (largely due to a lack of knowledge of English or French), and to a lesser extent in numeracy and problem solving (Parisa Mahboubi, 2019[32]). However, the under-skilled challenge of immigrants disappears with time, partly thanks to policies such as language programmes – some of are provided sometimes by the foreign MNEs themselves (see also Chapter 4).

Large foreign MNEs in Canada operating in sectors relying on mid-skilled workers such as manufacturing or wholesale trade are more likely to face skills mismatches than small firms requiring high-skilled labour. There is no data on skill mismatches specific to foreign MNEs in Canada, but the Survey of Employers on Workers' Skills (SWES) 2021 shows that 56% of firms – 93% in the case of large firms – reported having employees who were not fully proficient to be able to perform their job at the required level. Of these firms, 58% reported that the skills that needed the most improvement were technical, practical or job specific. Skill gaps are widespread across sectors, but employment by foreign firms is relatively low in most affected sectors (Figure 3.11). Several sectors with large employment by foreign firms, including manufacturing, wholesale trade and mining, still face large skill gaps, in contrast with professional, scientific and technical services that report lower skill gap.

Figure 3.11. Skill mismatches are widespread across sectors in Canada

Share of businesses within industries that reported skill gaps, 2022

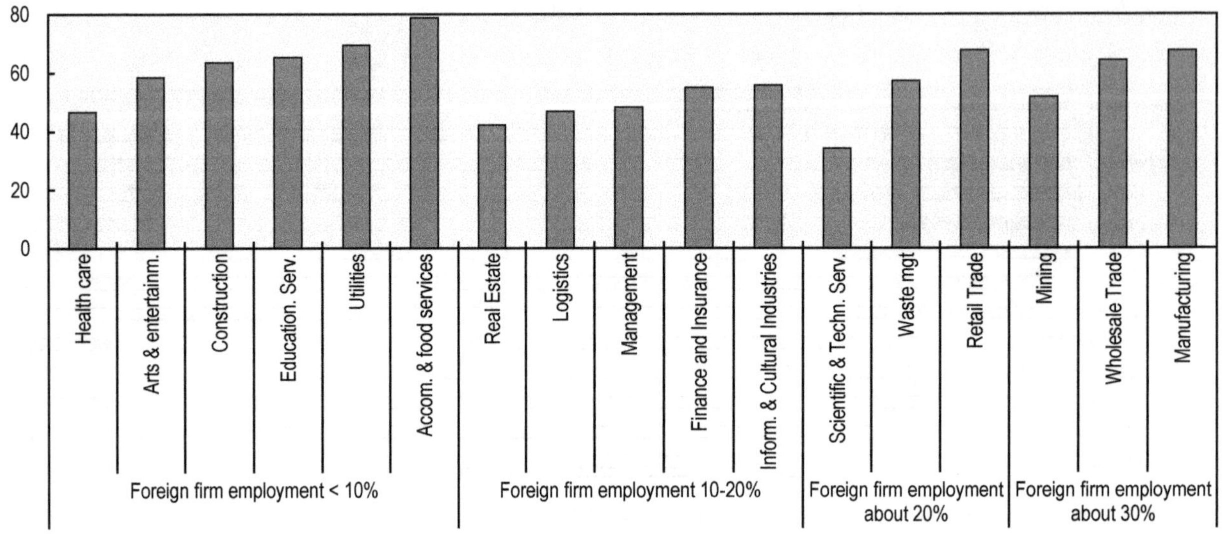

Note: Due to availability of data the share of employment in foreign firms is from 2019.
Source: OECD elaboration based on Statistics Canada (2022[25]), https://www150.statcan.gc.ca/n1/pub/18-001-x/18-001-x2022002-eng.htm and Statistics Canada (2023[2]), https://www150.statcan.gc.ca/t1/tbl1/en/tv.action?pid=3610062001

Foreign firms face skill shortages in computer science and in skilled trades that affect the attractiveness of Canada and future growth potential

Skills shortages are another key facet of skills imbalances in Canada that can affect the smooth operation of foreign firms and hamper their contribution to the labour market. In 2020, estimates of the unrealised value of skills vacancies in the Canadian economy amounted to 1.3% of the GDP (Gabler and Gormley, 2022[33]). According to the SWES 2021, conducted in 2022, almost half of firms in Canada (45%) experienced difficulties finding candidates who possessed the skills needed to do the job at the required level. For most firms (55%), the main reason was the lack of interested people for the type of vacant work. Other reasons were lower wages compared to other organisations (14%) – including in the United States where salaries tend to be higher, challenging working conditions (8%) and geographic location (5%). Large firms, among which many are MNEs, reported facing lower recruitment difficulties thanks to HR departments that are better equipped to recruit, hire, train, and retain workers (Statistics Canada, 2022[25]).

Both foreign and domestic firms in Canada face skill shortages across all sectors, but some sectors and skill types are more affected than others. Statistics Canada collects data based on the following type of skills: basic digital, computer science, IT, general data science & analytics, management, (international) business, skilled trades, and design. More than half of foreign firms with specific skills needs in manufacturing, utilities, management of companies, construction, transportation, and waste management face skills shortages (Figure 3.12). Especially in manufacturing, where foreign firms account for about one third of total employment, these shortages risk to undermine future growth potential in the Canadian economy: 43% of manufacturing firms claim having delayed or cancelled investment projects in Canada due to labour shortages while 15% are further considering moving production abroad (CME, 2022[34]).

Despite the prevailing skills shortage, foreign firms tend to be less severely affected by the lack of talent than domestic firms. In several sectors, including wholesale and retail trade, finance and insurance and mining, Canadian MNEs and non-MNEs are more likely to report skill shortages than foreign firms. For example, 6% of foreign firms in retail trade claim being affected by skill shortages whereas the share amounts to 83% of Canadian MNEs and 65% of non-MNEs (Figure 3.12). Such differences are likely to be driven by different skills needs between foreign MNEs and domestic firms due to different activities within sector, better recruitment strategies – including for attracting foreign workers, and higher wage offers.

Figure 3.12. Foreign and Canadian firms do not face the same skills shortages in all sectors

Skill shortages across sectors and firm-ownership category in Canada (% of firms within ownership category), 2019

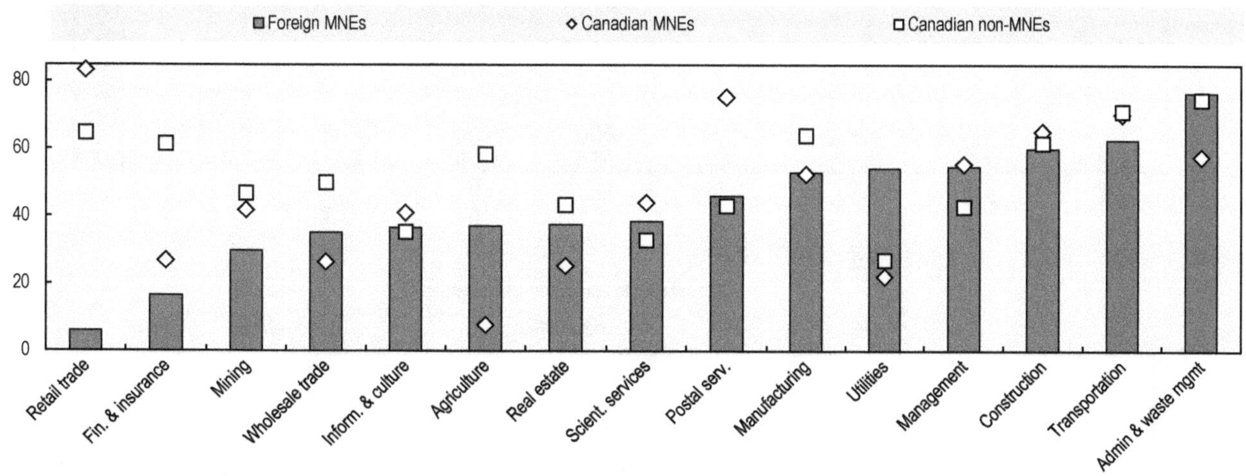

Note: This chart shows the share of firms reporting at least one shortage among 10 different skills. These skills include basic digital, computer science, IT, general data science & analytics, management, (international) business, skilled trades, and design. Shares are based on firms stating that a specific skill is relevant for their business. The chart is based on survey data from 2019.
Source: OECD elaboration based on Statistics Canada (2023[35]), https://doi.org/10.25318/3310030001-eng

Skilled trades and computer science are the skills in which foreign firms report the greatest shortages in the Canadian labour market. Almost half (46%) of foreign firms report skill shortages of skilled trades, followed by shortages in computer science (23%) and general data science and analytics (14%), while about 10% reveal shortages in design, IT, management, business and basic digital skills (Figure 3.13, Panel A). The severe shortage of skilled trades is exacerbated by demographic change affecting all firms. As to foreign firms, they face large shortages of skilled trades in sectors where they are large employers such as waste management and manufacturing, where they employ about one fifth and one third of the workforce respectively (Figure 3.13, Panel C). Projections show that about 700,000 skilled trades workers are expected to retire between 2019 and 2028, creating an ever-growing need to recruit and train more talent (Government of Canada, 2022[36]).

Skill shortages in computer and data science risk to affect the attractiveness of the Canadian tech industry and its absorptive capacity of FDI spillovers. These shortages are especially critical in advanced digital skills such as coding, web and app development, data visualisation and computer and data science (Mahboubi, 2022[37]). While the software and IT sector experienced the largest inflow of greenfield FDI in Canada over the past years, foreign firms claimed the largest shortage of tech related skills in these sectors (Figure 3.13, Panel B). Skills shortages in tech jobs are partly driven by strong competition for talent among STEM graduates from the United States, drawn by both significantly higher wages and more diverse work opportunities (Spicer, Olmstead and Goodman, 2018[38]).

Figure 3.13. Foreign MNEs in Canada flag the greatest skills shortages in skilled trades and computer science

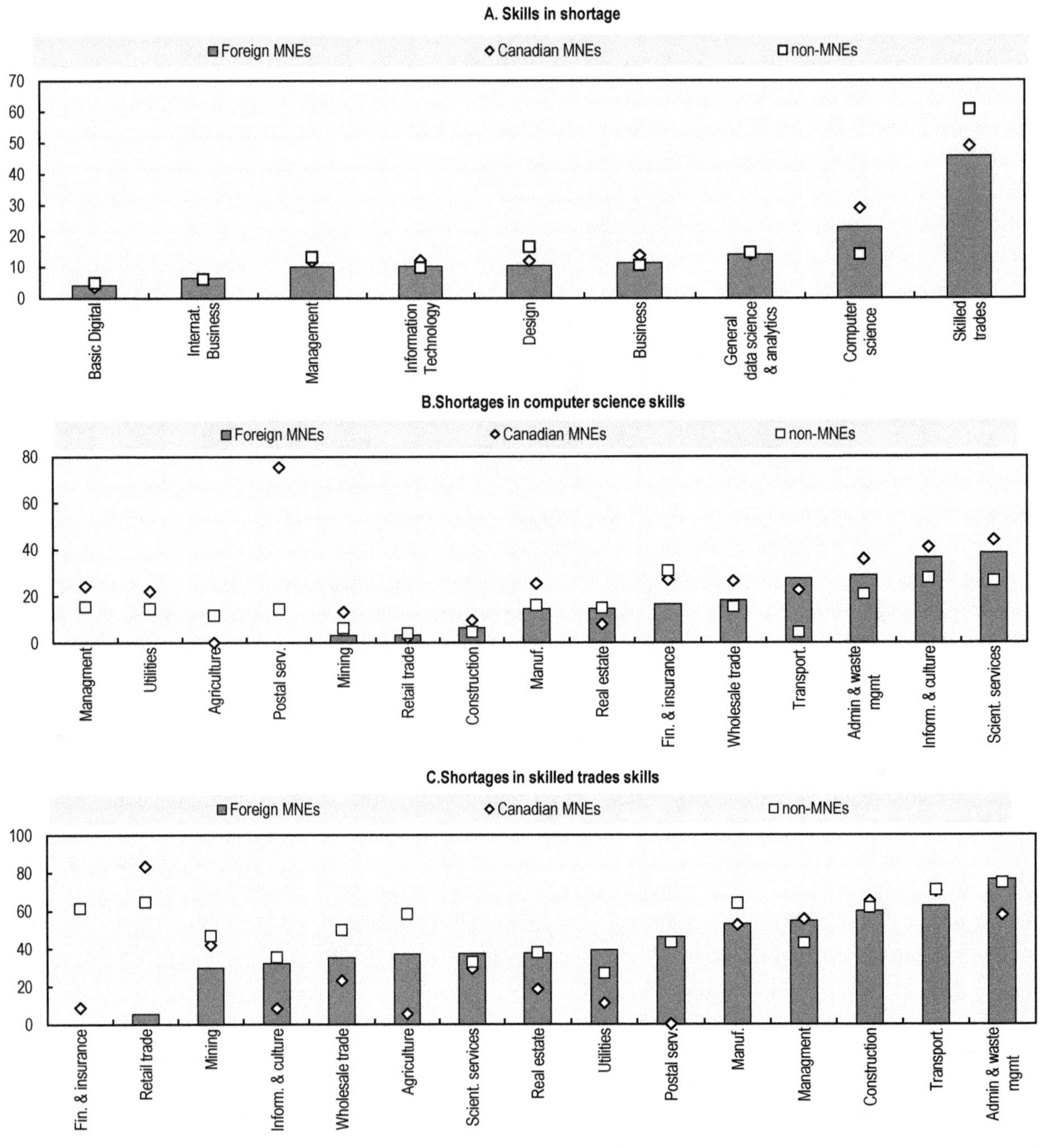

Note: Panel A: Share of firms reporting shortages in indicated skills. The total set of firms includes firms that claim listed skills as applicable in their business. Panel B and Panel C: Share of firms reporting shortages in computer science and skilled trades across different sectors. Panel A, B and C rely on survey data from 2019.
Source: OECD elaboration based on Statistics Canada (2023[35]), https://doi.org/10.25318/3310030001-eng

3.3.3. The Practices of foreign firms in Canada can contribute to lower skills imbalances

Foreign investment raises the demand for specific skills and occupations in Canada, but it can also increase the supply of adequate skills and thereby contribute to lower skills imbalances. In a context of tight labour markets, foreign and domestic firms in Canada are countering skill shortages and brain drain by providing higher wages and benefits, training staff, and offering more flexible work conditions. Employers in Canada that experienced labour shortages in 2022 were significantly more likely than unaffected peers to increase wages or benefits for existing (64%) or new employees (46%), to introduce flexible work arrangements (34%) or to foster the human capital of the workforce by providing on-the-job training (31%) or training employees to take other positions within the business (23%) (Figure 3.14).

Figure 3.14. Foreign firms rely mostly on wage increases to tackle skill shortages in Canada

Percentage of businesses planning to implement specific measures over the next 12 months, 2022

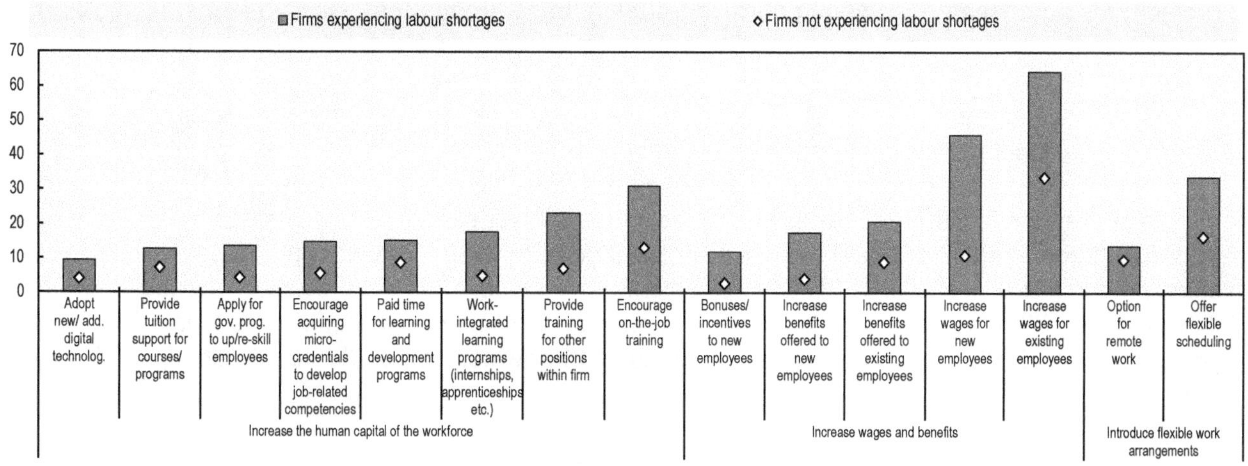

Note: This chart shows results from the Canadian Survey on Business Conditions, first quarter of 2022 with the sample (N=15,500) consisting of private sector businesses that do not plan to close over the next three months.
Source: OECD elaboration based on Statistics Canada (2022[39]), https://doi.org/10.25318/36280001202200700001-eng

Multinational companies in Canada tend to have more effective recruitment strategies

Canada's immigration programmes have been a key pull factor for many foreign firms, especially the Global Skills Strategy that help employers finding talented personnel more quickly. Foreign firms in Canada often have broader horizons and more elaborated strategies than domestic businesses in terms of where they can draw their talent, what training they provide and how they retain workers (OECD, 2022[7]). Foreign companies, and MNEs more broadly, tend to have more effective recruitment results due to their larger size, more extensive resources to offer financial incentives and more innovative recruitment strategies than non-MNEs. In 2019, large firms were generally more likely than small firms to have a targeted recruitment process (69% vs. 42%) and to offer additional financial incentives to recruit new employees (60% vs. 52%) (Statistics Canada, 2019[40]). Furthermore, many large MNEs have recently shifted their focus from pure qualifications-based hiring, i.e. based on education, to also hiring based on skills by removing degree requirements for several roles (World Economic Forum, 2023[41]).

Effective recruitment practices of large firms in Canada, including foreign MNEs, can help lowering the large skills imbalances, but there is also a risk that they contribute to the crowding out of small firms in local labour markets. Many Canadian SMEs revealed that they rely on local universities and colleges for talent attraction in the OECD Business Consultation on Sustainability Practices in Canada. Some SMEs also shared concerns of talent potentially moving to larger firms, presenting a challenge for their own employee retention strategies and an approach that lacks a coherent shift to give skill-based hiring as much leverage as qualifications-based hiring (OECD, 2022[7]).

Foreign companies can also leverage their international experience from other subsidiaries to attract and retain talent and, in turn, help increase the talent pool in the Canadian labour market. For example, in the manufacturing sector, where foreign firms account for around a third of jobs and flag significant skill needs, there is a particular drive to increase the talent pool through immigration and a more inclusive workplace. Canada is one of the most attractive destinations among OECD countries for highly educated workers (11th out of 38), entrepreneurs (4th out of 38), university students (5th out of 37) as well as startup founders (3rd out 24) and the economy relies substantially on the recruitment of foreign talent to tackle skills shortages (OECD, 2023[42]). In addition to foreign talent attraction, manufacturers opt for increasing employment of youth and underrepresented groups like women, based on their international experience, thereby supporting the integration of talent diversity in the Canadian labour market (see Chapter 4).

Foreign firms have been observed in nurturing a talent base among their locally hired staff, including in technologically intensive sectors where Canada lacks a comparative advantage or does not have a strongly established domestic industry. The OECD Business Consultation on Sustainability Practices in Canada shows that some foreign MNEs transfer their own existing staff from the headquarter or other subsidiaries to support their establishment in Canada, such as for specialised roles, providing them with an opportunity to transfer their knowledge and expertise to locally hired staff (Box 3.1). These interactions are crucial to stemming domestic skills shortages, especially for careers and industries that require digital and skilled trade talent. Additional evidence on knowledge spillovers shows that, in the medical devices sector, among a sampled pool of 272 Canadian company founders, 94 had previously worked for a foreign MNE (see also Chapter 2). In a case where 16 Canadian medical device companies in the Toronto area were acquired by MNEs, leaving senior talent founded 14 new companies (Matthews and Rice, 2022[43]).

Box 3.1. Specialised talent development practices in foreign MNEs in Canada

Several foreign MNEs in the OECD Business Consultation on Sustainability Practices in Canada have put in place specialised talent development practices. One large construction company expanded to Canada in 2005 and has since participated in tunnelling projects for both transport and utilities services. Canada has historically had fewer tunnelling operations than in Europe, which contributed to much of the company initial success on the market. During the company's first years in Canada, specialised engineers were largely made up of expatriates, having to fill talent needs which could not be found in Canada. Many of these included SEM tunnelling experts and TBM tunnel boring machine experts, many of which had over 30 years of experience. However, as the company's operations in Canada grew, it gradually began to have more Canadian employees in specialised positions, given the significant knowledge spillovers. Numerous Canadian employees that developed specialised skills at the company, especially around tunnelling, have brought these talents to local smaller design firms and larger Canadian firms.

Another example is an accounting software foreign firm. Establishing in 2018 as part of its first expansion into North America, it has since hired over 200 workers but have also transferred technical talent from headquarters, especially engineers, who have significant expertise in the company's tech infrastructure and internal systems, while being able to train and mentor Canadian engineers over time. By transferring more tenured employees to Canada during their growth phase, they have been able to bring people with advanced specialized knowledge of the company's software, services, business standards, processes, and best practices that they could not find in external candidates. This has allowed the company in Canada to stay connected to corporate culture and best practices of the source country, while developing and nurturing a distinct Canadian presence and talent base.

Source: OECD Business Consultation on Sustainability Practices in Canada (2022[71]).

Foreign firms in Canada leverage their training practices from a greater range of sources

Firms in Canada are behind most of their international peers in their spending on training and in hours of instruction, however. For example, Canadian firms spend 81% for each dollar that an American firm spends on training (Munro and Lamb, 2023[44]). Furthermore, 54% of Canadian workers participate in employer sponsored education and training, which is slightly less than their counterparts in New Zealand (62%), Australia (57%), and the United States (57%) (OECD, 2020[45]). Differences in recent training are significantly more pronounced, however, with 54% of Canadian workers reporting in December 2021 that they had not participated in any professional development opportunities during the past 12 months, versus 29% of American workers (D2L, 2022[46]). There is also inequitable distribution of training among employees, where it is more likely to be offered to higher-educated employees in management, professional and technical roles, and those who are in their core working years (25-54).

The reduced ability of firms in Canada to provide training compared with other countries may be linked to the lack of resources that Canadian SMEs have relative to larger firms. Although 68% of private sector employees in Canada worked in firms of less than 100 people, larger employers are as much as three times more likely to provide training than SMEs, and almost twice as likely to offer advanced technology adoption training, with 39% of large companies doing so, versus 21% of small companies. However, spending on training is also decreasing among large firms, while 81% of surveyed firms in the Business Council of Canada's membership base had spent over CAD 500 per employee on training in 2018, this had fallen to 65% of firms by 2022, possibly due to the COVID-19 pandemic (Munro and Lamb, 2023[44]).

Given that foreign firms tend to be larger than domestic non-MNEs, and have the ability to leverage training material, methods and staff from their global operations, they contribute positively to training and the development of talent in Canada. The OECD business consultation conducted for this study suggests that training and workforce development practices do not differ significantly between foreign and domestic firms in Canada, with a dependence on formal mechanisms of on-boarding training and locally hired human resources teams. Foreign firms often leverage their practices from a greater range of sources, however. This includes using elements from their country-of-origin operations providing international networking and mentoring opportunities, and a broader array of classroom and curriculum-based training modules for longer-term upskilling and employee development, especially for junior employees and recent graduates, such as through global training centres (Box 3.2). Investment in new or junior employees can lead to increased worker satisfaction, helping retain talent and reduce turnovers. Evidence shows that employees in Canada that received classroom training were 11% more productive than those that did not, although with limited effect on wages (Dostie, 2013[47]) (Dostie and Léger, 2014[48]).

Foreign firms are also more likely to provide technical apprenticeships or work-integrated learning opportunities, providing a pipeline of skills development for Canadian students and potential path to employment after graduation. The OECD Business Consultation on Sustainability Practices in Canada shows that many foreign firms draw talent from local universities and colleges, especially through work-integrated learning opportunities. They also work to leverage and develop talent bases that come from local universities through formalised training processes involving both on-the-job and more comprehensive classroom training. The Consultation indicates that foreign firms set up operations especially in regions where not only are there important market links, but also emerging talent pools through key universities, such as in Waterloo, Hamilton, Ottawa, and Vancouver (Box 3.2). This has potentially been having spillover effects. The percentage of large firms in Canada offering work-integrated learning (co-ops) increased from 72% in 2018 to 88% in 2022. Similarly, there has been a sharp rise of graduates with work-integrated-learning experience, with 63% of large firms in 2022 reporting that their entry-level employees have some industry experience against 24% in 2018 (Business Council of Canada, 2022[49]).

Box 3.2. Practices of foreign firms in Canada to develop and maintain talent

Examples of global training programmes by foreign MNEs

All junior-level hires of a foreign consulting firm in Canada since 2011, benefit from the company's two-week school in Europe, where new recruits can develop and present their own business cases and learn from others that are often outside of their own areas of specialisation. This training goes beyond a traditional textbook format and allows beneficiaries to learn from a simulation of their actual work ahead. A medium-sized foreign climate control and building automation company, enhances the skills of its employees worldwide and in Canada through an online learning platform that provides horticulture and building automation courses for designers, installers, and sales staff, while also pairing staff with plant scientists for further knowledge transfer opportunities. The learning platform has also been used by external customers, such as vocational schoolteachers, and employees of other companies, including growers, building operators and dealers.

Examples of foreign MNEs' partnerships with local universities

A foreign ICT multinational, which has been expanding rapidly in the Ottawa and Toronto regions, collaborates with IT and engineering faculties across Canada, taking 450 students per year through co-op programs, in addition to providing various scholarships, bursaries and technical development workshops for students. The company's *co-op jobs* strategy is to rely on, attract and train existing local talent, and contribute to an ecosystem of talent that can eventually also benefit other firms. A foreign vehicle technology company established a subsidiary in Canada in 2016, with a product and service focus on cybersecurity. The company has leveraged its proximity to the University of Waterloo to achieve a co-operative education partnership, employing 50+ co-op students in the last seven years, and converting four of these to permanent employment after graduation.

One ICT multinational launched a five-year partnership in 2021 to enhance Carleton University's Institute for Data Science and its cross-disciplinary AI and Data Science programmes. Alongside joint research and educational initiatives between the company and the university, the company provides Carleton students with apprenticeships through the company's end-to-end co-creation model to accelerate digital transformation. This is part of a wider, longstanding collaboration that the MNE has had with Canadian universities, largely through its Advanced Studies programme, active in Canada since 1990, which directly engages with universities in collaborative projects with the company's staff, students, and educators.

One leading dedicated pure-play semiconductor foundry expanded to Canada in 2007, through the opening of a design center, initially with 20 employees, having tripled to almost 60 today. With the growth of a domestic talent base being vital for the future of the semiconductor industry in Canada, many of the design centre's design and layout engineers come from around the world. In recent years, the center has increased its focus on sourcing domestic talent and transferring knowledge to them internally. To achieve this, they look towards top semiconductor engineering programmes at Canadian universities, inviting students for internships to hone their skills in an industrial R&D environment. To further encourage learning in semiconductor design and layout, the company launched a University Programme that provides, through select service partners, broad educational access for students, faculty, and researchers to the process design kit of the industry's most successful fin field-effect transistor technology, enabling students to design their projects into a modern process. This programme will likely be introduced into several partner Canadian universities, providing specialised upskilling for engineering students in an emerging sector.

Source: OECD Business Consultation on Sustainability Practices in Canada (2022[7]), Carleton University (2023[50]), IBM (2023[51])

References

Adalet McGowan, M. and D. Andrews (2017), "Skills mismatch, productivity and policies: Evidence from the second wave of PIAAC", *OECD Economics Department Working Papers*, No. 1403, OECD Publishing, Paris, https://doi.org/10.1787/65dab7c6-en. [30]

Aguzzoli, R. and J. Geary (2014), "An 'emerging challenge': The employment practices of a Brazilian multinational company in Canada", *Human Relations*, Vol. 67/5, pp. 519-632, https://doi.org/10.1177/0018726713497523. [21]

Baldwin, J. and W. Gu (2005), *Global Links: Multinationals, Foreign Ownership, and Productivity Growth in Canadian Manufacturing*, Statistics Canada, https://www150.statcan.gc.ca/n1/en/pub/11-622-m/11-622-m2005009-eng.pdf?st=D2-aTkNu. [10]

Becker, B. et al. (2020), "FDI in hot labour markets: The implications of the war for talent", *Journal of International Business Policy*, Vol. 3/2, pp. 107-133, https://doi.org/10.1057/s42214-020-00052-y. [28]

Business Council of Canada (2022), *Empowering People for Recovery and Growth: 2022 Skills Survey Report*, https://thebusinesscouncil.ca/report/empowering-people-for-recovery-and-growth/#:~:text=The%202022%20edition%20of%20the,to%20the%20COVID%2D19%20pandemic. [49]

Carleton University (2023), *IBM-Carleton Partnership*, https://carleton.ca/ips/partnerships-in-action/ibm/. [50]

CME (2022), *2022 Labour and skills survey*, https://cme-mec.ca/initiatives/2022-labour-skills-survey/ (accessed on 25 July 2023). [34]

Criscuolo, C. et al. (2020), "Workforce composition, productivity and pay: the role of firms in wage inequality", *OECD Economics Department Working Papers*, No. 1603, OECD Publishing, Paris, https://doi.org/10.1787/52ab4e26-en. [16]

D2L (2022), *Enabling Upskilling at Scale: Adapting to Meet the Needs of the Working Learner*, D2L Corporation, https://www.d2l.com/resources/assets/enabling-upskilling-at-scale/. [46]

Dostie, B. (2013), "Estimating the Returns to Firm-Sponsored On-the-Job and Classroom Training", *Journal of Human Capital*, Vol. 7/2, pp. 161-189, https://doi.org/10.1086/671186. [47]

Dostie, B. and P. Léger (2014), "Firm-Sponsored Classroom Training: Is It Worth It for Older Workers?", *Canadian Public Policy*, Vol. 40/4, pp. 377-90. [48]

Financial Times (2023), *FDI Markets: the in-depth crossborder investment monitor from the Financial Time*, https://www.fdimarkets.com/ (accessed on 30 January 2023). [5]

Gabler, N. and B. Gormley (2022), *Lost Opportunities: Measuring the Unrealized Value of Skill Vacancies in Canada*, https://fsc-ccf.ca/research/lost-opportunities-measuring-the-unrealized-value-of-skill-vacancies-in-canada/ (accessed on 28 July 2023). [33]

Government of Canada (2022), *Government of Canada bolsters the skilled trades sector by investing in training*, https://www.canada.ca/en/employment-social-development/news/2022/04/government-of-canada-bolsters-the-skilled-trades-sector-by-investing-in-training.html (accessed on 3 August 2023). [36]

Huang, X. (2016), "Exporter Wage Premium: A Plant-Level Analysis with Canadian Linked Employer-Employee Data", *SSRN Electronic Journal*, https://doi.org/10.2139/ssrn.2797712. [8]

IBM (2023), *IBM Canada Advanced Studies*, https://www-40.ibm.com/ibm/cas/canada/. [51]

Levesque, C. et al. (2015), "Labour relations policies: A three-country study of power dynamics", *Journal of Industrial Relations*, pp. 187-209, https://doi.org/10.1177/0022185614564377. [20]

Mahboubi, P. (2022), *The Knowledge Gap: Canada Faces a Shortage in Digital and STEM Skills*, https://www.cdhowe.org/sites/default/files/2022-08/Commentary_626.pdf. [37]

Matthews, M. and F. Rice (2022), *Context Matters: Strengthening the Impact of Foreign Investment on Domestic Innovation*, Information and Communications Technology Council (ICTC). Ottawa, Canada., https://www.digitalthinktankictc.com/ictc-admin/resources/admin/fdi-ip-canadian-innovation-2022.pdf. [43]

Munro, D. and G. Lamb (2023), *Employer-Sponsored Training: A picture of skills training opportunities provided*, Future Skills Centre, https://fsc-ccf.ca/research/employer-sponsored-skills-training/. [44]

OECD (2023), *Adult education level* (indicator), https://doi.org/10.1787/36bce3fe-en (accessed on 24 July 2023). [26]

OECD (2023), *Inward activity of multinationals by industrial sector - ISIC Rev 4*, https://stats.oecd.org/Index.aspx?DataSetCode=AMNE_IN (accessed on 5 May 2023). [3]

OECD (2023), *Job Quality Database*, https://www.oecd.org/statistics/job-quality.htm. [13]

OECD (2023), *Talent Attractiveness: How does your country compare in each dimension?*, https://www.oecd.org/migration/talent-attractiveness/how-does-your-country-compare-in-each-dimension.htm (accessed on 1 August 2023). [42]

OECD (2022), *Business Consultation on Sustainability Practices in Canada*. [7]

OECD (2022), *FDI Qualities Policy Toolkit*, OECD Publishing, Paris, https://doi.org/10.1787/7ba74100-en. [6]

OECD (2022), *Skills for jobs - Mismatch by country in 2019*, https://stats.oecd.org/Index.aspx?DataSetCode=S4J2022_MISMATCH. [29]

OECD (2020), *Education at a Glance 2020: OECD Indicators*, OECD Publishing, Paris, https://doi.org/10.1787/69096873-en. [45]

OECD (2020), *Workforce Innovation to Foster Positive Learning Environments in Canada*, Getting Skills Right, OECD Publishing, Paris, https://doi.org/10.1787/a92cf94d-en. [24]

OECD (2019), *FDI Qualities Indicators: Measuring the sustainable development impacts of investment*, OECD, Paris, http://www.oecd.org/fr/investissement/fdi-qualities-indicators.htm (accessed on 6 February 2023). [4]

OECD (2019), *Negotiating Our Way Up: Collective Bargaining in a Changing World of Work*, https://doi.org/10.1787/1fd2da34-en. [17]

OECD (2019), *Negotiating Our Way Up: Collective Bargaining in a Changing World of Work*, OECD Publishing, Paris, https://doi.org/10.1787/1fd2da34-en. [15]

OECD (2019), "Non-standard forms of work and pensions", in *Pensions at a Glance 2019: OECD and G20 Indicators*, OECD Publishing, Paris, https://doi.org/10.1787/5ffa7926-en. [12]

OECD (2017), *Board-level employee representation*. [22]

OECD (2011), *OECD Guidelines for Multinational Enterprises, 2011 Edition*, OECD Publishing, Paris, https://doi.org/10.1787/9789264115415-en. [23]

Parisa Mahboubi (2019), *Bad Fits: The Causes, Extent and Costs of Job Skills Mismatch in Canada*. [32]

Pohler, D. and C. Riddell (2018), "Multinationals' Compliance with Employment Law: An Empirical Assessment Using Administrative Data from Ontario, 2004 to 2015", *ILR Review*, Vol. 72/3, pp. 606-635, https://doi.org/10.1177/0019793918788837. [19]

Series, T. (ed.) (2011), *Breau, S., & Brown, W. M. (2011). Global links: Exporting, Foreign direct investment, and wages: Evidence from the Canadian manufacturing sector*, Statistics Canada, https://www150.statcan.gc.ca/n1/en/pub/11-622-m/11-622-m2011021-eng.pdf?st=v58B7v9J. [9]

Setzler, B. and F. Tintelnot (2021), "The Effects of Foreign Multinationals on Workers and Firms in the United States", *The Quarterly Journal of Economics*, Vol. 136/3, pp. 1943-1991, https://doi.org/10.1093/QJE/QJAB015. [11]

Spicer, Z., N. Olmstead and N. Goodman (2018), *Reversing the Brain Drain: Where is Canadian STEM Talent Going?*. [38]

Statistics Canada (2023), *Activities of multinational enterprises in Canada, Canadian and foreign multinationals, by province, sector and industry, establishment level*, https://www150.statcan.gc.ca/t1/tbl1/en/tv.action?pid=3610062001 (accessed on 5 May 2023). [2]

Statistics Canada (2023), *Activities of multinational enterprises in Canada, foreign multinationals, by ultimate investor country and industry*, https://www150.statcan.gc.ca/t1/tbl1/en/tv.action?pid=3610058201 (accessed on 5 May 2023). [1]

Statistics Canada (2023), *Labour force characteristics, monthly, seasonally adjusted and trend-cycle, last 5 months*, https://www150.statcan.gc.ca/t1/tbl1/en/tv.action?pid=1410028701. [31]

Statistics Canada (2023), *Required skills, by industry and enterprise size*, https://www150.statcan.gc.ca/t1/tbl1/en/tv.action?pid=3310029901 (accessed on 28 July 2023). [27]

Statistics Canada (2023), *Skill shortages, by industry and enterprise size (Table 33-10-0300-01)*, https://doi.org/10.25318/3310030001-eng. [35]

Statistics Canada (2023), *Table 14-10-0070-01 Union coverage by industry, annual (x 1,000)*, https://doi.org/10.25318/1410007001-eng. [18]

Statistics Canada (2022), *Determinants of skill gaps in the workplace and recruitment difficulties in Canada*, https://www150.statcan.gc.ca/n1/pub/18-001-x/18-001-x2022002-eng.htm (accessed on 24 July 2023). [25]

Statistics Canada (2022), *Employer responses to labour shortages*, Economic and Social Reports, https://doi.org/10.25318/36280001202200700001-eng. [39]

Statistics Canada (2019), *Employment at multinational enterprises in Canada*, https://www150.statcan.gc.ca/n1/en/pub/13-605-x/2019001/article/00012-eng.pdf?st=pXHjbpa2. [14]

Statistics Canada (2019), *Measures taken to overcome skill shortages, by industry and enterprise size (Table 33-10-0301-01)*, https://doi.org/10.25318/3310030101-eng. [40]

World Economic Forum (2023), *5 ways a 'skills-first' approach unlocks access to future jobs*, https://www.weforum.org/agenda/2023/01/5-ways-skills-first-approach-unlocks-access-to-jobs-davos-2023/ (accessed on 1 August 2023). [41]

Notes

[1] Analysis using the Survey of Employers of Workers Skills 2021 shows that firms with a higher percentage of workers aged 50 years and older were less likely to experience skills gaps, potentially because older workers are more likely to be experienced and, in turn, proficient at their jobs (Statistics Canada, 2022[25]).

4 The contribution of FDI to diversity and inclusion in the labour market

This chapter examines the contribution of FDI to the creation of a more diverse and inclusive Canadian workforce, focusing on women, Indigenous peoples, immigrants, and persons with disabilities. The chapter relies on a variety of national and international statistics and on the OECD business consultation on sustainability practices of domestic and foreign firms in Canada.

4.1. Summary of key findings

A workforce that reflects variety in gender, sexual orientation, ethnicity, race, religion, abilities is a key resource for an economy. A diverse workforce is not only ethically desirable, but also offers a richer talent pool and a wider range of perspectives. This in turn can improve problem solving, responsiveness to consumer needs and overall business performance. Canada has one of the highest female labour market participation rates in the OECD area (75.6%), but significant gender inequalities remain in terms of time spent in unpaid work, pay and professional development. Indigenous peoples participate less in the labour market and are predominantly employed in low-wage sectors and occupations. They are also less likely to have a tertiary education. Immigrants make a large contribution to the Canadian labour market, supporting labour force growth and filling labour shortages in many sectors, but they face challenges in relation to their skill utilisation. People with disabilities are less likely to find a job than people without disabilities, and face systematic barriers to employment, including stigma, stereotypes, physical and logistical barriers.

FDI and foreign companies could further influence the creation of a more diverse and inclusive labour market in Canada for women, Indigenous peoples, immigrants, and persons with disabilities. FDI stocks are largely concentrated in the primary sector (particularly in mining and oil and gas extraction), business and support services (i.e. management of companies and enterprises), manufacturing, finance and real estates, and wholesale and retail trade. Less than one-third of women and just over one-third of Indigenous peoples, immigrants, and persons with disabilities work in these sectors. New establishments of foreign companies (i.e., greenfield FDI) are also mainly concentrated and create more job opportunities in the primary, manufacturing, and trade sectors. The impact of FDI can vary across the vulnerable groups. For instance, FDI in mining may create many jobs for Indigenous peoples given the geographic location of oil and gas sites but less for women or persons with disabilities.

The results of an OECD business consultation conducted for this study suggest that Canadian companies may be more aware of the importance and committed to promoting diversity in the workplace than affiliates of foreign multinational enterprises (MNEs). This is reflected in the fact that Canadian companies that participated in the consultation have a higher share of women, Indigenous peoples and persons with disabilities than foreign companies, as well as a higher share of managers among these vulnerable employee groups. On the other hand, the foreign companies surveyed have a larger share of foreign workers, including foreign managers.

The OECD business consultation also shows that a higher share of the Canadian companies surveyed use inclusive workplace practices (e.g. inclusive hiring strategies, diversity training) than foreign companies. The foreign companies, however, seem to attach more importance to training than the domestic companies consulted, in line with existing international evidence. A higher proportion of the foreign companies offer formal training and they also have a higher proportion of people from vulnerable groups who have received training. The consultation is not based on a representative sample of companies, however, and therefore further investigation is needed to assess the impact of FDI and the practices of foreign firms in the area of diversity and inclusion. This would require adequate statistics at the intersection of foreign ownership and diversity and inclusion in the workplace.

Policy considerations

- Continued policy efforts and gender mainstreaming in all policy areas, including investment, will be crucial to achieve a diverse and inclusive labour market. Women, Indigenous peoples, immigrants and persons with disabilities face various barriers and discrimination in the labour market. The strong commitment of successive Canadian governments has enabled important steps forward, but further efforts by all policy actors will be crucial to eliminate persisting barriers.
- Improving the representation of vulnerable groups in sectors where Canada attracts or wants to attract more investment will be crucial to ensure that employment opportunities created by foreign companies are fairly shared among all workers, including those from vulnerable groups. Invest in Canada can actively work with other government entities to ensure that solutions are designed to increase the participation of vulnerable groups in these priority sectors, including by providing data and monitoring the impact of FDI.
- Canada can play an important role in conveying to foreign investors the importance of values such as diversity and inclusion of vulnerable workers in the labour market. The OECD business consultation shows that Canadian companies have a more diverse workforce and use more inclusive workplace practices than foreign companies, probably because values such as diversity and inclusion of vulnerable people are embedded in their corporate culture. Canadian IPAs can play a role by organising or participating in information campaigns, initiatives and events, or by prioritising investments that attach greater importance to diversity and the inclusion of vulnerable people.
- Some of the existing programmes and incentives to attract foreign companies could be linked to diversity and inclusion objectives to support the spread of more inclusive workplace practices. However, it is important that such programmes and incentives are designed in a transparent manner and that their costs and benefits are regularly evaluated.
- Canadian IPAs could collaborate with other government authorities to help design training programmes for workers from vulnerable groups involving foreign companies. The results of the study show that foreign companies attach more importance to training and use more elaborate training practices to develop skills and retain talent (Chapter 3). They are also better able to identify the skills required by the labour market.

4.2. Diversity and inclusion in the Canadian labour market: an overview

4.2.1. Gender inequalities persist in the labour market

Canada has one of the highest female labour market participation rates in the OECD area, at 75.6% for the population aged 15 to 64, similar to other economies with a strong commitment to gender equality such as Sweden, Norway, Finland and Denmark (Figure 4.1, Panel A) (Box 4.1). Moreover, the gender gap in labour force participation is among the lowest in the OECD area (5.5% compared to 9.8% in the OECD average). Labour market participation rates, however, tend to be lower among women from Indigenous and immigrant groups (Statistics Canada, 2022[1]; Statistics Canada, 2023[2]).

Women spend fewer hours than men in paid work. About 24% of women work part-time, compared to 13% of men. The percentage of women who work part-time is similar to the OECD average (24.7%), while that of men is higher (about 10% in the OECD average). In contrast, women devote more time than men to unpaid work, i.e. domestic work, childcare and care of the elderly. They spend on average 223 minutes per day on unpaid work, 75 minutes more than men. The gap is lower than the OECD average of 127 minutes and similar to countries such as Finland (78 minutes), Norway (59 minutes), and Denmark (57 minutes) (OECD Gender Portal, (2023[3]).

Figure 4.1. Canada has a high female labour force participation, but a significant gender wage gap

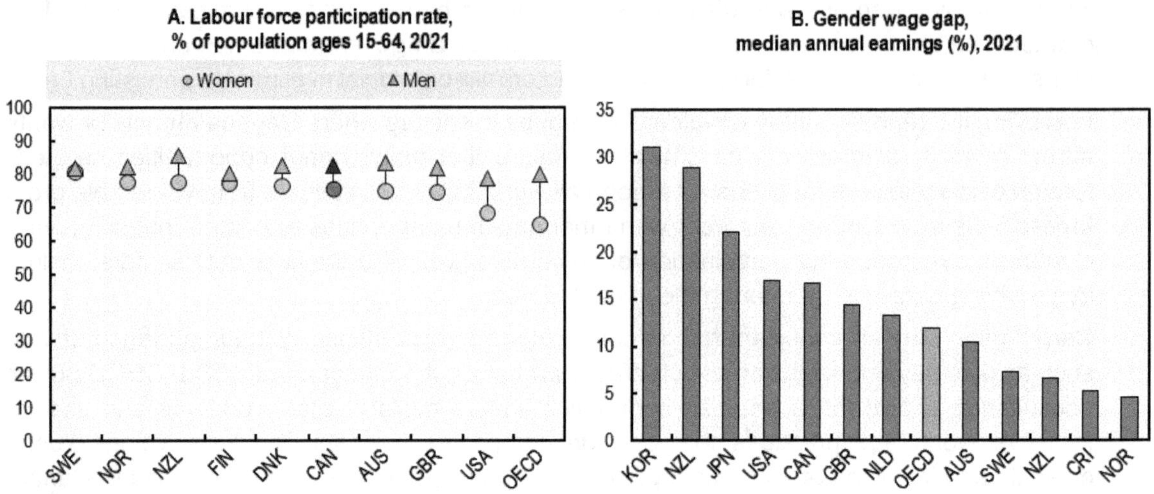

Source: OECD (2023[3]), Gender Portal, https://www.oecd.org/gender/data/.

Box 4.1. Terminology and concepts

Gender: Gender refers to the personal and social identity of an individual as a man, woman or non-binary person. Gender is a different concept from sex at birth, which is understood primarily in terms of physical and biological characteristics (e.g. chromosomes). Although referring to different concepts, the two terms are often used interchangeably, especially in statistical definitions. This report also uses them interchangeably and the term gender essentially refers to the binary difference between men and women. Although LGBT (lesbian, gay, bisexual and transgender) people are also subject to discrimination in the labour market, this report focuses solely on women. This is largely explained by the lack of labour market statistics on LGBT people.

Indigenous peoples: Indigenous or Aboriginal peoples are terms that refer to the original peoples of North America and their descendants. The Canadian Constitution (Constitution Act, 1982, Section 35 (2)) recognises three groups of Indigenous peoples: Indians (more commonly called First Nations), Inuit and Métis. These are three distinct peoples with unique histories, languages, cultural practices and spiritual beliefs. Indigenous peoples also include those who are registered under the Indian Act of Canada (Registered Indians) or persons who belong to a First Nation or Indian band that has signed a treaty with the Crown (Treaty Indians). For First Nations, a further differentiation is whether individuals live on or off the reserve. Definitions of Indigenous groups can change in the various Canadian statistical sources due to the blurred boundaries of Indigenous groups.

Immigrant status: Immigrant status indicates whether the person is a non-immigrant, an immigrant or a non-permanent resident of Canada. A non-immigrant person is a person born in Canada (and therefore with Canadian citizenship). An immigrant person is a person born outside Canada with permanent resident (or landed immigrant) status. A recent immigrant is a person who has obtained a permanent resident status up to five years prior to a particular census year (e.g., 2021). A non-permanent resident is a person from another country with a usual place of residence in Canada who holds a work or study permit or who has applied for refugee status. The terms foreign national and foreign worker refer to both immigrants and non-permanent residents in this report. Not all foreign workers can be considered 'vulnerable' workers and some of them may be highly educated and have highly paid jobs.

Disability: According to the Canadian Survey of Disability (CSD), disability is the result of the interaction between a person's functional limitations and barriers in the environment, including social and physical barriers that make daily functioning more difficult. The CSD covers various types of disabilities, including those related to development, memory, dexterity, learning, seeing, hearing, mental health, mobility, flexibility and pain. The CSD also classifies four classes of disability severity, based on the intensity and frequency of activity limitations: mild, moderate, severe and very severe.

Source: OECD elaboration based on Statistics Canada (2021[4]), Gender of person, https://www23.statcan.gc.ca/imdb/p3Var.pl?Function=DEC&Id=410445; Statistics Canada (2022[5]), Indigenous peoples and communities, https://www.rcaanc-cirnac.gc.ca/eng/1100100013785/1529102490303, Statistics Canada (2017[6]), 2016 Census of Population: Immigration and ethnocultural diversity, https://www12.statcan.gc.ca/census-recensement/2016/ref/98-501/98-501-x2016008-eng.cfm; Statistics Canada (2022[7]), Measuring disability in Canada, https://www150.statcan.gc.ca/n1/pub/11-627-m/11-627-m2022062-eng.htm.

Women and men are employed in different sectors and professions. About 90% of women work in services, compared to 70% of men. They are concentrated in health and social care, educational services, retail trade, professional, scientific, and technical services, finance and insurance. Only 6% of women work in manufacturing (compared to 12% of men), just over 2% in construction (compared to 13% of men) and about 2% in agriculture and forestry, mining and energy (compared to 7% of men) (Statistics Canada, 2023[8]). Women are also more likely to be in lower-skilled occupations, such as administrative, service support and paraprofessional occupations, while many more men are in managerial, professional and technical occupations (Statistics Canada, 2023[9]).

The gender wage gap persists in Canada, regardless of how it is measured. For full-time employees, the difference between women's and men's median annual earnings relative to men's median annual earnings is 16.6%. This figure places Canada among the ten OECD countries with the worst gender wage gap (Figure 4.1, Panel B). Examining the hourly rate, a measure that takes into account the fact that men work more hours than women, shows that women earn on average about 89 cents for every Canadian dollar earned by a man (Government of Canada, 2021[10]). Recent research has shown that about three quarters of the wage gap between men and women with similar qualifications relates to differences within firms. This mainly reflects differences in tasks and responsibilities and, to a lesser extent, differences in pay for jobs of equal value. The remaining quarter of the wage gap between men and women stems from the concentration of women in low-wage companies and sectors (OECD, 2023[11]).

In Canada, as in all OECD countries, women are under-represented in managerial and leadership positions. This is due to the so-called 'glass-ceiling', an invisible barrier explained by demographic characteristics (e.g., gender, race) rather than skills or performance (OECD, 2017[12]). In Canada, about 36% of managers are women, a slightly higher proportion than the OECD average of 33.7% (Figure 4.2).

The share of women on company boards is even lower, at around 20% in private companies and around 25% in listed companies (Statistics Canada, 2022[13]).

Figure 4.2. The share of female managers is above the OECD average

Share of female managers (%), 2021

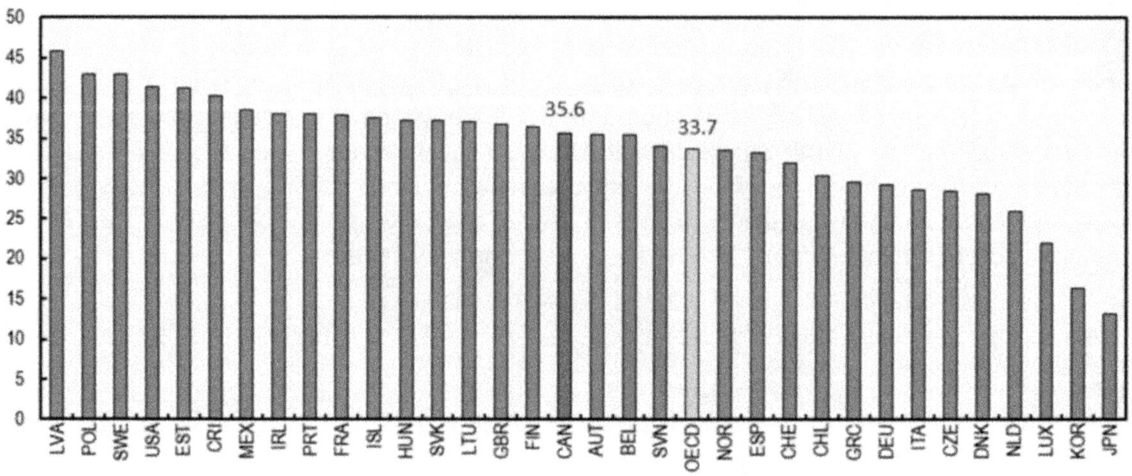

Source: OECD (2023[3]), Gender Portal, https://www.oecd.org/gender/data/.

In the field of education, women have long surpassed men: 75% of women aged 25-34 have a tertiary degree in Canada, compared to 58% of men OECD (2023[3]). The figure for women puts Canada in second place after Korea in the OECD area. At the same time, gender differences persist in academic achievement. OECD PISA tests show that girls' reading skills exceed those of boys in Canada, as well as in all OECD countries (as shown by the negative difference between boys' scores and girls' scores) (Figure 4.3, Panel A). However, boys perform better in mathematics (as indicated by the positive difference between boys' scores and girls' scores), although the gap with girls is smaller than in the OECD average.

Women and men also differ in their choice of fields of study. In graduate studies, women tend to choose business, administration and law, health and welfare and social sciences, while a much higher proportion of men is found in engineering and ICT studies (Figure 4.3, panel B). Recent estimates show that among high school graduates in Canada, women are 29.8 % less likely than men to enrol in a post-secondary STEM programme immediately after graduation (Chan, Handler and Frenette, 2021[14]). Furthermore, among young STEM graduates (aged 25-34), men are more likely than women to work in STEM occupations (Statistics Canada., 2017[15]). These gender gaps in academic fields are reflected in the workforce and perpetuate gender inequalities in pay and career progression.

Figure 4.3. Girls have higher scores than boys in reading but lower scores in mathematics and select less engineering and ICT as study subjects

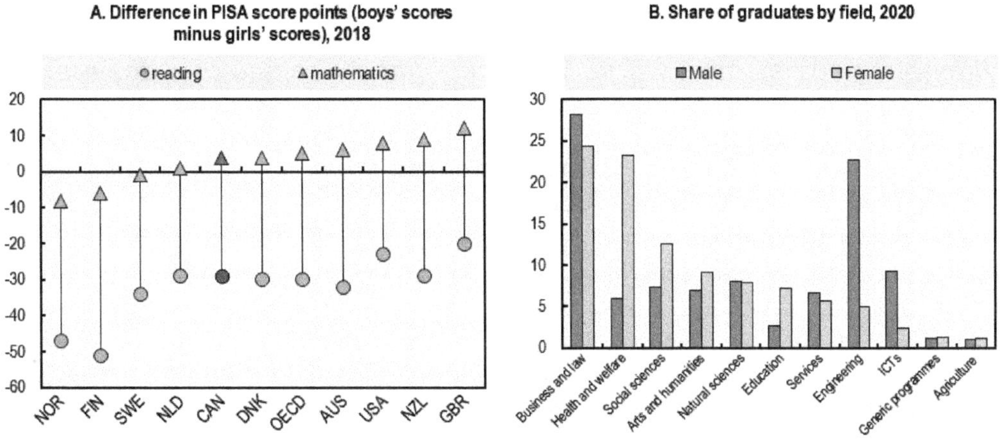

Source: OECD (2018[16]), PISA Database, https://www.oecd.org/pisa/data/2018database/https://www.oecd.org/pisa/data/2018database/.

Box 4.2. A conceptual framework to study the impact of FDI on vulnerable workers

The FDI Qualities Initiative provides a framework for analysing the impact of foreign direct investment (FDI) on the sustainable development of host countries. It comprises the FDI Qualities Indicators, the FDI Qualities Policy Toolkit and the Council Recommendation on FDI Qualities. All three pillars have a gender dimension. The FDI Qualities Indicators on gender help assess the impact of FDI on gender equality outcomes in the labour market (e.g., female labour force participation, gender wage gap). The gender component of the Policy Toolkit provides governments with policy guidance and best practices for attracting and retaining sustainable investment that supports gender equality. In addition, the OECD Council Recommendation on FDI Qualities offers a concise set of key policy principles to improve the positive contribution of international investment to the SDGs, including SDG 5 on gender equality.

The gender dimension of the FDI Qualities Initiative offers a useful conceptual framework to study the impact of FDI also on other groups of vulnerable workers, such as immigrants, Indigenous peoples and persons with disabilities. This is because these vulnerable groups face discrimination and barriers in the labour market similar to those faced by women. For example, in most countries these groups of vulnerable workers tend to work in lower-paying sectors and are paid less for jobs of equal value than non-vulnerable reference groups (e.g. non-immigrants). The mechanisms through which FDI can promote or hinder their integration into the labour market are also similar. In particular, FDI may encourage or impede the integration of these vulnerable workers into the labour market by influencing the development of sectors or activities in which these people tend to be employed. FDI may also support or hinder the economic inclusion of these groups through the activities and practices of affiliates of foreign MNEs in host countries. For example, foreign affiliates can create good employment opportunities for vulnerable workers and support their professional development through training and inclusive workplace practices.

Source: OECD (2019[17]), FDI Qualities Indicators: Measuring the sustainable development impacts of investment, https://www.oecd.org/fr/investissement/fdi-qualities-indicators.htm; OECD (2022[18]), FDI Qualities Indicators 2022, https://www.oecd.org/investment/fdi-qualities-indicators.htm; OECD (2022[19]), FDI Qualities Policy Toolkit, https://doi.org/10.1787/7ba74100-en.; OECD (2022[20]), Recommendation of the Council on Foreign Direct Investment Qualities for Sustainable Development, https://legalinstruments.oecd.org/en/instruments/OECD-LEGAL-0476

4.2.2. Indigenous peoples have worse labour market outcomes than the rest of the population

The Indigenous population in Canada has historically had lower labour force participation rates and employment rates than the non-Indigenous population (OECD, 2019[21]) (Box 4.1). Data from 2022 show that labour force participation of Indigenous people between 15 and 64 years old is about 75%, 7 percent points lower than non-Indigenous people (Figure 4.4, Panel A). There are however significant differences between Indigenous groups, geographical areas, and gender. Employment rates tend to be higher among Métis than Inuit and First Nations peoples. The gaps in employment rates between Indigenous and non-Indigenous populations are lower in the Central provinces (Quebec and Ontario) and higher in the Atlantic region (provinces of Newfoundland and Labrador, Nova Scotia, New Brunswick, and Prince Edward Island) (Statistics Canada, 2023[22]). In addition, employment rates of Indigenous women are lower than those of Indigenous men. Geography is one factor contributing to labour market gaps between Indigenous and non-Indigenous populations: most Indigenous peoples live in remote locations, which offer fewer employment opportunities, while the majority of non-Indigenous people live in or close to urban centres (OECD, 2019[21]).

Figure 4.4. Indigenous peoples participate less in the labour force and are paid less

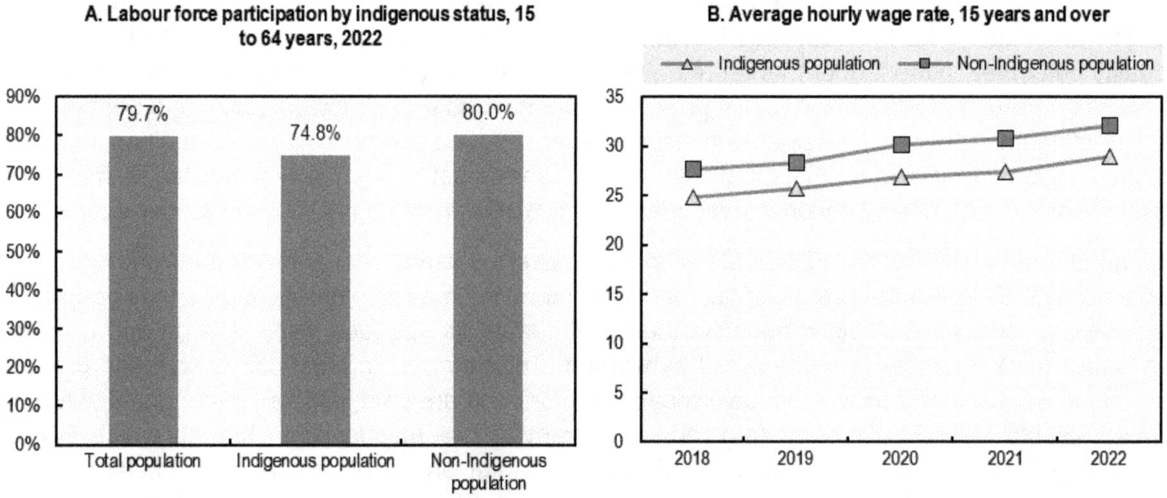

Note: Indigenous population includes persons who reported having an Indigenous identity, that is, First Nations (North American Indian), Métis or Inuk (Inuit), or those who reported more than one identity. Excluded from the survey's coverage are persons living on reserves and other Indigenous settlements in the provinces, as well as those living in the territories.
Source: Panel A: OECD elaboration based on Statistics Canada (2023[22]), https://doi.org/10.25318/1410036501-eng; Panel B: Statistics Canada (2023[23]), https://doi.org/10.25318/1410037001-eng

Indigenous peoples tend to concentrate in certain sectors and occupations. They are more likely to work in wholesale and retail trade, health care and social assistance, construction, manufacturing (food industries), educational services, than non-Indigenous peoples. Conversely, they are under-represented in professional, scientific, and technical services, which typically require post-secondary education and pay better. The share of Indigenous employment in public administration is also high, and the gap with respect to non-Indigenous peoples has narrowed over time (Statistics Canada, 2023[24]). At the occupational level, large shares of Indigenous peoples are in sales and service occupations; trades, transport and equipment operators; education, law and social and community government services; and business, finance and administration occupations. In addition, Indigenous people are less likely to have managerial positions and natural and applied sciences occupations than non-Indigenous peoples, which tend to pay higher salaries (Statistics Canada, 2023[24]).The concentration of the Indigenous population in lower-paying sectors and occupations largely explains the wage gap with the Indigenous population (Figure 4.4, Panel B). The average hourly wage of Indigenous and non-Indigenous people has increased in recent years, but the hourly wage gap has remained almost unchanged at around 10%.

Inequalities in the labour market between the Indigenous and non-Indigenous population can be explained by different levels of education, particularly at the tertiary level. Indigenous peoples in Canada have lower education rates than the total population. In the population aged 25-64, the percentage of Indigenous people with tertiary education is 16%, compared to 36% of the total population. Furthermore, the gap with the non-Indigenous population appears to be greater in the northern regions and rural areas, where education offerings are more limited (OECD, 2019[21]). Studies also point to a significant literacy, numeracy and technology skills gap to the disadvantage of the Indigenous population, which largely explain the observed wage differentials (Hu, Daley and Casey, 2017[25]).

4.2.3. Immigrants, temporary foreign workers and international students make an important contribution to the Canadian labour market, but some challenges remain

Canada has historically been an immigration destination. In 2021, more than 8.3 million people, 23% of the total population in Canada, were or had been permanent resident in Canada, the highest proportion of the population since 1921 (Statistics Canada, 2022[26]) (Box 4.1). The share of recent immigrants (people who obtained permanent resident status in the past 5 years) has also increased significantly in recent years: over 1.3 million new immigrants settled permanently in Canada from 2016 to 2021, the highest number of recent immigrants recorded in a Canadian census (Statistics Canada, 2021[27]). The share of non-permanent residents (people coming to Canada temporarily on work or study permits or as asylum seekers) amounted to 2.5% in 2021.

In international comparison, immigrants in Canada are well integrated economically. Labour market outcomes of foreign-born are good, partly as a result of the large share of highly educated immigrants. The labour participation rate for the population aged 15-64 is slightly higher for the foreign-born than for native-born (80% for the foreign-born compared to 79% for natives) (Figure 4.5). Labour force participation rates of foreign-born also tend to exceed those of native-born in OECD countries with large recent inflows of labour migrants, especially in Southern, Central and Eastern European countries (Poland, Hungary, Portugal, Czechia) and other so-called settlement countries such as New Zealand and the United States. The opposite is observed for longer-standing European destinations and Nordic countries (Sweden, Norway, Finland, France, Belgium), mainly due to high levels of inactivity among foreign-born women. Employments rates of foreign-born are very similar to those of native-born, close to 73% (OECD, 2021[28]). Immigrants in Canada also show a high level of social inclusion. They report very high levels of life satisfaction and the best health status in the entire OECD (OECD, 2019[29]; OECD/EU, 2018[30]).

Figure 4.5. In Canada, the labour force participation of the foreign-born is comparable to that of the native-born

Labour force participation (%) by place of birth, 15-64 year-olds, 2021

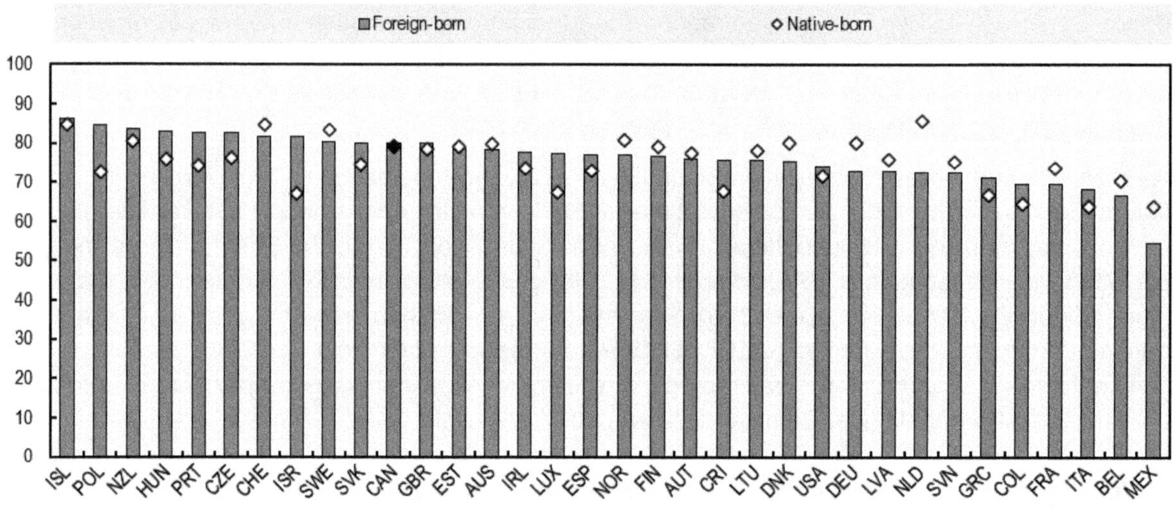

Source: OECD (2021[28]), https://stats.oecd.org/https://stats.oecd.org/

Immigrants, particularly recent immigrants whose age structure is younger than the general population, make an important contribution to Canada's labour market. The labour force participation rate for the population over the age of 15 is higher for recent immigrants than for Canadian-born and all immigrants, and this difference has increased in recent years. However, labour force participation for the population aged 25-54 remains higher for Canadian-born than for immigrants and especially for recent immigrants (in 2022, 90% for Canadian-born, 87% for all immigrants and 85% for recent immigrants) (Figure 4.6).According to Statistics Canada, from 2016 to 2021, immigrants accounted for four-fifths of labour force growth (Statistics Canada, 2022[31]). This is also consistent with the majority of recent immigrants, about 56%, being admitted under the economic category, that is based on their potential economic contribution.

Figure 4.6. The labour force participation rate is higher for recent immigrants than for Canadian-born

Labour force participation rate (%), over 15 years old

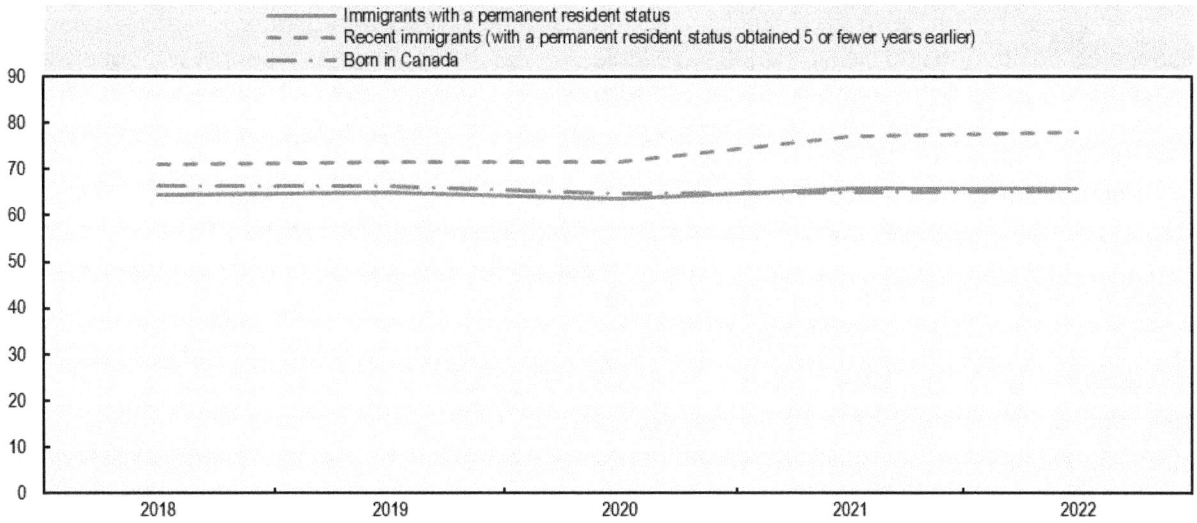

Note: See Box 4.1 for terminology and definitions.
Source: OECD elaboration based on Statistics Canada (2023[32]), https://doi.org/10.25318/1410008301-eng

Recent immigrants fill labour shortages in many sectors. Since 2010, the share of new immigrants grew fast in accommodation and food services sector, in the professional services sector, and in the manufacturing and transport sectors (Statistics Canada, 2022[33]). Nevertheless, recent immigrants face challenges in relation to their skill utilisation. From 2001 to 2016, the percentage of university-educated recent immigrants aged 25 to 34 years working in jobs requiring a university degree decreased from 46% to 38%. In comparison, the percentage of Canadian-born workers with a bachelor's degree in jobs requiring a university degree remained close to 60% (Statistics Canada, 2022[33]). The complexity of the process of recognition of the foreign qualifications of immigrants can create challenges in integrating immigrants into the labour market. This process is different in each province and territory, and for each profession. It is particularly challenging for applicants in regulated occupations (Brosseau, 2020[34]).

Temporary foreign workers and international students have also been instrumental in filling labour shortages. The number of temporary foreign workers increased sevenfold, from 111,000 in 2000 to 777,000 in 2021. The increase has been particularly significant in low-skilled sectors such as agriculture, accommodation and food services, administrative and support services, waste management and remediation, but also in some high-skilled activities such as professional, scientific, and technical services and the information and cultural industries. The number of international students has also increased significantly and reached 807,750 students in 2022, up from 214,000 a decade earlier, according to Immigration, Refugees and Citizenship Canada. Both temporary foreign workers and international students are moving to permanent residency in increasing numbers. About 25% of temporary foreign workers who arrived in Canada between the late 2000s and early 2010 became permanent residents within five years of obtaining their first work permit. One-third of international students who arrived between the late 2000s and early 2010 became permanent residents within 10 years of arriving in Canada (Statistics Canada, 2022[33]).

4.2.4. People with disabilities have fewer job opportunities

According to Statistics Canada's Canadian Survey of Disability (CSD) (2017[35]), 22% of the Canadian population aged 15 years and over have one or more disabilities (Morris et al., 2018[36]). Disability is more likely in older people and women. Moreover, the types of disability (e.g., pain-related, mobility, mental health) and their severity also vary significantly between age groups and gender. Disability affects the likelihood of finding a job and the type of jobs available. Research has shown that people without disabilities are more likely to be employed than those with disabilities (Turcotte, 2015[37]; Matthew et al., 2015[38]). According to the CSD (2017[35]), among those aged 25-64, three out of five (59%) people with disabilities are employed compared to four out of five (80%) of those without disabilities. In addition, the employment rate was lower among people with more severe types of disability (Figure 4.7). Regardless of the level of disability severity, the employment rates of people with disabilities were higher for those with post-secondary education than for those with a high school diploma or less. Canada's employment rate of persons with disabilities is higher than the OECD 2019 average of 42% (OECD, 2022[39]).

The types of jobs available to people with disabilities vary compared to people without disabilities. Part-time work is more common among people with disabilities: 23% among people with mild disabilities, 29% among people with more severe disabilities, compared to 18.8% among people without disabilities. In addition, most people with disabilities work in less remunerative services sectors (health care and social assistance, public administration and retail trade) and are under-represented in manufacturing, agriculture, mining and construction. The over-representation of people with disabilities in part-time jobs or in certain sectors can be explained to some extent by some constraints they may have (e.g. some people with disabilities may not be able to work full-time). Research suggests, however, that people with disabilities face systematic barriers to employment. These include stigma and stereotypes, lack of training on how to employ and manage people with disabilities, lack of employees with disabilities as role models or mentors, and other logistical difficulties related, for example, to the lack of affordable housing near jobs (Canadian Human Rights Commission, 2017[40]; Canadian Heritage, 2020[41]). Moreover, Statistics Canada estimates that among people with disabilities aged 25-64 who were not employed and not attending school, two out of five (39%) showed significant potential to work. Many of these were young people and women (Morris et al., 2018[36]).

Figure 4.7. The employment rate of persons with disabilities decreases with the severity of the disability

Employment of Canadian population aged 25 to 64 years, by disability status and severity (%), 2016

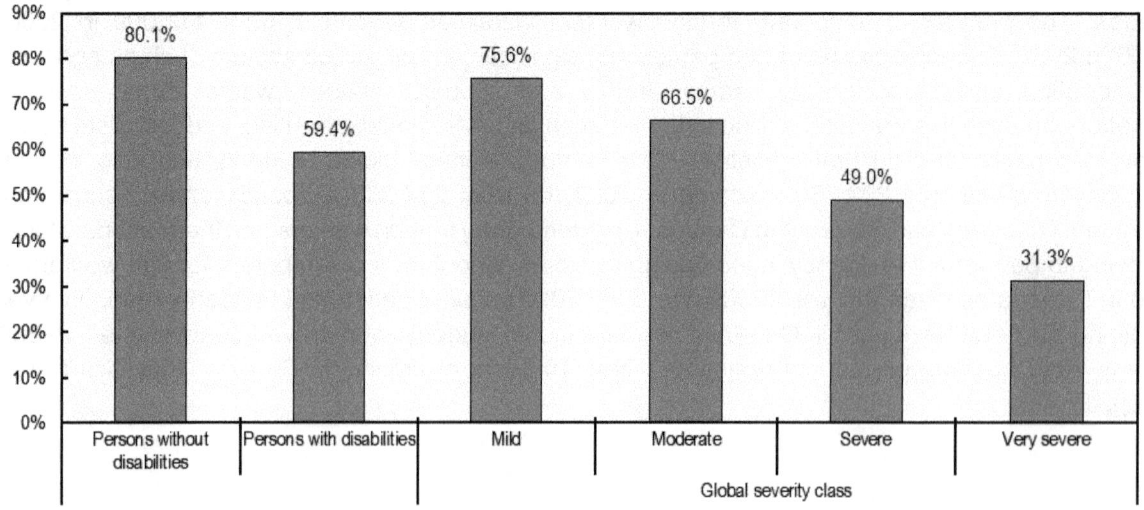

Source: OECD elaboration based on Statistics Canada (2021[42]), https://doi.org/10.25318/4110004901-eng

4.3. The role of FDI for diversity and inclusion

4.3.1. FDI is prevalent and creates more jobs in sectors where vulnerable people are less represented

FDI can contribute to the integration of vulnerable workers into the local labour market by supporting the development of sectors and activities in which these categories of workers are employed. As discussed in the first part of this chapter, women, Indigenous peoples, foreign workers (i.e. foreign nationals with permanent resident status or study/work-visa status), particularly immigrants, and persons with disabilities tend to be over-represented in low value-added service sectors, such as health and social care, educational services, wholesale and retail trade, and public administration (Table 4.1). Conversely, they are under-represented in higher value-added service activities (professional and business services), manufacturing, construction, and the primary sector (agriculture, mining and oil and gas extraction, and utilities).

Sectors where those vulnerable groups are concentrated tend to attract lower shares of foreign investment. According to Statistics Canada, FDI stocks in Canada is largely concentrated in the primary sector, particularly mining and oil and gas extraction, business and other support services (i.e. management of companies and enterprises)[1], manufacturing, finance, and wholesale and retail trade. Less than one-third of women and slightly more than one-third of Indigenous peoples, immigrants, and persons with disabilities work in those sectors. New establishments of foreign companies (i.e., greenfield FDI) are also mainly concentrated in the primary sector (mining and oil and gas extraction and utilities), manufacturing, and business and other support activities. In addition, more than two-thirds of the jobs created by these new foreign establishments are in manufacturing and business and other support services. This suggests that greater participation of women, Indigenous peoples, immigrants and persons with disabilities in sectors receiving more FDI could enable them to take even more advantage of the job opportunities created by foreign firms. However, FDI impact can vary across vulnerable groups and by sector. For example, mining is likely to remain a male-dominated sector, and jobs in sectors like mining and construction are not necessarily feasible options for persons with disabilities – depending on the type of disability. On the other hand, FDI in mining may create many jobs for Indigenous peoples given the geographic location of most mines and oil and gas sites (Box 4.3).

Table 4.1. FDI is prevalent and creates more jobs in sectors where vulnerable people are less represented

	Employment (% total)						
	Women	Indigenous peoples	Immigrants	Persons with disabilities	Inward FDI stocks (%)	Greenfield FDI (%)	Jobs created by greenfield FDI (%)
Agriculture, natural resources and utilities	2%	6%	3%	4%	11%	34%	5%
Construction	2%	9%	6%	7%	1%	2%	3%
Manufacturing	6%	8%	11%	8%	18%	33%	43%
Wholesale and retail trade	12%	16%	14%	15%	11%	0%	0%
Transportation and warehousing	2%	6%	6%	5%	2%	3%	5%
Finance and real estate	9%	4%	8%	4%	16%	3%	6%

Professional, scientific and technical services	9%	4%	9%	7%	4%	0%	0%
Business and other support services	3%	4%	5%	7%	31%	17%	33%
Educational services	13%	6%	6%	8%	0%	0%	0%
Health care and social assistance	25%	15%	12%	13%	0%	0%	0%
Information, culture and recreation	3%	3%	2%	2%	2%	9%	5%
Accommodation and food services	4%	6%	8%	5%	0%	0%	0%
Public administration	7%	7%	4%	8%	0%	0%	1%
Other services	4%	4%	6%	7%	0%	0%	0%

Note: Data on employment refer to 2022 for women and Indigenous peoples, 2015 for immigrants, 2016 for persons with disabilities. Data on Inward FDI stocks refer to 2021. Greenfield FDI is the sum of greenfield FDI between 2003 and 2022. Jobs created by greenfield FDI is the sum of all jobs created by greenfield FDI between 2003 and 2022.
Source: OECD elaboration based on Statistics Canada Labour Force Characteristics (2023[8]), https://doi.org/10.25318/1410002301-eng; Employment by Indigenous group and industry (2023[24]), https://doi.org/10.25318/1410036601-eng; 2016 Census of Population (2016[43]), https://www12.statcan.gc.ca/census-recensement/2016/index-eng.cfm; Immigration (2022[26]), https://www150.statcan.gc.ca/n1/pub/12-581-x/2022001/sec2-eng.htm; Canadian Survey on Disability (2017[35]), https://www150.statcan.gc.ca/n1/pub/71-607-x/71-607-x2019035-eng.htm; International investment position (2022[44]), https://doi.org/10.25318/3610000901-eng.; Financial Times (2023[45]), https://www.fdimarkets.com/.

4.3.2. Foreign and domestic firms surveyed have similar shares of vulnerable employees

The activities and practices of locally established affiliates of MNEs (henceforth foreign companies) can support the integration of vulnerable groups into the workforce and contribute to a more diverse labour market. A business consultation conducted by the OECD in the third quarter of 2022 sheds light on the workforce characteristics and diversity and inclusion practices of 24 Canadian and 33 foreign companies in Canada (Chapter 1, Annex 1.A). Canadian companies that participated in the consultation have on average slightly higher proportions of women, Indigenous peoples, and persons with disabilities than their foreign peers (Figure 4.8, Panel A). On the other hand, the foreign companies have on average higher shares of foreign workers (i.e., foreign nationals with permanent resident status or study/work-visa status). In total, however, the Canadian and foreign companies surveyed have a similar share of employees from vulnerable groups. The results also show that, regardless of ownership, the companies consulted from the service sector have on average a higher proportion of women, while the companies in the natural resources sector have higher proportions of Indigenous peoples.

Although the results are not generalisable to all domestic and foreign companies in Canada, they seem in line with existing evidence. Recent studies have shown that corporate culture is an important factor in explaining companies' performance and practices with respect to gender inclusion. Companies from countries that are more gender-equal tend to have higher shares of female employees and to adopt more gender-inclusive work practices (Kodama, Javorcik and Abe, 2018[46]; Tang and Zhang, 2021[47]). While these studies focus on gender equality, corporate culture is likely to play an important role with respect to the inclusion of other vulnerable groups. Given the importance of the socio-economic inclusion of vulnerable groups for Canada and the active commitment of successive governments in this direction, Canadian companies seem to be more aware of the importance of having a more diverse workforce than companies from other countries, which may explain the slightly higher shares of women, Indigenous peoples and persons with disabilities among the Canadian firms surveyed. On the other hand, the presence of higher shares of foreign workers in the foreign companies can be explained by the fact that foreign companies often transfer foreign staff from their home countries especially in the early stages of business, as well as by their more international working environment, which attracts more international workers and students.

The higher representation of women in the services companies surveyed is not surprising, as women are predominantly employed in services (around 90% of women). Similarly, the higher share of Indigenous peoples in surveyed natural resource companies is in line with the higher representation of these groups in the primary sector, compared to non-Indigenous peoples (6% of Indigenous peoples as opposed to 4% of non-Indigenous peoples). This is explained by the fact that Indigenous peoples live predominantly in non-urban areas and by their close ties to land and natural resources (Box 4.3).

Figure 4.8. Foreign firms surveyed have slightly lower shares of women, Indigenous peoples and persons with disabilities, but have higher shares of foreign workers

Average share of employees by vulnerable group and ownership (% total employees)

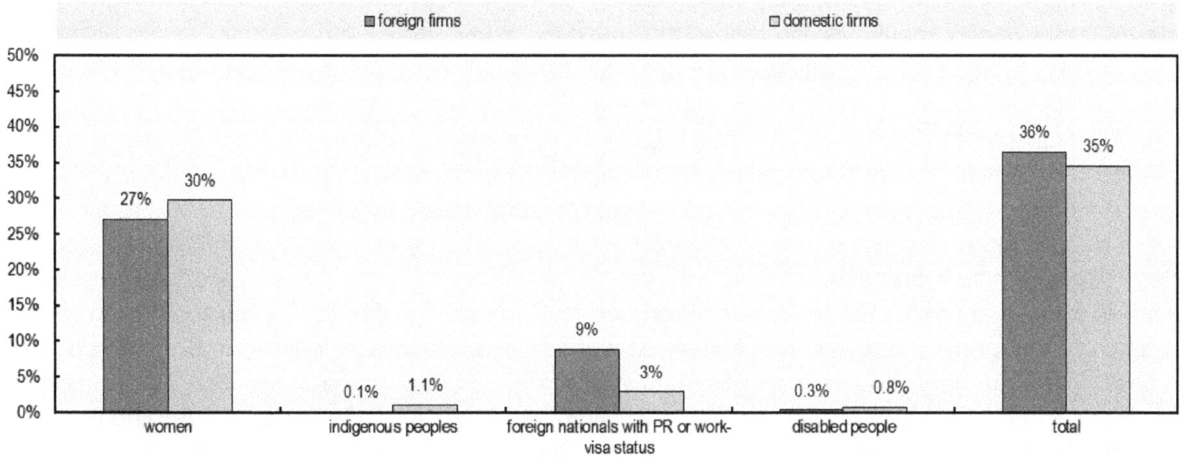

Source: OECD Business Consultation on Sustainability Practices in Canada (2022[48]).

Box 4.3. Indigenous peoples, land and natural resources

Land and the natural resources that cover it (fisheries, forestry, mining, water) are a key economic asset and the right to land can generate revenue and increase economic opportunities. Land, however, is not only an economic resource for Indigenous peoples, but is linked to traditional knowledge, spiritual beliefs, cultural reproduction and ensures the preservation of their traditional way of life. Access to land and resources has historically been limited and unequal for Indigenous peoples across Canada. Treaties are a key mechanism for Indigenous peoples to secure ownership of land. Benefit-sharing agreements, known in Canada as Impact and Benefit Agreements (IBAs), have been an important tool in minimising the environmental and socio-economic impacts of resource exploitation by corporations on the territories and lands inhabited by Indigenous peoples. Through these agreements, corporations offer Indigenous peoples environmental impact assessments and monitoring, as well as financial compensation, job creation and eventual environmental restoration in exchange for the development of their projects. IBAs often also include incentives for Indigenous communities, such as preferential hiring, priority bidding for local entrepreneurs and businesses, heritage protection and social support programmes. However, such agreements are not mandatory for companies. Moreover, they are confidential and parties entering new negotiations may not be aware of precedent negotiations, which may weaken Indigenous communities' claims. As of 2019, impact assessment introduced by the Impact Assessment Act (which replaced the environmental assessment under the former 2012 Canadian Environmental Assessment Act), provides another key tool for the prevention of adverse environmental effects on Indigenous peoples' territories from projects on federal lands. Budget 2024 launched the

Indigenous Loan Guarantee Programme to unlock access to capital for Indigenous communities and help remove barriers to Indigenous equity investment in natural resources and energy projects.

Source: OECD (2019[21]), Linking Indigenous Communities with Regional Development in Canada, https://doi.org/10.1787/3203c082-en.; Government of Canada (2022[49]), Impact Assessment Process Overview, https://www.canada.ca/en/impact-assessment-agency/services/policy-guidance/impact-assessment-process-overview.html

4.3.3. Foreign firms surveyed have lower shares of managers among women, Indigenous peoples and persons with disabilities

The OECD business consultation finds that the domestic companies have a higher share of managers among women, Indigenous peoples, and persons with disabilities than foreign companies, while the foreign companies surveyed have a higher share of managers among foreign workers (Figure 4.9, Panel A). This seems to be consistent with the fact that these vulnerable groups are more represented in their respective workforces. Moreover, the share of managers among all vulnerable employees is higher in domestic than in foreign companies surveyed (17% in domestic firms compared to 13% in foreign firms). Overall, the results still hold when comparing foreign and domestic companies in the same sector and covered by the survey. Moreover, both domestic and foreign firms in construction and services report higher shares of managers from vulnerable categories, particularly women and foreign workers. The results also show that the share of managers among women and foreign workers is significantly higher in SMEs (i.e., companies with less than 250 employees), regardless of ownership. At the same time, only large (domestic) companies report having Indigenous and persons with disabilities among their managers. The results also show that the share of firms with a woman among the owners is higher in foreign firms and SMEs (Figure 4.9, Panel B).

Recent studies emphasise the importance of corporate culture as a crucial factor for a more diverse workforce, even in middle and senior management positions (Kodama, Javorcik and Abe, 2018[46]; Tang and Zhang, 2021[47]). Considering these findings, the higher percentages of female managers in the Canadian companies may be attributed to a greater awareness and focus on inclusion and empowerment of women. Some similarities are also found between the results of the OECD business consultation and those of another recent survey conducted by McKinsey & Company (2019[50]) of 100 Canadian companies and organisations (which, however, does not distinguish between domestic and foreign companies). The McKinsey & Company survey finds that SMEs in Canada have a higher representation of women in middle and senior management positions than large organisations, which is also reflected in the OECD business consultation. According to McKinsey & Company report, the less hierarchical structure of SMEs poses fewer obstacles to the advancement of women. The report also concludes that neither staff turnover nor the desire for promotion lead to the under-representation of women in management roles. In fact, the results show that women and men leave their organisations and declare their desire for promotion at similar rates.

There is limited evidence on the impact of foreign ownership on female entrepreneurship. OECD research has shown that differences with respect to women's participation in ownership between FDI-engaged (foreign) and non-FDI-engaged (domestic) enterprises tend to be statistically insignificant (OECD, 2019[17]; 2022[18]). In contrast, firm size appears to be an important factor in explaining women's representation in ownership. Some evidence shows that women-owned firms tend to be smaller in size than their male counterparts (OECD, 2017[12]). This is consistent with the findings of the OECD's business consultation that a larger share of women-owned firms are found among SMEs, although most of the surveyed SMEs were foreign and, in turn, may not be representative of female participation in ownership in SMEs.

Figure 4.9. Foreign firms have higher shares of managers among foreign workers, but lower shares among women, Indigenous peoples, and people with disabilities

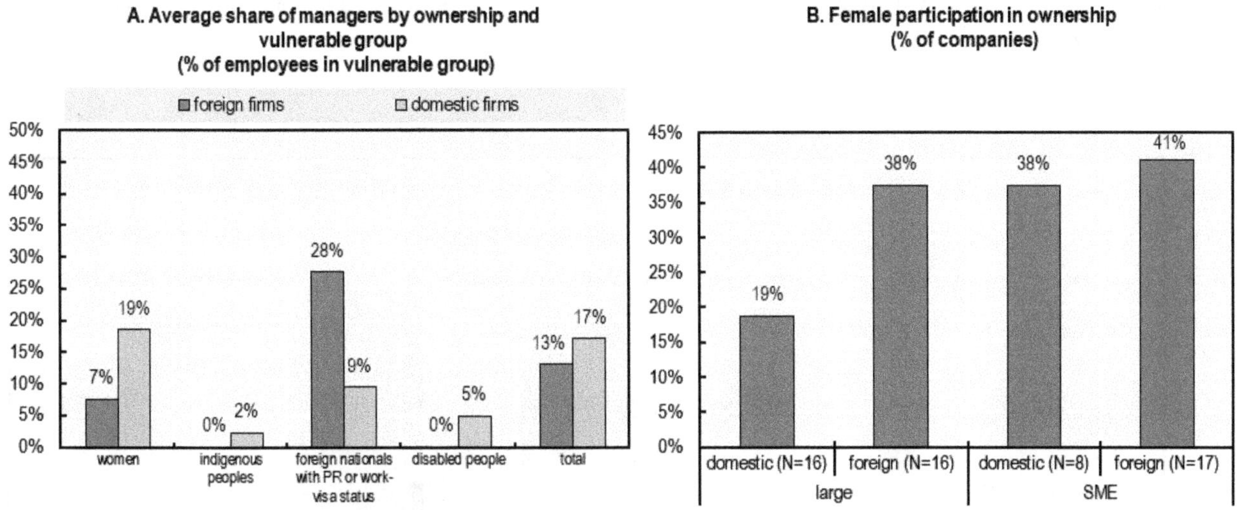

Note: SMEs are companies with less than 250 employees.
Source: OECD Business Consultation on Sustainability Practices in Canada (2022[48]).

4.3.4. Formal training is more likely to be offered by foreign companies surveyed, including to employees from vulnerable groups

Training is key to increasing performance, improving corporate culture and reducing turnover. It is also an effective tool to promote the integration of vulnerable employees and support their professional development in the company. About 83% of domestic and 90% of foreign companies that participated in the OECD business consultation offer formal training to their employees. Formal training can take different forms, ranging from induction training, i.e. introducing new employees to their new job role, technical skills training (e.g., on how to use a machine or software), management and leadership skills training and so on (diversity training and skills development programmes aimed at specifically vulnerable groups are discussed in the next session). The results also show that the foreign companies have a higher percentage of employees who have received training for all categories of vulnerable workers except for Indigenous peoples, which is not surprising considering that the percentage of Indigenous peoples in their workforce is very low (Figure 4.10). The results are still valid when comparing foreign and domestic companies in the same sector, with a few exceptions (domestic firms have higher shares of women who received training than foreign firms in mining, and higher shares of employees with disabilities who received training in construction and services). Overall, 31% of vulnerable workers receive some form of training in foreign companies, compared to 20% in domestic companies.

Evidence, observed in many countries, indicates that foreign firms are more likely to provide training to their employees than domestic firms. This result is often explained in light of the fact that firms that engage in FDI (and exports) tend to be larger, more technologically advanced and employ a higher share of skilled workers on average than domestic firms (OECD, 2019[17]; 2022[18]). However, although a higher share of vulnerable workers receive training in foreign firms, this does not seem to lead to better professional development prospects for these groups, as evidenced by the lower shares of managers among these vulnerable groups in the foreign firms surveyed. This suggests that professional development and career opportunities for these vulnerable employees are not directly related to their skills and motivation, a finding highlighted in particular for women (2019[50]).

Figure 4.10. Foreign firms surveyed have higher shares of vulnerable employees who have received training

Average share of employees who received training by ownership and vulnerable group (% of employees in vulnerable group)

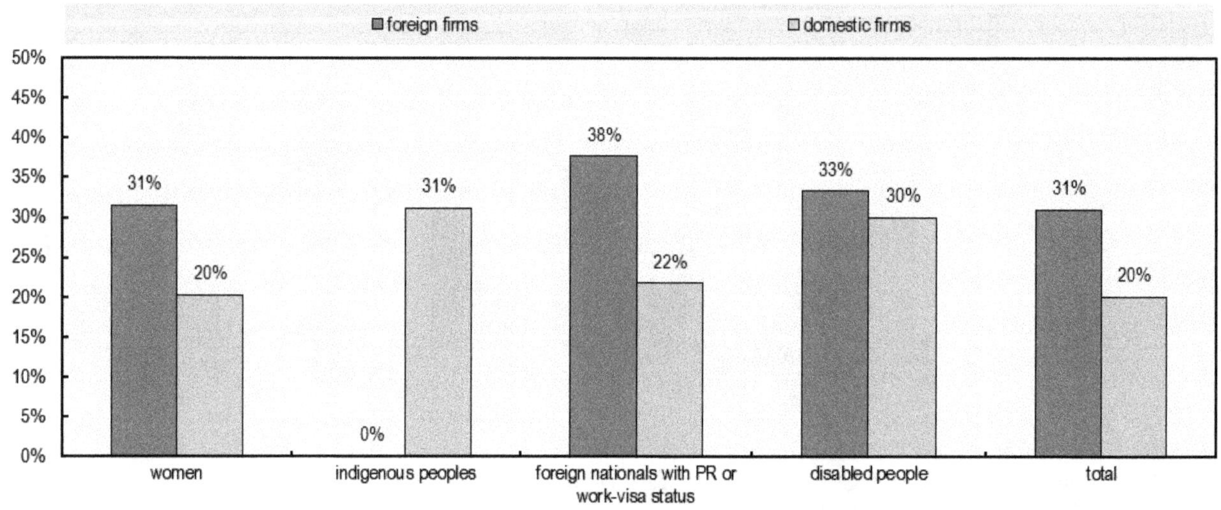

Source: OECD Business Consultation on Sustainability Practices in Canada (2022[48])

Box 4.4. Skills development and career support programmes for vulnerable groups: examples of practices from foreign MNEs

Scholarships for Indigenous engineering students and women

A foreign aerospace and defence services company offers scholarships to support Indigenous peoples and women. As part of an Indigenous workforce development programme, in collaboration with the Canadian Council for Aboriginal Business (CCAB) of which it is a member, the company offers one scholarship per year to Indigenous engineering students at the University of Victoria and a one-semester internship, with the possibility of being hired by the company at the end of the internship. The company also has a mentorship programme for women, the aim of which is to support the entry of women into senior roles, where women currently account for just under a quarter of positions.

Efforts to support emerging female and Indigenous talent

One foreign ICT and telecommunications multinational partners with various schools throughout Canada with the intent to target and develop relationships with groups such as females and Indigenous students in STEM, scheduling workshops with them and conducting tours of the company sites, to attract them as potential employees. The company has supported Carleton University's Women in Engineering & IT group through speaking opportunities and visibility within the campus community to highlight career opportunities for women. The company has also sponsored one of largest all-female hackathons, at Western University, and challenged participants to build a platform for mentors and mentees to connect to encourage more women to step into the STEM field. The company has also established a women's employee resource group that allows its female staff to network and benefit from mentorship events, such as those around career advancement and the future of women in leadership.

Training and support for underrepresented groups from the high school level

One foreign manufacturer and distributor of nitrogen and hydrogen products for agricultural, industrial and clean energy use, offers annual scholarships to students from underrepresented groups, particularly women and Indigenous students, in communities near its plants in Medicine Hat, Alberta and Courtright, Ontario, enabling them to pursue degrees in STEM subjects at local universities. The company has also supported high school events such as 'STEM for a Day', which introduces students to STEM career options, and organisations such as Careers: The Next Generation, which connects high school students with paid internships. Through engagements with high school students, the company supports exposure to STEM careers for a more diverse audience before the university level, where STEM programmes are more likely to be dominated by male students.

Source: OECD Business Consultation on Sustainability Practices in Canada (2022[48]), HerVolution (2023[51]), STEMing UP, https://www.hervolution.org/steming-up-program/;

4.3.5. A larger share of Canadian firms surveyed use inclusive workplace practices

Companies can actively promote diversity in their workforce through a range of inclusive workplace practices. These include inclusive recruitment strategies, ranging from drafting inclusive job descriptions, to setting targets/quotas for vulnerable employees, to recruitment programmes that focus on underrepresented groups, to scholarships and internships for vulnerable groups that lead to potential hires. (Box 4.4). Another form of inclusive practices is diversity training aimed at eliminating stereotypes and raising staff awareness of the importance of diversity in the workforce, and skills training programmes for employees from vulnerable groups with the aim of encouraging their professional development (Box 4.5). Finally, the provision of diversity-friendly infrastructures is also important to remove barriers and create a level playing field for all employees. These include, for example, flexible working hours, extended leave policies for parents, return-to-work programmes after maternity leave, pay equity and pay transparency initiatives; and so on.

According to the results of the OECD business consultation, a higher percentage of Canadian companies report using inclusive workplace practices in all three categories considered (Figure 4.11). This is consistent with the fact that domestic companies have a higher proportion of employees and managers from these vulnerable groups than foreign companies. Overall, the results hold also when comparing Canadian and foreign companies in the same sector. They also show that, regardless of ownership and sector, large companies are more likely to adopt inclusive workplace practices than SMEs. These results seem to provide further confirmation that the inclusion of vulnerable people is an important value in the corporate culture of Canadian companies. It is also not surprising that large companies are more proactive in implementing inclusive corporate policies, given their greater resources and the stronger institutional pressures they may be exposed to.

Figure 4.11. A larger share of domestic firms surveyed use inclusive workplace practices in all three categories

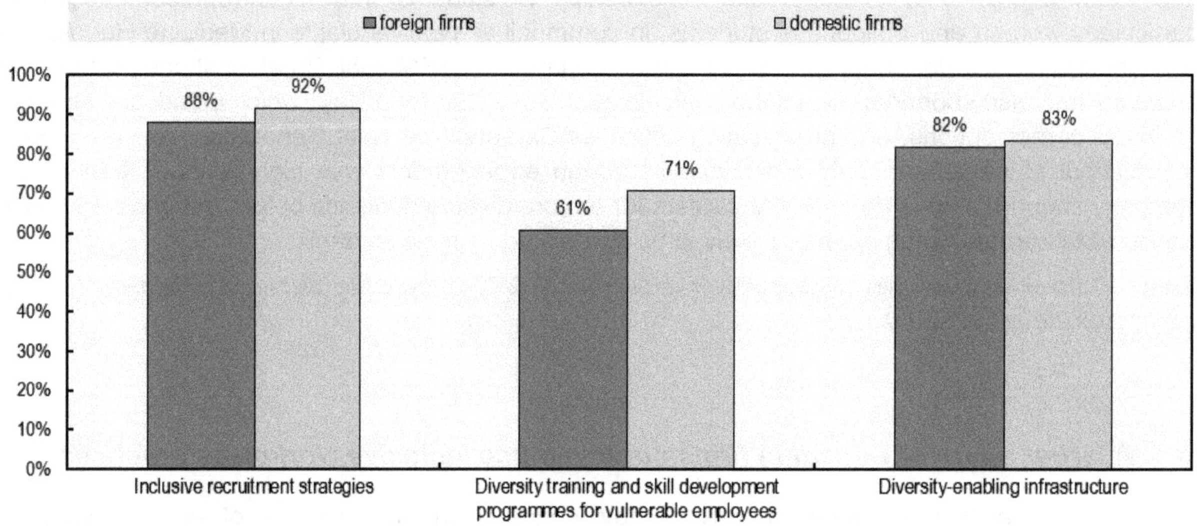

Source: OECD Business Consultation on Sustainability Practices in Canada (2022[48]).

Box 4.5. Hiring practicies to enhance diversity in the workforce: examples of practices from foreign MNEs

Inclusive rehiring schemes

One foreign car manufacturer recently implemented a plan to reopen in 2021 after a two-year closure, giving priority to hiring women. Working with the labour union, Unifor, the company ensured that half of its 1200 new hires were women, by targeting job ads to women, lifting manufacturing experience requirements, and focusing on other acquired workplace skills, while ensuring that half of candidate evaluators were women.

Neurodiversity Centres of Excellence

One MNE has launched Neurodiversity Centres of Excellence in 19 cities in eight countries, including Canada, that help companies and organisations recruit, onboard and develop neurodiverse talent. These centres design inclusive recruitment processes and work environments for neurodiverse candidates and employees through upskilling and process redesign. These Centres of Excellence have recorded a 92% retention rate for neurodiverse employees hired through the programme worldwide. In addition, the MNE hosts a larger neurodiversity community of over 1,200 employees globally who self-identify as neurodiverse across all grades and service lines. The MNE has already supported several large organisations in creating neurodiverse talent, including in Canada.

Source: OECD Business Consultation on Sustainability Practices in Canada (2022[48]),

References

Brosseau, L. (2020), *Recognition of the Foreign Qualifications of Immigrants*, Library of Parliament Background Papers, https://lop.parl.ca/staticfiles/PublicWebsite/Home/ResearchPublications/BackgroundPapers/PDF/2020-86-e.pdf. [34]

Canadian Heritage (2020), *Systemic barriers to the full socio-economic participation of persons with disabilities and the benefits realized when such persons are included in the workplace*, https://www.canada.ca/content/dam/pch/documents/corporate/transparency/open-government/literature-review/Lit-Review-Systemic-Barriers-eng.pdf. [41]

Canadian Human Rights Commission (2017), *Roadblocks on the career path: Challenges faced by persons with disabilities in employment*, https://www.chrc-ccdp.gc.ca/sites/default/files/publication-pdfs/ottawaiti7-2565385-v7-report_on_employment_and_persons_with_disabilitie_final-s.pdf. [40]

Chan, P., T. Handler and M. Frenette (2021), *Gender differences in STEM enrolment and graduation: What are the roles of academic performance and preparation?*, https://doi.org/10.25318/36280001202101100004-eng. [14]

Financial Times (2023), *FDI Markets: the in-depth crossborder investment monitor from the Financial Times*, https://www.fdimarkets.com/. [45]

Government of Canada (2022), *Impact Assessment Process Overview*, https://www.canada.ca/en/impact-assessment-agency/services/policy-guidance/impact-assessment-process-overview.html. [49]

Government of Canada (2021), *Government of Canada announces that the Pay Equity Act will come into force on August 31, 2021*, https://www.canada.ca/en/employment-social-development/news/2021/07/government-of-canada-announces-that-the-pay-equity-act-will-come-into-force-on-august-31-2021.html. [10]

HerVolution (2023), *STEMing UP*, https://www.hervolution.org/steming-up-program/;. [51]

Hu, M., A. Daley and W. Casey (2017), "Literacy, Numeracy, Technology Skill and Labour Market Outcomes among Indigenous Peoples in Canada", https://doi.org/10.3138/cpp.2017-068. [25]

Kodama, N., B. Javorcik and Y. Abe (2018), "Transplanting corporate culture across international borders: Foreign direct investment and female employment in Japan", *The World Economy*, Vol. 41/1, pp. 1148–1165, https://ideas.repec.org/a/bla/worlde/v41y2018i5p1148-1165.html. [46]

Matthew, T. et al. (2015), *A Profile of the Labour Market Experiences of Adults with Disabilities among Canadians Aged 15 Years and Older*, Canadian Survey on Disability Reports. Statistics Canada Cataloge, https://publications.gc.ca/site/eng/9.802571/publication.html. [38]

McKinsey & Company (2019), *The present and future of women at work in Canada*, https://www.mckinsey.com/featured-insights/gender-equality/the-present-and-future-of-women-at-work-in-canada. [50]

Morris, S. et al. (2018), *A demographic, employment and income profile of Canadians with disabilities aged 15 years and over, 2017*, https://www150.statcan.gc.ca/n1/pub/89-654-x/89-654-x2018002-eng.htm. [36]

OECD (2023), *Gender Portal*, https://www.oecd.org/gender/data/. [3]

OECD (2023), *Public Investment in Bulgaria: Planning and Delivering Infrastructure*, OECD Public Governance Reviews, OECD Publishing, Paris, https://doi.org/10.1787/b73ef3b4-en. [11]

OECD (2022), *Business Consultation on Sustainability Practices in Canada*. [48]

OECD (2022), *Disability, Work and Inclusion: Mainstreaming in All Policies and Practices*, OECD Publishing, Paris, https://doi.org/10.1787/1eaa5e9c-en. [39]

OECD (2022), *FDI Qualities Policy Toolkit*, OECD Publishing, Paris, https://doi.org/10.1787/7ba74100-en. [19]

OECD (2022), "Making the most of public investment to address regional inequalities, megatrends and future shocks", *OECD Regional Development Papers*, OECD Publishing, Paris, https://doi.org/10.1787/8a1fb523-en. [18]

OECD (2022), *Recommendation of the Council on Foreign Direct Investment Qualities for Sustainable Development*, https://legalinstruments.oecd.org/en/instruments/OECD-LEGAL-0476. [20]

OECD (2021), *Employment, unemployment, and participation rates by place of birth and sex*, https://stats.oecd.org/. [28]

OECD (2019), *FDI Qualities Indicators: Measuring the sustainable development impacts of investment*, https://www.oecd.org/fr/investissement/fdi-qualities-indicators.htm. [17]

OECD (2019), *Linking Indigenous Communities with Regional Development in Canada*, OECD Rural Policy Reviews, OECD Publishing, Paris, https://doi.org/10.1787/3203c082-en. [21]

OECD (2019), *Recruiting Immigrant Workers: Canada 2019, Recruiting Immigrant Workers*, OECD Publishing, Paris, https://doi.org/10.1787/4abab00d-en. [29]

OECD (2018), *PISA Database*, https://www.oecd.org/pisa/data/2018database/. [16]

OECD (2017), *The Pursuit of Gender Equality: An Uphill Battle*, OECD Publishing, Paris, https://doi.org/10.1787/9789264281318-en. [12]

OECD/EU (2018), *Settling In 2018: Indicators of Immigrant Integration*, OECD Publishing, Paris, https://doi.org/10.1787/9789264307216-en. [30]

Statistics Canada (2023), *Table 14-10-0023-01 Labour force characteristics by industry, annual (x 1,000)*, https://doi.org/10.25318/1410002301-eng. [8]

Statistics Canada (2023), *Table 14-10-0083-01 Labour force characteristics by immigrant status, annual*, https://doi.org/10.25318/1410008301-eng. [32]

Statistics Canada (2023), *Table 14-10-0085-01 Labour force characteristics of immigrants by sex and age group, annual*, https://doi.org/10.25318/1410008501-eng. [2]

Statistics Canada (2023), *Table 14-10-0297-01 Labour force characteristics by occupation, annual, 1987 to 2018, inactive (x 1,000)*, https://doi.org/10.25318/1410029701-eng. [9]

Statistics Canada (2023), *Table 14-10-0365-01 Labour force characteristics by region and detailed Indigenous group*, https://doi.org/10.25318/1410036501-eng. [22]

Statistics Canada (2023), *Table 14-10-0366-01 Employment by Indigenous group and industry (x 1,000)*, https://doi.org/10.25318/1410036601-eng. [24]

Statistics Canada (2023), *Table 14-10-0370-01 Average hourly and weekly wages and average usual weekly hours by Indigenous group, inactive*, https://doi.org/10.25318/1410037001-eng. [23]

Statistics Canada (2022), *Immigrants make up the largest share of the population in over 150 years and continue to shape who we are as Canadians*, https://www150.statcan.gc.ca/n1/daily-quotidien/221026/dq221026a-eng.htm. [31]

Statistics Canada (2022), *Immigration*, https://www150.statcan.gc.ca/n1/pub/12-581-x/2022001/sec2-eng.htm. [26]

Statistics Canada (2022), *Immigration as a source of labour supply*, https://www150.statcan.gc.ca/n1/daily-quotidien/220622/dq220622c-eng.htm. [33]

Statistics Canada (2022), *Indigenous peoples and communities*, https://www.rcaanc-cirnac.gc.ca/eng/1100100013785/1529102490303. [5]

Statistics Canada (2022), *Measuring disability in Canada*, https://www150.statcan.gc.ca/n1/pub/11-627-m/11-627-m2022062-eng.htm. [7]

Statistics Canada (2022), *Table 33-10-0501-01 Representation of women and men on boards of directors and in officer positions, by firm attributes*, https://doi.org/10.25318/3310050101-eng. [13]

Statistics Canada (2022), *Table 36-10-0009-01 International investment position, Canadian direct investment abroad and foreign direct investment in Canada, by North American Industry Classification System (NAICS) and region, annual (x 1,000,000)*, https://doi.org/10.25318/3610000901-eng. [44]

Statistics Canada (2022), *Table 98-10-0451-01 Labour force status by highest level of education, Indigenous identity, age and gender: Canada, provinces and territories, census metropolitan areas and census agglomerations with parts*, https://doi.org/10.25318/9810045101-eng. [1]

Statistics Canada (2021), *Focus on Geography Series, 2021 Census of Population*, https://www12.statcan.gc.ca/census-recensement/2021/as-sa/fogs-spg/page.cfm?topic=9&lang=E&dguid=2021A000011124. [27]

Statistics Canada (2021), *Gender of person*, https://www23.statcan.gc.ca/imdb/p3Var.pl?Function=DEC&Id=410445. [4]

Statistics Canada (2021), *Table 41-10-0049-01 Disability status, disability severity class and labour force status by Aboriginal identity, age group and sex*, https://doi.org/10.25318/4110004901-eng. [42]

Statistics Canada (2017), *2016 Census of Population: Immigration and ethnocultural diversity*, https://www12.statcan.gc.ca/census-recensement/2016/ref/98-501/98-501-x2016008-eng.cfm. [6]

Statistics Canada (2017), *Canadian Survey on Disability (CSD)*, https://www150.statcan.gc.ca/n1/pub/71-607-x/71-607-x2019035-eng.htm. [35]

Statistics Canada (2016), *2016 Census of Population*, https://www12.statcan.gc.ca/census-recensement/2016/index-eng.cfm. [43]

Statistics Canada. (2017), *Is field of study a factor in the earnings of young bachelor's degree holders?*, https://www12.statcan.gc.ca/census-recensement/2016/as-sa/98-200-x/2016023/98-200-x2016023-eng.cfm. [15]

Tang, H. and Y. Zhang (2021), "Do Multinationals Transfer Culture? Evidence on Female Employment in China", *Journal of International Economics*, Vol. 133, https://www.sciencedirect.com/science/article/pii/S0022199621000982. [47]

Turcotte, M. (2015), *Persons with Disabilities and Employment*, Insights on Canadian Society. Statistics Canada Catalogue no. 75-006-X., https://www150.statcan.gc.ca/n1/en/pub/75-006-x/2014001/article/14115-eng.pdf?st=ehUFDqwn. [37]

Notes

[1] 'Business and other support services' comprises establishments coded to 'Management of companies and enterprises' and to 'Administrative and support, waste management and remediation services'. Inward FDI stock refers to 'Management of companies and enterprises'. Most FDI in this category is redistributed to other companies within the corporate group, which are associated with other sectors, such as mining, oil and gas extraction and manufacturing.

5 The contribution of FDI to the green transition

This chapter examines the contribution of FDI to Canada's green transition, using project-level FDI data and the OECD business consultation on sustainability practices of domestic and foreign firms in Canada.

5.1. Green transition in Canada: challenges and opportunities

5.1.1. Economic activity in Canada is carbon- and energy-intensive

As the fourth largest producer of crude oil and the sixth largest producer of natural gas in the world, Canada emits more carbon dioxide (CO_2) relative to its GDP than all other OECD economies (Figure 5.1, Panel A). Its weather and geography contribute to large energy requirements to heat homes in winter and to transport people and goods across large distances, driving up energy intensity of GDP to the second highest in the OECD (Figure 5.1, Panel B). Both carbon- and energy-intensity have declined by around 30% over the last three decades, suggesting that Canada has made progress in decoupling carbon emissions and economic growth. Indeed, replacement of coal-fired power with natural gas and hydroelectric power, and energy-efficiency improvements in homes and some heavy industries helped reduce the emission-intensity of energy in the past two decades. While the emission cuts are impressive in Canada, the speed of emission decline was only around half of the OECD average over the last decade. Moreover, according to recent evidence, reductions in carbon- and energy-intensities were offset by increased emissions from population and economic growth (OECD, 2023[1]).

Figure 5.1. Economic activity in Canada is carbon- and energy-intensive

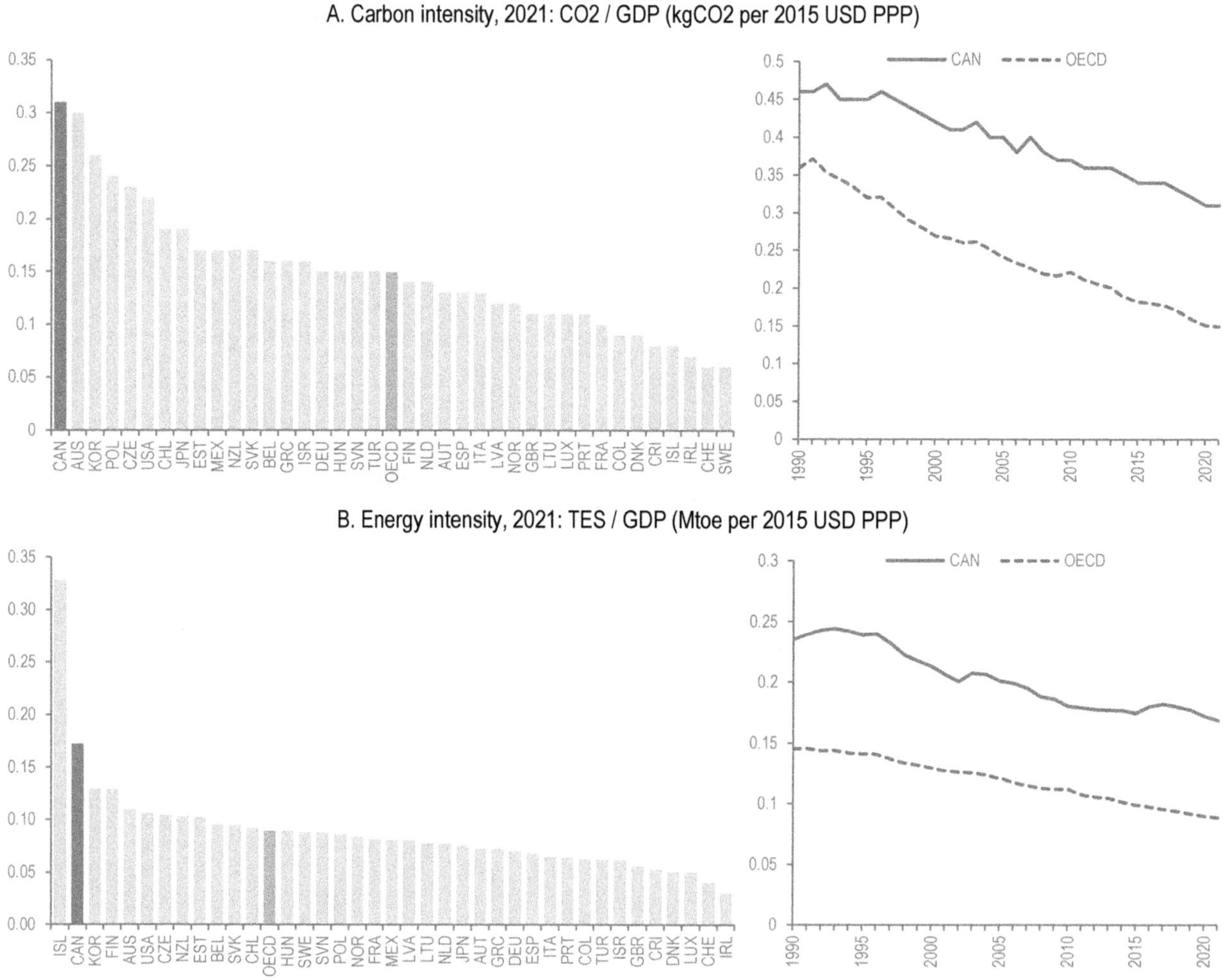

Source: IEA (2023), GHG from Energy Statistics database (2023[2]), https://www.iea.org/data-and-statistics

Box 5.1. Terminology and concepts

Greenhouse gas (GHG) emissions: total greenhouse gas emissions from fuel combustion including carbon dioxide (CO_2), methane (CH_4) and nitrous oxide (N_2O). CO_2 is the primary GHG responsible for global warming.

Carbon intensity: The ratio of carbon emissions and gross domestic product (GDP), expressed as kilogrammes of CO_2 per 2015 US$ calculated using purchasing power parities (e.g. kgCO_2 per 2015 USD PPP).

Energy intensity: the ratio between total energy supply (TES) and GDP, expressed in megajoules per 2015 USD calculated using purchasing power parities (MJ per 2015 USD PPP). Total energy supply means the overall supply of energy for all activities on the territory of the country, but excluding international marine and aviation bunkers (i.e. TES = production + imports - exports - international marine and international aviation bunkers).

Low-carbon technology: a technology that helps reduce carbon emissions by either (1) reducing energy use (e.g. energy-saving); (2) reducing or eliminating carbon emissions from production or use (e.g. renewable energy, green hydrogen); (3) removing carbon from the atmosphere (e.g. carbon capture); or (4) conserving resources (e.g. recycling). For the purpose of this report, the terms green and low-carbon are used interchangeably.

Renewable energy: energy from sources that are naturally replenishing. It generally is considered to include six renewable-power generation sectors: geothermal, marine/tidal, small hydroelectric, solar, wind, and the combined sector biomass and waste. Clean energy and renewable energy are used interchangeably for the purpose of this report.

Green hydrogen: hydrogen can be burnt to generate energy or combined with water to produce electricity without emitting any pollutants or GHGs. Green hydrogen is produced by splitting water into hydrogen and oxygen using renewable electricity (i.e. electrolysis), while grey hydrogen is produced with fossil fuels and blue hydrogen combines fossil fuels and carbon capture. Possible uses for hydrogen include power generation and electricity grid stabilisation, fuel for heavy manufacturing processes in industries (e.g. steel, cement, chemicals), and fuel cells for electric vehicles and heavy transport (e.g. shipping).

Green FDI: New cross-border investment projects (or expansions of existing projects) in environmental technologies. The definition is assigned on a project basis in the Financial Times FDI Markets database of greenfield investments, and encompasses a wide-range of technologies and solutions (e.g. energy-saving, waste-reducing, zero-emission, sequestration) across all major sectors of the economy. Beyond the renewable energy sector, some examples include energy storage systems, recycling solutions (e.g. packaging, textiles, auto-parts, electronic scrap, etc.), and digital solutions in support of the transition (e.g. platforms for carbon accounting or environmental commodity trading).

5.1.2. The energy sector is key for Canada's green transition

Given its rich endowments of fossil fuel energy resources and its large energy needs, burning fossil fuels for energy use is the main source of Canada's carbon footprint, reaching 80% of its greenhouse gas (GHG) emissions in 2020. Oil and gas extraction alone are responsible for over a quarter of Canada's emissions (26%), but energy consumption by other sectors also contributes heavily to Canada's carbon footprint, with residential and transport use accounting for almost half of Canada's overall GHG emissions (Figure 5.2). Manufacturing and construction account for just under a fifth of GHG emissions, when combining direct emissions from industrial processes (8%) and indirect emissions from energy use (9%). Compared to other OECD economies, the share of emissions from energy use is relatively high, while industrial processes tend to be relatively cleaner. To further advance Canada's green transition, the shift away from carbon-intensive energy generation to clean energy generation must accelerate significantly, alongside the electrification of key sectors like transport, buildings and industry. Significant investment will be needed to upgrade and adapt grids to accommodate greater demand for clean electricity and more generation from intermittent renewable energy sources (OECD, 2023[1]).

Figure 5.2. Energy use is the main source of Canada's GHG emissions

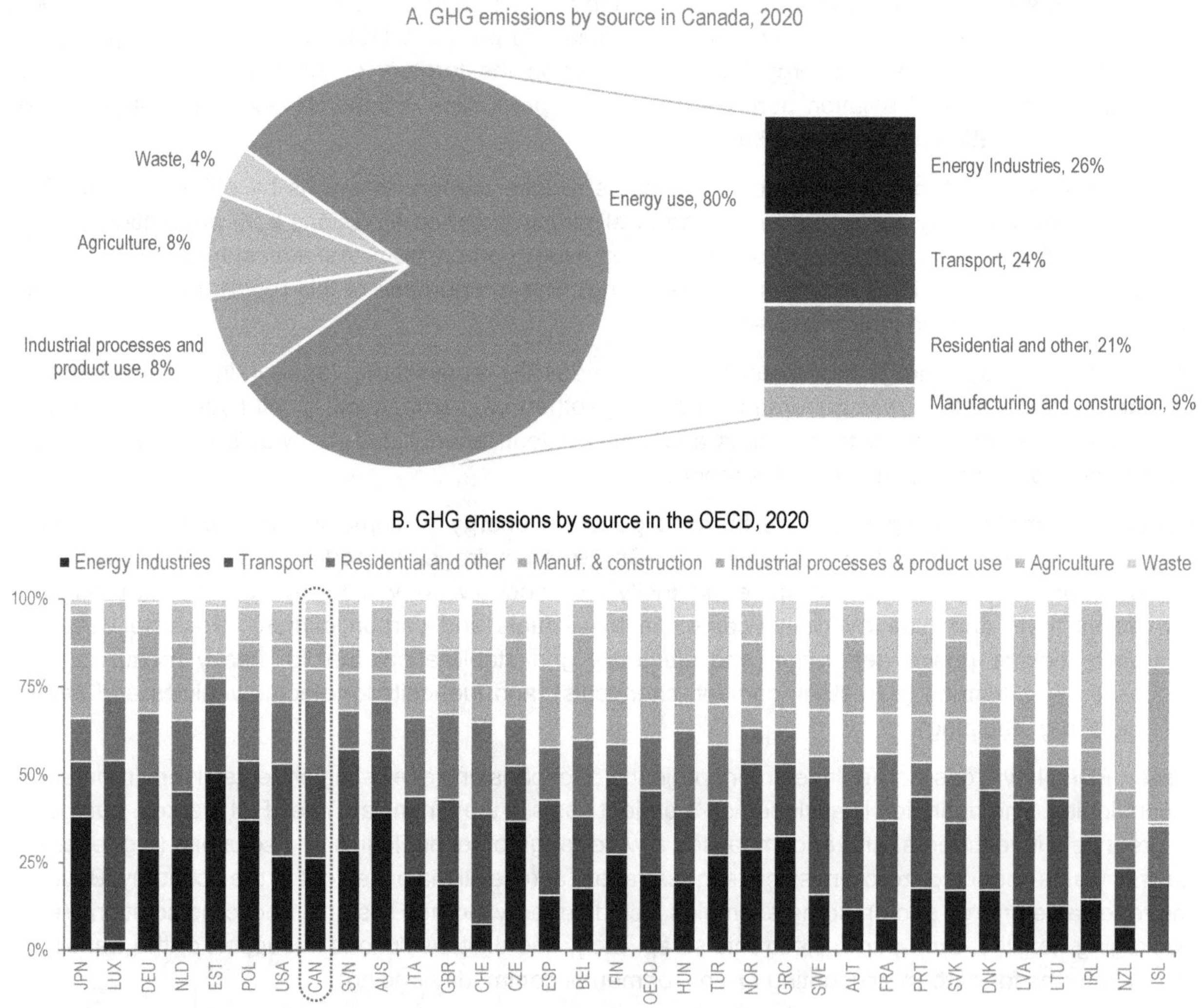

Note: Emissions exclude land use, land use change and forestry (LULUCF). Blue shaded areas represent energy use in related sectors.
Source: Authors' elaboration based on OECD Air and Climate, Environment Statistics database (2023[3]), http://dotstat.oecd.org/

While energy use is responsible for the bulk of Canada's emissions (primarily due to fuel and heat consumption), electricity is greener in Canada than in many other OECD countries, with approximately 82% generated from non-emitting sources (Figure 5.3). Thanks to abundant hydroelectric capacity in British Columbia, Quebec, Manitoba and Ontario, and retirement of coal in Ontario and Alberta (expected by the end of 2023), emissions from the electricity sector declined 41% in the past decade despite a 12% increase in generation (IEA, 2023[4]). Yet, substantial variation remains at the sub-national level

(Figure 5.4). Provinces like Quebec, Manitoba, and Newfoundland and Labrador generate more than 85% of their power from their abundant hydro resources, while Nova Scotia, Saskatchewan and Alberta still rely on fossil fuels for over three-quarters of their electricity, and on coal for over 35%. Ontario and New Brunswick have managed to decarbonise electricity substantially by exploiting nuclear as well as hydro power, and Prince Edward Island generates close to 100% of its electricity from wind power. In the northern territories, the situation is also varied with Yukon benefitting from vast hydroelectric capacity, which accounts for 80% of its power, while the energy mix is evenly split across hydro and fossil fuels in the Northwest Territories, and virtually oil-based in Nunavut.

The federal government aims to drive remaining net emissions from electricity generation to zero by 2035 (Environment and Climate Change Canada, 2022[5]). To achieve this objective, new sources of clean electricity will be needed beyond hydropower. It is likely that Canada's provinces and territories will increasingly exploit wind and solar power potential in coming years, given the relatively low capital and operational costs of these technologies. From 5% of total supply in 2019, the Canada Energy Regulator (CER) projects that solar and wind power will together comprise 15% of electricity generated in Canada in 2035.

Figure 5.3. Electricity generation is greener in Canada than in most other OECD countries

Electricity generation by energy source, 2021

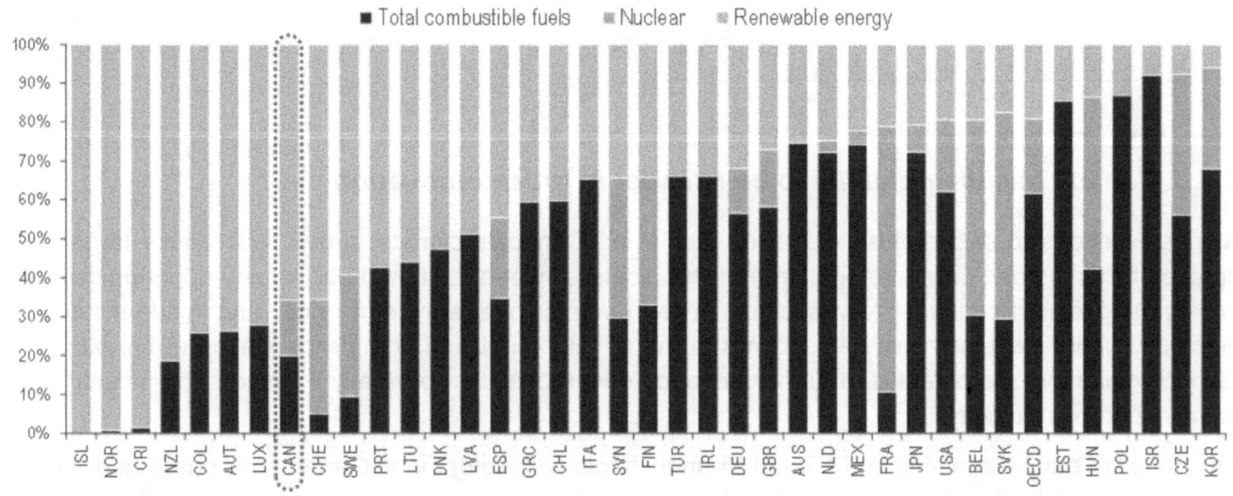

Note: Renewable energy includes biomass, geothermal, hydro, solar, tidal and wind. Combustible fuels include coal, oil and natural gas.
Source: Authors' elaboration based on IEA Electricity Information database (2023[4]), https://www.iea.org/data-and-statistics

Figure 5.4. Electricity generation varies considerably across Canadian provinces

Energy generation by province, 2021

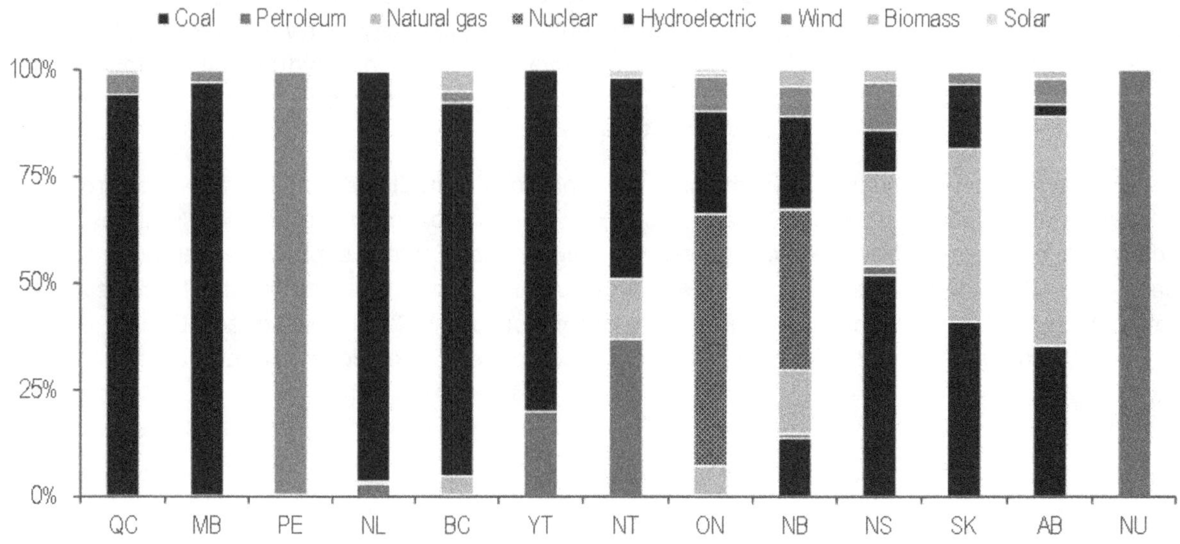

Note: Renewable energy includes biomass, geothermal, hydro, solar, tidal and wind. Combustible fuels include coal, oil and natural gas.
Source: Authors' elaboration based on Canada Energy Regulator (2023[6]), https://www.cer-rec.gc.ca/en/data-analysis/energy-markets/provincial-territorial-energy-profiles/index.html

5.1.3. Canada has the potential to be a leader in green innovation

Alongside efforts to decarbonise electricity, achieving Canada's climate targets will require large-scale uptake of existing and new, strategic green technologies. Indeed, as noted above, key opportunities lie in accelerating electrification of key sectors, improvements in energy efficiency, and modernisation of electricity grids. R&D-intensive investments in the development and commercialisation of breakthrough technologies have the potential to further advance decarbonisation of heavy transport and industry, and achieve carbon neutrality.

As a result of early leadership in R&D and clean technology development, Canada has positioned itself as a global leader in the development and deployment of new green technologies, like carbon capture utilisation and storage (CCUS) and hydrogen fuel cell. Canada has the potential to play a critical role in the large-scale adoption of these technologies, and application across an array of sectors that have been most challenging to decarbonise, such as steel, cement and heavy transport (Box 5.2). For example, Canada is home to one-fifth of the world's large-scale CCUS projects in operation, and more than half of fuel cell buses deployed around the world contain Canadian fuel cell powertrain technology (Natural Resources Canada, 2020[7]).

Governments play an important role in reducing barriers to R&D and mitigating risks specific to green R&D. The knowledge and learning benefits of R&D and early deployment of technologies cannot be fully commercially captured by companies who bear the costs of R&D as there are spillover benefits to other developers. This acts as a disincentive to socially optimal levels of investment in these areas. Public spending on green R&D is therefore warranted to address this market failure and can catalyse greater private sector investment in these technologies. Canada is among the OECD countries with highest public spending on R&D in low-carbon technologies, which amounted to around half a percent of GDP in 2021, compared to 0.3% for the OECD average (Figure 5.5). This is in contrast with broader (public and private) spending on R&D across sectors which is low in Canada (1.7% of GDP) relative to OECD peers (2.7% on average). Among green technologies, energy efficiency, nuclear energy and renewable energy attract the largest shares of public R&D, although fossil fuels still attract a sizeable share of public R&D spending (14%).

Figure 5.5. Public spending on green R&D is high in Canada

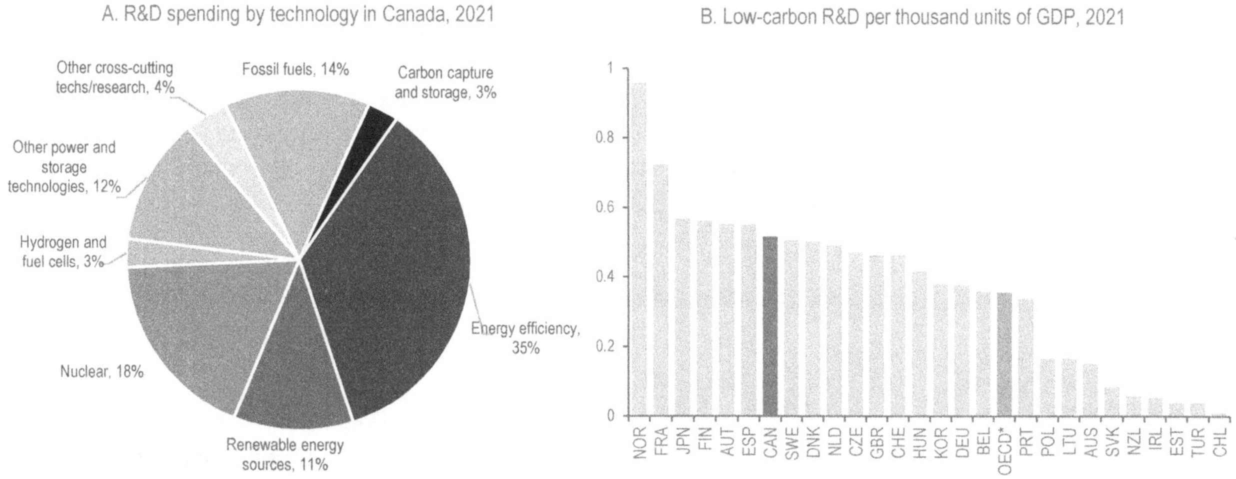

Note: Low-carbon includes all categories shown in the pie chart with the exception of fossil fuel technologies. OECD Average includes the 28 countries for which there is data.
Source: Authors' elaboration based on IEA Energy Technology R&D database (2023[8]), https://www.iea.org/data-and-statistics

Box 5.2. Canada is a global leader in hydrogen and fuel cell technologies

Hydrogen is essential to decarbonising the top third of Canada's most energy-intensive and hard-to-abate end-use applications, as the leading candidate to replace coal in steelmaking, oil and gas for industrial heating, and liquid fuels in transport. Fuel cell technologies are being used to enhance the performance of clean energy systems by helping to balance fluctuations in energy loads, and can help grow the renewable energy sector. Paired with carbon capture and sequestration, hydrogen can also help the traditional energy sector transition into low emissions energy.

Canada has played an important role in the development of the growing global hydrogen economy, and been a pioneer in fuel cell technology. Canada continues to be an R&D and technology leader in the sector, with over 100 companies in the sector which generated CAD 527 million in revenues in 2021, CAD 125 million in R&D expenditure, and employed 4291 people in 2021 (CHFCA, 2022[9]).

Early success in small hydrogen projects (such as the Raglan Mine and Bella Coola HARP project) has led to larger, more integrated projects and reduced reliance on diesel in remote locations. In Alberta, carbon is captured during hydrogen production at the North West Sturgeon Refinery, and Suncor Energy has partnered with ATCO to produce more than 300,000 tonnes per year of low-carbon hydrogen. An investment decision for the project is expected by 2024, and it could be operational by 2028. Fort Saskatchewan is also home to a blending pilot project by ATCO, which would allow ATCO to deliver a blend of natural gas containing up to 5% hydrogen into part of Fort Saskatchewan's residential natural gas distribution network. Air Products announced that it plans to build a CAD 1.3 billion facility in Edmonton that will produce hydrogen derived from natural gas, with operations expected to start in 2024. In Ontario, the Enbridge-Cummins energy storage facility can store excess renewable energy as hydrogen. In early 2022, Enbridge Gas and Cummins completed a project to blend this hydrogen into the Enbridge Gas natural gas network in Ontario. In Quebec, construction has been completed on the world's largest proton-exchange membrane electrolyser. The 20-megawatt (MW) electrolyser will take advantage of Quebec's hydroelectric resources to produce green hydrogen. CF industries provided input to provincial hydrogen strategies in both Ontario and Alberta, while also contributing to public-private feasibility study partnerships, such as for the development of a low-carbon hydrogen hub in Medicine Hat, Alberta.

According to Canada's 2020 Hydrogen Strategy, the demand for hydrogen in global energy systems is projected to experience a tenfold increase in demand over the next three decades. Canada has unique competitive and comparative advantages that position the country to become a world-leading producer, user, and exporter of clean hydrogen, as well as hydrogen technologies and services. If Canada fully seizes the opportunity presented by hydrogen, it could lead to more than 350,000 sector jobs and direct revenues of over CAD 50 billion per year by 2050 (Government of Canada, 2020[10]).

Source: OECD Business Consultation on Sustainability Practices in Canada (2022[11])

5.2. The contribution of FDI to the green transition

Foreign direct investment (FDI) has the potential to contribute financial and technological resources to accelerate the green transition (OECD, 2022[12]). For example, through research collaborations, joint ventures and by contributing to clean-tech clusters and innovation hubs, FDI can help advance the development and commercialisation of innovative green technologies and solutions across a wide range of applications. The carbon intensity of foreign investments depends on a range of investor characteristics, including the technologies they use, the energy they consume, the products and services they offer, and their corporate cultures and environmental policies and practices. Governments have the potential to influence carbon intensity of FDI by putting in place appropriate policies and incentives that encourage investors to internalise the carbon-related costs of their operations.

5.2.1. There is scope for reducing carbon-intensity of foreign companies in some key sectors

The relationship between foreign firm operations and carbon-intensity in Canada is not clear-cut. When considering the overall economy, output of foreign firms appears less carbon-intensive than domestic output, generating 60% lower emissions per unit of output, on average (Figure 5.6). Carbon-intensity of domestic firms is also on the high side of the distribution relative to other OECD economies. This high domestic carbon-intensity is primarily driven by the coke and refined petroleum sector in which domestic firms emit six times more CO_2 per unit of output than their foreign peers (Figure 5.7, Panel A). In other sectors (except for electricity and gas), foreign firms are at least as carbon-intensive as domestic peers, and significantly more so in mining, transport, chemicals and pharmaceuticals. The low carbon-intensity of foreign firms in the oil sector suggests that foreign firms adopt more energy efficient technologies in refining crude oil and may contribute to emissions reductions in this highly carbon-intensive sector.

Figure 5.6. Foreign firms are less carbon-intensive than domestic firms on average

Carbon intensity of output by ownership (mtCO2 per million US$)

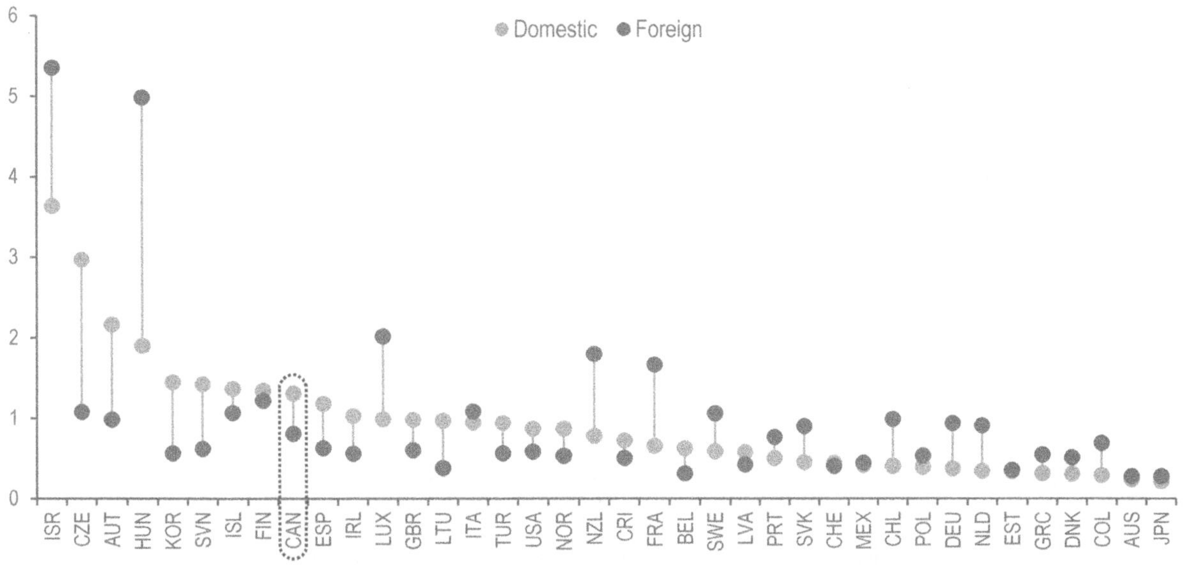

Note: Data points are constructed by averaging CO_2 emissions per unit of output of foreign and domestic enterprises across 34 sectors, weighted by the share of CO_2 emissions generated in the corresponding sectors (so that sectors that are more carbon-intensive get more weight).
Source: Authors' elaboration based on IMF Climate Change Indicators Dashboard (2023[13]), https://climatedata.imf.org/pages/go-indicators

A closer look at estimates of the share of direct carbon emissions of foreign companies in each industry, for Canada and the OECD average, helps shed light on the industries in which foreign firms play the most significant role in carbon emissions (Figure 5.7, Panel B). In the case of Canada, foreign firms account for over three quarters of emissions in chemicals and pharmaceuticals, finance and insurance, electrical equipment and motor vehicles, which is significantly higher than the OECD average for these sectors (39-61%). Other sectors in which foreign firms have a large carbon footprint, well above the OECD average, include mining and quarrying (68%), computer and electronics (61%), and IT and information services (59%). This is also the result of foreign firms' large economic footprint in these sectors and does not necessarily imply that Canada performs worse than other OECD countries in these sectors. Nevertheless, particularly for sectors in which carbon intensity of foreign firms is also relatively high like in mining and chemicals, it does suggest that there remains scope for improving energy and carbon performance of foreign firms in Canada, and further increasing its contribution to decarbonisation.

Figure 5.7. FDI remains relatively carbon-intensive in mining, transport and chemicals

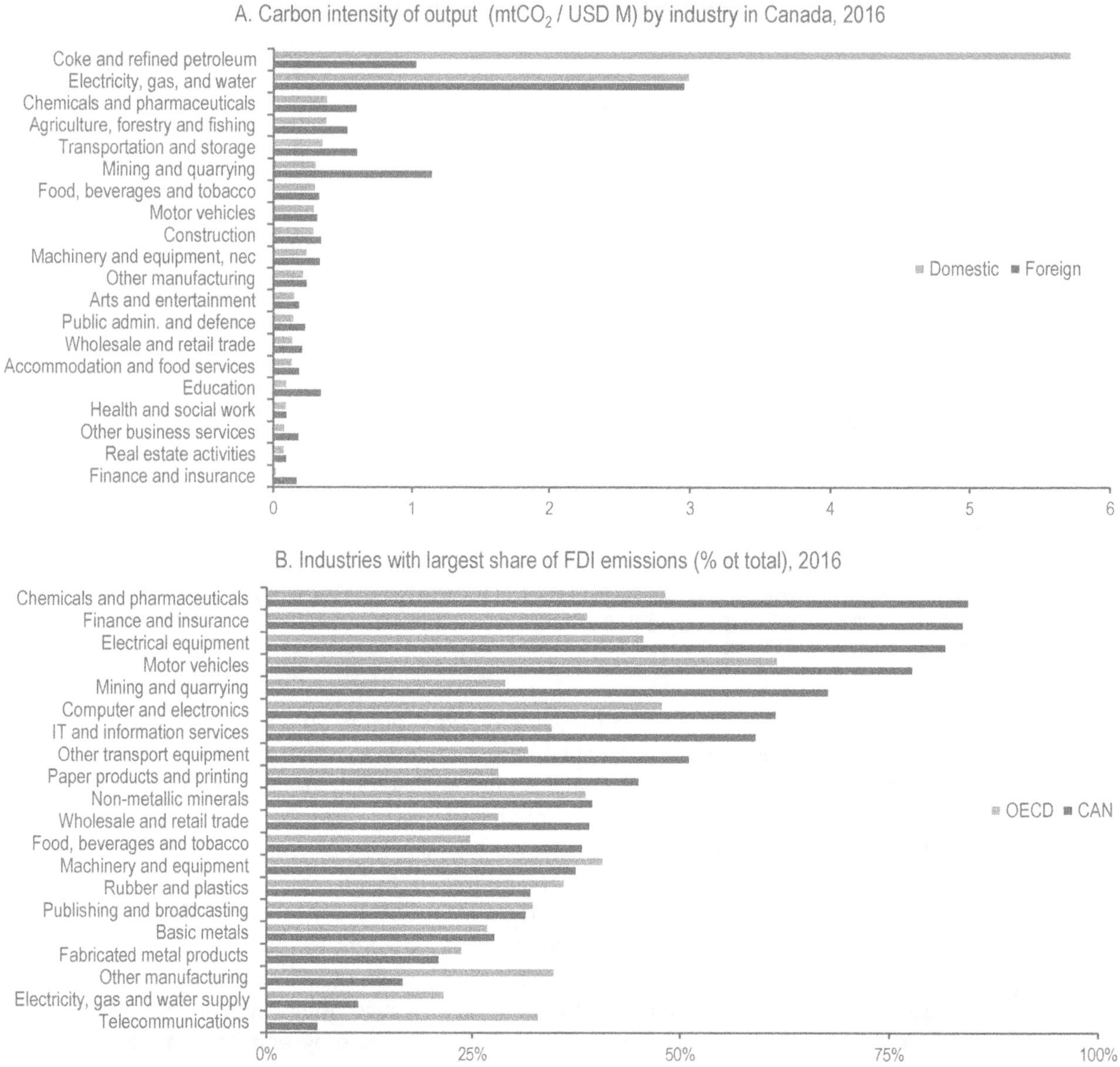

Note: Panel A covers 20 sectors that account for 93% of Canada's overall CO_2 emissions. Panel B considers total emissions and total output across all 34 sectors for which there is data.
Source: Authors' elaboration based on IMF Climate Change Indicators Dashboard (2023[13]), https://climatedata.imf.org/pages/go-indicators

5.2.2. Green FDI remains modest relative to peers

Green or low-carbon technologies, by definition, reduce the CO_2 emissions associated with economic activity in any sector and are therefore key drivers of the carbon intensity of investments, including FDI (Box 5.1). As multinationals are leading players in capital- and emissions-intensive activities like energy, mining, industry and transport, they can make an important contribution to furthering electrification and energy efficiency, or developing altogether new breakthrough technologies for emissions reductions (Box 5.3 provides an example for the transport sector). Indeed it is estimated that FDI accounted for 30% of global new investments in renewable energy in 2020, and that it has shifted considerably away from fossil fuels over the last decade (OECD, 2022[14]).

In Canada, FDI in environmental technologies (henceforth, 'green FDI') has been fairly volatile, fluctuating between 1% and 16% of new (or greenfield) FDI project announcements entering the country over the last two decades (Figure 5.8, Panel B). In absolute terms, green FDI project announcements in Canada have also been volatile with a strong increase from 2005-2011 due to large renewable energy projects but lower green FDI inflows in more recent years. In terms of sector distribution, three quarters of green FDI project announcements into Canada have been in renewable energy, and over a fifth have been in manufacturing activities related to green technologies and products, including electronic components (12%), engines and turbines (5%) and metals (3%). Other green activities that have attracted somewhat more limited FDI include recycling (3%) and green R&D (1%) (discussed in greater detail in the next section).

Accumulated green FDI project announcements over the last two decades accounts for around 6% of overall greenfield FDI, compared to 16% for the OECD average (Figure 5.8, Panel C). Comparing accumulated green FDI flows across countries shows that Canada received comparable amounts as an average OECD country such as France or Türkiye. Canada received however less than half as much green FDI as Germany, Italy, Spain, or Chile. The United States, the United Kingdom and Australia are the main green FDI recipients in the OECD, receiving jointly more than 50% of all green FDI in the OECD.

As mentioned above, the majority of this FDI has been in renewable energy (5%), primarily in wind power, followed by solar and biomass, while hydro power attracts less than 1% of green FDI. This suggests that FDI has the potential to support the expansion of solar and wind capacity in Canada, and therefore to help drive remaining net emissions from electricity generation to zero. Yet, when considering the energy sector more generally, fossil fuels still dominate FDI in Canada, accounting for 25% of overall accumulated greenfield investments and 84% of FDI in the energy sector (Figure 5.8, Panel D). In contrast, in the OECD, fossil fuels account for around 13% of greenfield FDI, and 47% of FDI in the energy sector. This evidence suggests that there remains considerable scope for enhancing the direct contribution of FDI to decarbonisation in Canada, by increasing FDI attraction in green technologies.

The majority of cross-border investments in green technologies in Canada are made by investors from the USA (37%), France (12%), Germany (11%), and the UK (10%), followed by other OECD economies (25%) like Japan and Australia (Figure 5.9). In contrast 87% of investments originating from the Netherlands are in fossil fuels, compared to less than 1% in green technologies. Moreover, the USA invests disproportionately more in oil and gas (19%) than it does in green technologies (5%), while the reverse is true for the UK, France and Germany, from which 12% of their combined investments are in green technologies, compared to 5% in fossil fuels. Non-OECD countries (primarily China and India) invest primarily in sectors that are neither green nor carbon-intensive (90%).

Figure 5.8. Green FDI remains modest while fossil fuels dominate energy FDI

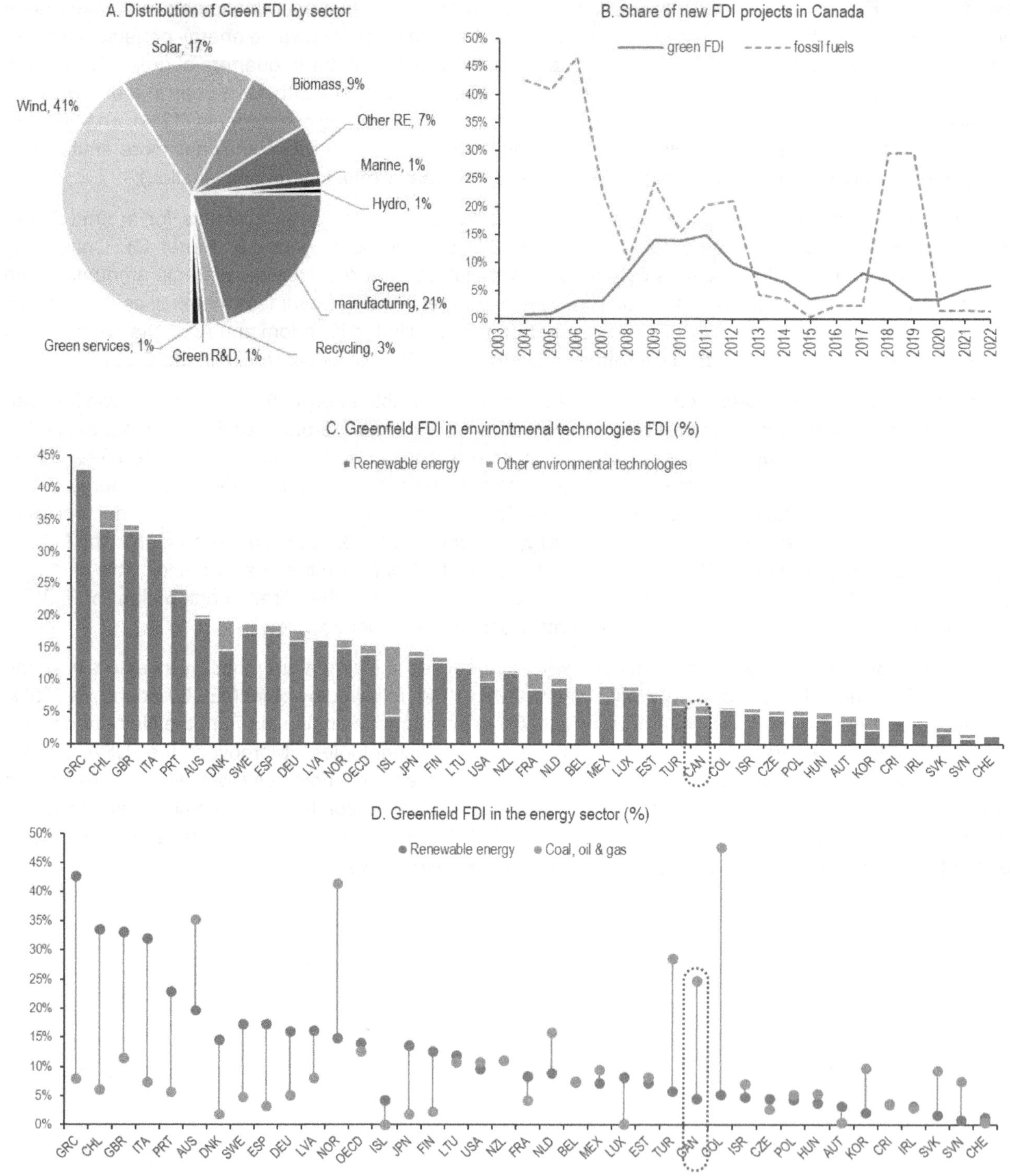

Note: Figures include all announced and opened investment projects over 2003-2023q1.
Source: Authors' elaboration based on Financial Times FDI Markets database (2023[15]), https://www.fdimarkets.com/

Figure 5.9. Green investors in Canada are mainly from USA, UK, France and Germany

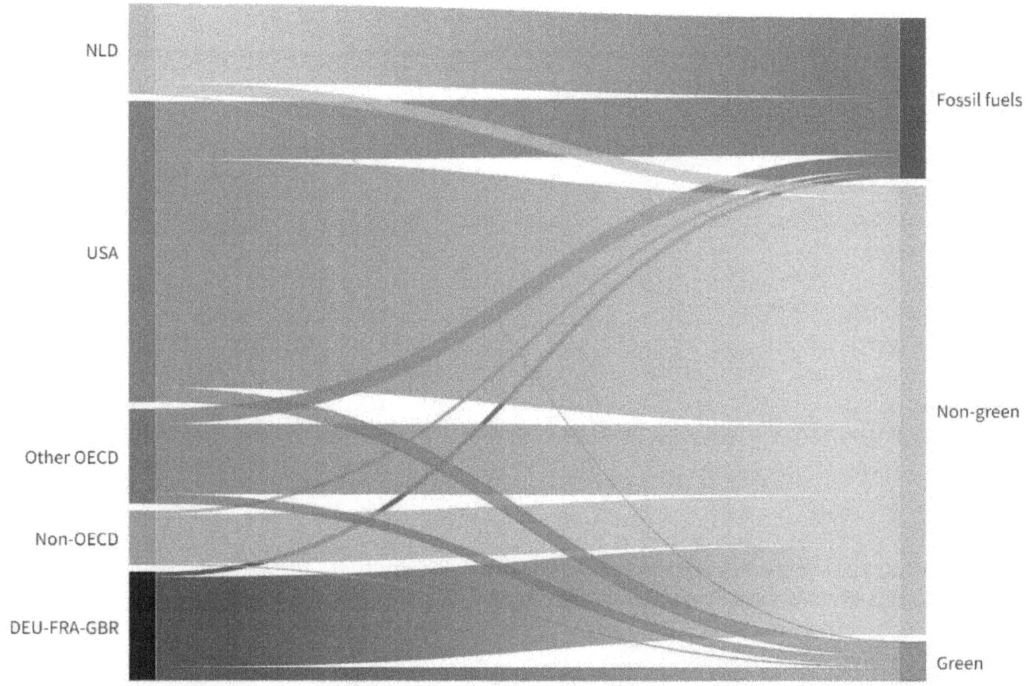

Note: Figures include all announced and opened investment projects over 2003-2023q1.
Source: Authors' elaboration based on Financial Times FDI Markets database (2023[15]), https://www.fdimarkets.com/

Green FDI is unevenly distributed across Canadian provinces (Figure 5.10). Economically larger provinces like Ontario, Alberta, and Quebec jointly account for 70% of new FDI inflows since 2003, and 80% of green FDI inflows. A few economically smaller provinces like Nova Scotia and Manitoba, also attract high shares of green FDI entering Canada. As a result, in these provinces FDI has the potential to make relatively larger contributions to decarbonisation. On the other hand, British Columbia, which alone attracts just under a fifth of greenfield projects in the country, attracts considerably less green FDI (7%), while fossil fuels account for 55% of FDI in the province. This is in stark contrast with the province's highly decarbonised power sector and suggests that green FDI is somewhat below its potential. Newfoundland and Saskatchewan also experience low levels of green FDI, despite considerable investment opportunities in clean energy and plant-based protein, respectively Canada's three territories, attract negligeable levels of greenfield, including in green technologies. Attracting greater FDI in newer clean energy technologies, such as heat pumps and small modular reactors, could help Nunavut address some of its energy-related challenges, and lower emissions generated in the region.

Figure 5.10. Green FDI is unevenly distributed across provinces

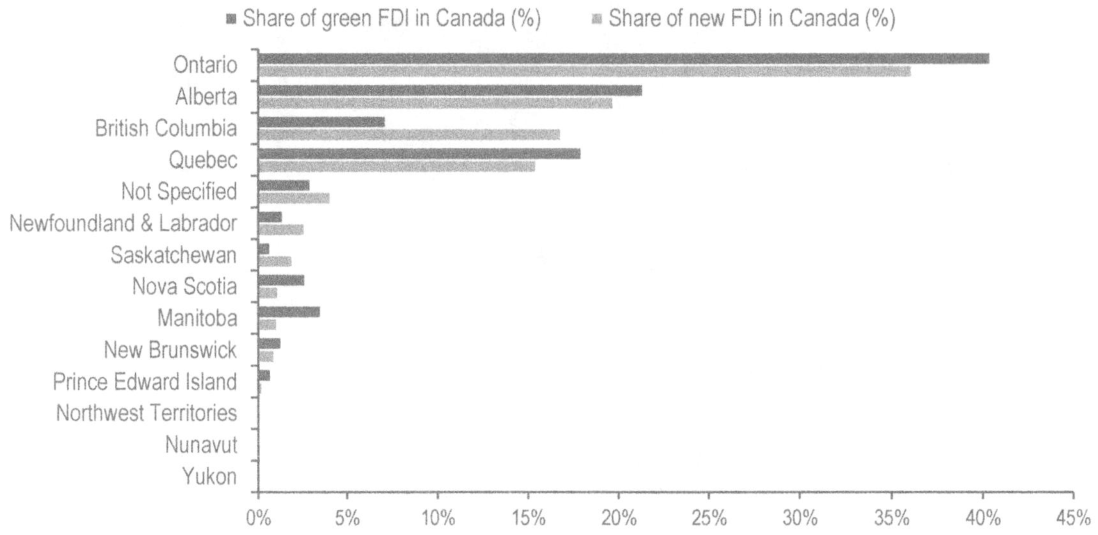

Note: Figures include all announced and opened investment projects over 2003-2023q1.
Source: Authors' elaboration based on Financial Times FDI Markets database (2023[15]), https://www.fdimarkets.com/

Box 5.3. Foreign firms contribute to generate innovative solutions to decarbonise Canada's transport sector

One Canadian company is specialised in the design of ultra-high-speed zero-emission transportation technology and vehicles. The vehicles designed by the company would have the potential to travel four times as fast as conventional high-speed rail (over 1000 km/h), providing a clean alternative to road and air travel and freight, and delivering on Canada's emission reduction targets. The company has partnered with a number of foreign and domestic private and public sector actors to develop, test and demonstrate its hyperloop technology. For example, it partnered with a French company for the research, development, and production of new cabin and vehicle thermal systems designed specifically for its hyperloop system to ensure safety, efficiency, and passenger comfort.

One foreign company is a major supporter of the global 10% sustainable aviation fuel (SAF) target by 2030, catalysing various government, air operators and supply chain partners to reach this goal. In 2015, the company launched an aviation biofuel project in collaboration with the Canadian aviation industry, along with several Canadian research institutes. This collaboration aimed to transform waste from the Canadian forest industry into SAF, exploiting the potential of Canada's natural resources.

Source: OECD Business Consultation on Sustainability Practices in Canada (2022[11])

5.2.3. The contribution of FDI to green R&D is below potential

The premise behind FDI spillovers is that multinational firms have access to innovative technologies and operating procedures, which, if applied, could help raise environmental performance overall and induce the broader uptake of low-carbon technologies. The realisation of these spillovers hinges on the transfer of knowledge from foreign to domestic firms, through their market interactions and through the mobility of workers. The spillover potential varies across technology and spillover channels.

In the case of Canada, domestic innovation potential with respect to green technologies is already very high, with Canada leading innovations and knowhow in a number of breakthrough zero-emission technologies. Nevertheless, FDI can contribute to advancing the development and commercialisation of these technologies across a wide range of applications through research collaborations, joint ventures and by contributing to clean-tech clusters and innovation hubs. Currently, the contribution of FDI to green R&D is in line with the OECD average, with accumulated FDI projects of around USD 170 million (or 8.4 per thousand units of GDP), but much lower than OECD peers like Denmark (100), the Netherlands and (27) the United Kingdom (24), which tend to have higher overall contribution of FDI to GDP (Figure 5.11). When considering total FDI in R&D activities in Canada, the share that is devoted to green R&D is especially low (0.3% compared to 3% for the OECD). This is contrast with the high domestic spending in green R&D relative to other forms of R&D. In other words, the contribution of FDI to green R&D is below its potential.

Figure 5.11. FDI's contribution to green R&D is modest

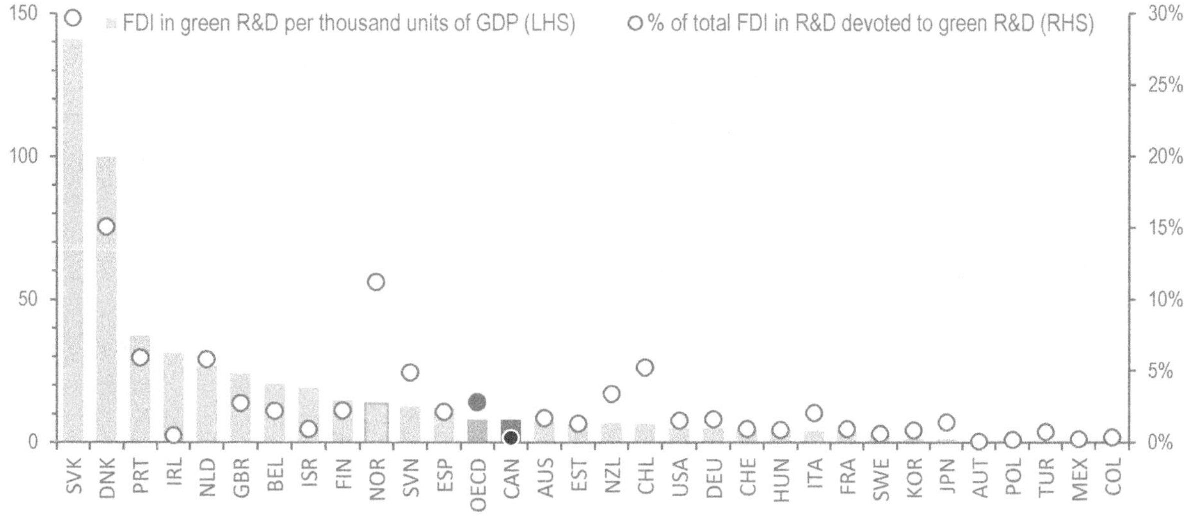

Note: Figures include all announced and opened investment projects over 2003-2023q1.
Source: Authors' elaboration based on Financial Times FDI Markets database (2023[15]), https://www.fdimarkets.com/

5.2.4. FDI generates a growing number of green jobs

FDI can contribute to the green transition by creating green jobs and helping develop green skills. In Canada, FDI creates approximately 670 green jobs per year on average, or 33 jobs per million workers, which is very close to the OECD average (38) and to peers like the USA (31) and France (32), but considerably lower than OECD peers that attract more FDI in environmental technologies like Chile (154) the UK (97), and Australia (87). Relative to the size of investments, FDI-induced direct job creation in Canada is approximately 0.6 jobs per million USD invested, which reflects the relatively high capital intensity of these investments (Figure 5.12).

A closer look at the FDI-induced job creation over time shows that, while job creation in the renewable energy sector has been modest over the last two decades, averaging around 1% of total jobs created by FDI, there has been a reduction in jobs created by carbon-intensive industries like fossil fuels, which averaged 6% up until 2012, but dropped to 1% over the last decade (Figure 5.13). This reflects a gradual shift in FDI away from fossil fuels. When considering green technologies more generally, the extent of job creation has been more volatile, reaching a peak of 13% of overall jobs created by FDI in 2010, and averaging 3% thereafter. The share of green jobs created by FDI appears to be on an upward trend since the outbreak of the COVID-19 pandemic, suggesting that green sectors are resilient to global economic shocks, and that FDI is shifting toward greener industries.

Figure 5.12. There is potential for increasing direct jobs created by green FDI

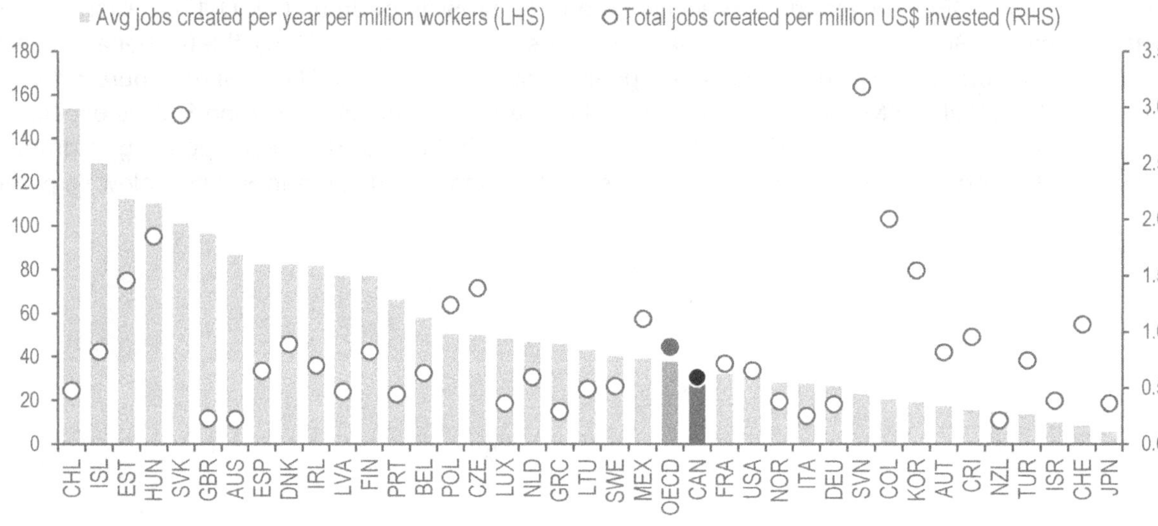

Note: Figures include all announced and opened investment projects over 2003-2023q1.
Source: Authors' elaboration based on Financial Times FDI Markets database (2023[15]), https://www.fdimarkets.com/

Figure 5.13. FDI-induced green jobs are resilient to economic shocks, and expected to rise

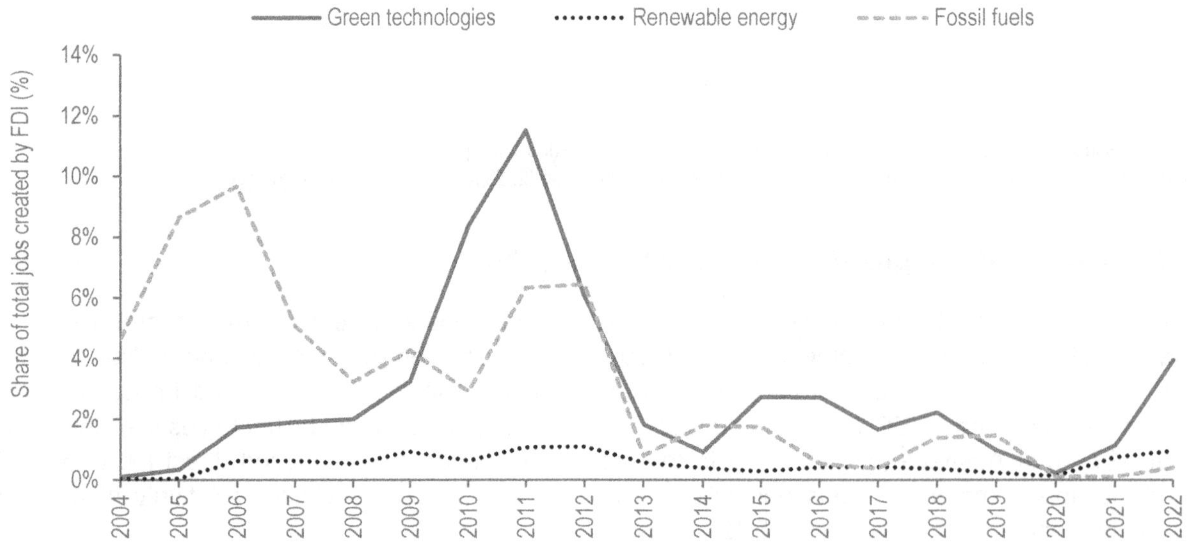

Note: The time series are constructed as two-year moving averages based on all announced and opened greenfield FDI projects.
Source: Authors' elaboration based on Financial Times FDI Markets database (2023[15]), https://www.fdimarkets.com/

5.2.5. Environmental practices do not vary substantially by firm ownership

An OECD business consultation of 24 domestic and 33 foreign-owned companies in Canada offers some insights on the environmental practices of companies operating in Canada (Chapter 1, Annex 1.A). Although the results of the business consultation cannot be generalised, as the sample of companies is not representative, they do provide some novel qualitative information on the green practices of companies in Canada, which is not available from other statistical sources. According to the results, the vast majority of companies, whether foreign or domestic, incorporate some form of environmental or climate considerations in their strategic objectives and performance targets (Figure 5.14). The most commonly cited objectives and targets relate to GHG emissions (71-73%), energy use (64-67%) and waste minimisation (58-63%). In most cases, the difference in likelihood of addressing environmental issues across foreign and domestic firms is relatively small, although the domestic companies surveyed are somewhat more concerned with waste minimisation and recycling, while foreign companies are relatively more concerned with water pollution. However, the water pollution focus of the foreign companies surveyed could reflect their specific industries.

Perhaps motivated by cost concerns, energy saving improvements are the most widespread measures implemented by the surveyed foreign (67%) and domestic companies (64%) in Canada to improve their environmental performance (Figure 5.15). Relative to domestic peers, the foreign companies surveyed are more likely to upgrade machinery and vehicles, and to implement measures to control air pollution, possibly as a result of greater access to more advanced green technologies and equipment. In contrast, the domestic firms are more likely to offer training to employees on environmental issues, and to generate renewable energy for own-use onsite. This may suggest that the potential for FDI-induced knowledge transfer on environmental and energy-saving practices through worker training and mobility remains limited.

Figure 5.14. Surveyed foreign and domestic firms adopt similar approaches to environmental management

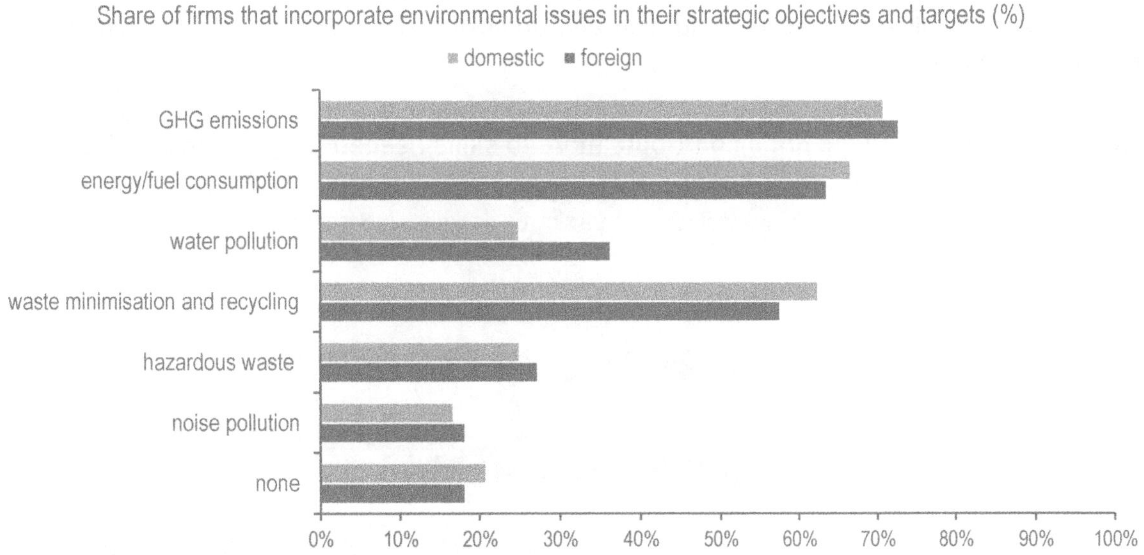

Note: A total of 24 domestic and 33 foreign companies participated in the business consultation.
Source: OECD Business Consultation on Sustainability Practices in Canada (2022[11]).

Figure 5.15. Surveyed foreign firms are more likely to upgrade machinery and control air pollution but less likely to train staff or generate renewable energy on-site

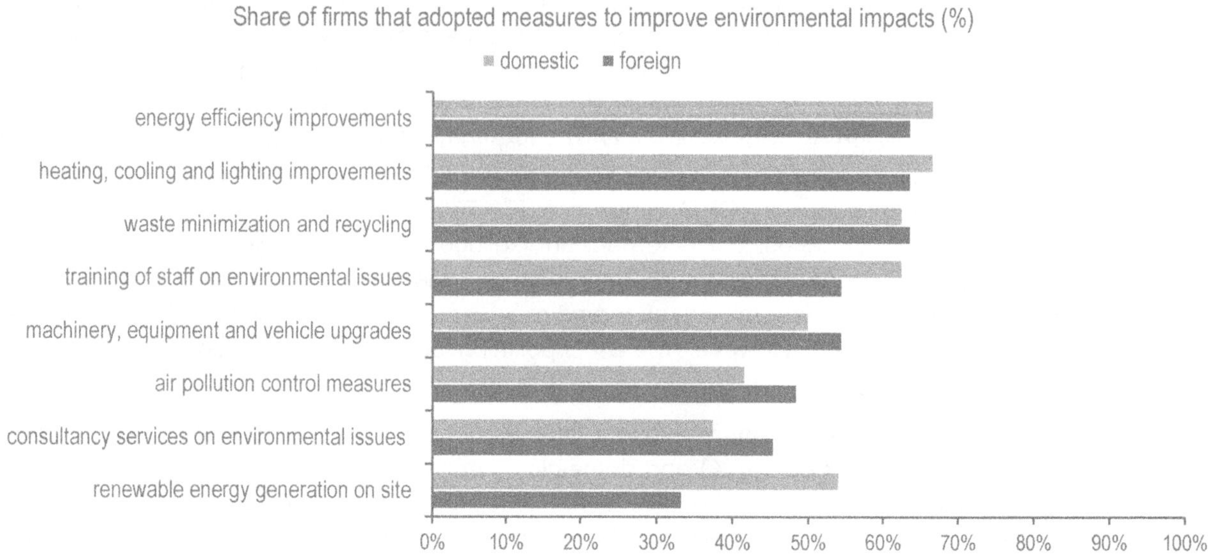

Note: A total of 57 companies participated in the survey.
Source: OECD Business Consultation on Sustainability Practices in Canada (2022[11]).

The results also reveal that the majority of both foreign and domestic firms surveyed (55%) offer training on environmental management, including issues relating to mitigating environmental risks. Possibly motivated by cost reasons, domestic firms are more likely to offer training related to energy-saving practices (54% compared to 42%), while foreign firms are significantly more likely to offer training related to the use of green technologies (45% compared to 29%). This seems to suggest that foreign firms may contribute to fostering skills needed for the green transition. However, it is again important to highlight that the industry sample difference between foreign and domestic firms surveyed can explain some of the observed difference.

Figure 5.16. Surveyed foreign firms contribute more to skills needed for green technologies

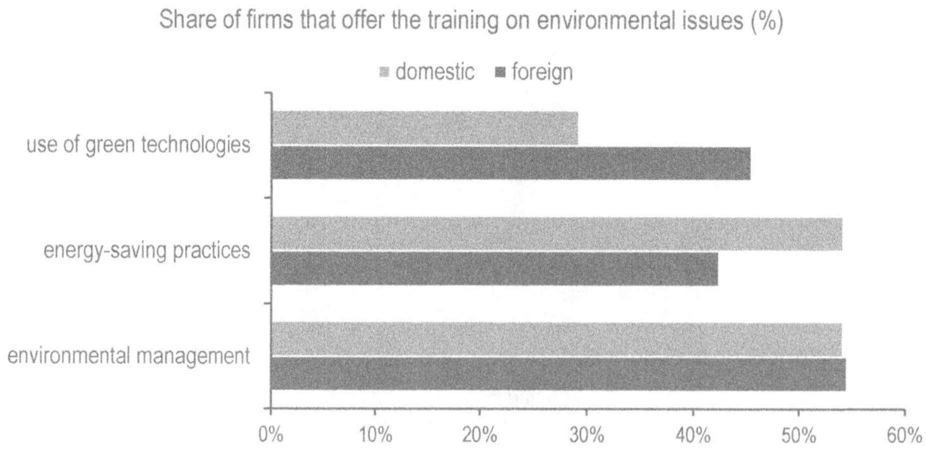

Note: A total of 57 companies participated in the survey.
Source: OECD Business Consultation on Sustainability Practices in Canada (2022[11]).

References

Becker, B. et al. (2020), "FDI in hot labour markets: The implications of the war for talent", *Journal of International Business Policy*, Vol. 3/2, pp. 107-133, https://doi.org/10.1057/s42214-020-00052-y. [16]

BloombergNEF (2022), . [21]

Brosseau, L. (2020), *Recognition of the Foreign Qualifications of Immigrants*, Library of Parliament Background Papers, https://lop.parl.ca/staticfiles/PublicWebsite/Home/ResearchPublications/BackgroundPapers/PDF/2020-86-e.pdf. [19]

Canada Energy Regulatory (2023), *Provincial and Territorial Energy Profiles*, https://www.cer-rec.gc.ca/en/data-analysis/energy-markets/provincial-territorial-energy-profiles/index.html. [6]

CHFCA (2022), *Canadian Hydrogen and Fuel Cell Sector Profile: Final Report - June 202*, https://www.chfca.ca/wp-content/uploads/2022/08/CHFCA-Sector-Profile-2022-Final-2.pdf. [9]

Environment and Climate Change Canada (2022), *A Clean Electricity Standard*, https://www.canada.ca/en/environment-climate-change/services/canadian-environmental-protection-act-registry/achieving-net-zero-emissions-electricity-generation-discussion-paper.html. [5]

Financial Times (2023), *FDI Markets: the in-depth crossborder investment monitor from the Financial Times*, https://www.fdimarkets.com/. [15]

Government of Canada (2020), *Hydrogen Strategy for Canada: Seizing the Opportunities for Hydrogen*, https://natural-resources.canada.ca/climate-change-adapting-impacts-and-reducing-emissions/canadas-green-future/the-hydrogen-strategy/23080. [10]

IEA (2023), *Electricity Information: Electricity and Heat Generation*, http://iea.org. [4]

IEA (2023), *Energy Technology R&D*, https://www.iea.org/data-and-statistics. [8]

IEA (2023), *GHG Emissions from Energy*, https://www.iea.org/data-and-statistics. [2]

IMF (2023), *Climate Change Dashboard*, https://climatedata.imf.org/pages/go-indicators. [13]

Invest in Canada (n.d.), *Hyrdogen*, https://www.investcanada.ca/industries/hydrogen. [20]

Natural Resources Canada (2020), *HYDROGEN STRATEGY FOR CANADA: Seizing the Opportunities for Hydrogen*, https://natural-resources.canada.ca/sites/nrcan/files/environment/hydrogen/NRCan_Hydrogen-Strategy-Canada-na-en-v3.pdf. [7]

OECD (2023), *Environment Statistics: Air and Climate*, http://dotstat.oecd.org/. [3]

OECD (2023), *OECD Economic Surveys: Canada 2023*, OECD Publishing, Paris, https://doi.org/10.1787/7eb16f83-en. [1]

OECD (2022), *Business Consultation on Sustainability Practices in Canada*. [11]

OECD (2022), *Disability, Work and Inclusion: Mainstreaming in All Policies and Practices*, OECD Publishing, Paris, https://doi.org/10.1787/1eaa5e9c-en. [18]

OECD (2022), *FDI Qualities Indicators 2022*, https://www.oecd.org/investment/fdi-qualities-indicators.htm. [14]

OECD (2022), *FDI Qualities Policy Toolkit*, OECD Publishing, Paris, https://doi.org/10.1787/7ba74100-en. [17]

OECD (2022), *FDI Qualities Policy Toolkit*, OECD Publishing, Paris, https://doi.org/10.1787/7ba74100-en. [12]

www.ingramcontent.com/pod-product-compliance
Lightning Source LLC
Chambersburg PA
CBHW061221240926
51846CB00006B/1298